Greek Phrase Book

Greek translation by
Maria Waring

Phonetic transcription by
Dr Henry Waring

Greek
Phrase Book

Edmund Swinglehurst

NEWNES·BOOKS

NEWNES·BOOKS

First published in 1981 by
The Hamlyn Publishing Group Limited
Published in 1983 by Newnes Books,
84-88, The Centre, Feltham, Middlesex, England.

© Copyright The Hamlyn Publishing Group Limited 1981
and Newnes Books, a division of
the Hamlyn Publishing Group Limited 1983.

Second Impression 1984.

ISBN 0 600 34137 2

Printed in Great Britain.

Distributed in the U.S. by
Larousse & Co. Inc., 572 Fifth Avenue, New York,
New York 10036.

Contents

Introduction

The Newnes Greek Phrase Book is designed to help the reader who has no previous knowledge of the language. With its aid he should be able to make himself readily understood on all occasions and to cope with the host of minor problems — and some major ones — that can arise when on holiday or travelling in Greece and Cyprus.

The key to successful speech in a foreign language is pronunciation, and an outline of the principles of vowel and consonant sounds and their usage in Greek is to be found at the beginning of this book. This is followed by a section dealing with the essential elements of Greek grammar. A close study of these two sections and constant reference to them will be of the utmost value: with the pattern of sentence construction in mind and a feeling for the sound of the language, the reader will be well equipped to use the phrases in this book.

These are set out in logical order, beginning with the various means of travel and entry to the country. The section on accommodation covers the whole range from hotels and private houses and villas to youth hostels and camping sites. Particular attention is paid in the chapter on eating and drinking to the speciality dishes of Greece and the different kinds of Greek wines. Shopping, too, is covered in detail; whether the reader wishes to buy some of the fine Greek leather products, or equip his self-catering apartment with a week's supply of groceries, he will find a selection of appropriate phrases easy to refer to and simple to use.

Entertainment, sightseeing, public services, and general conversations in the hotel bar are all covered, and there is an important section on looking after your money. In addition to carefully chosen phrases, each section includes an appropriate vocabulary which is as comprehensive as possible, and at the end of the book there are quick-reference metric conversion tables for the more important temperatures, weights and measures and an index to all the phrases.

The Newnes Greek Phrase Book will not only enable the traveller to handle any situation with confidence but will help to make his stay in Greece a more enjoyable one.

Guide to Greek Pronunciation

This is intended for people with no previous knowledge of Greek and is based on English pronunciation. This means that it is not entirely accurate but the reader who pays careful attention to this section should, with practice, be able to make himself understood reasonably well in Greek.

The Greek Alphabet

LETTER		NAME	USUALLY REPRESENTED IN THE IMITATED PRONUNCIATION BY
Α	α	alfa	a
Β	β	veeta	v
Γ	γ	ghama	gh, y
Δ	δ	dhelta	dh
Ε	ε	epseelon	e
Ζ	ζ	zeeta	z
Η	η	eeta	ee
Θ	θ	theeta	th
Ι	ι	yota	ee
Κ	κ	kapa	k
Λ	λ	lamdha	l
Μ	μ	mee	m
Ν	ν	nee	n
Ξ	ξ	ksee	ks
Ο	ο	omeekron	o
Π	π	pee	p
Ρ	ϱ	ro	r
Σ	σ, ς	seeghma	s
Τ	τ	taf	t
Υ	υ	eepseelon	ee

Φ	φ	fee	f
X	χ	khee	kh
Ψ	ψ	psee	ps
Ω	ω	omegha	o

The Vowels

SYMBOL	APPROXIMATE PRONUNCIATION	LETTER	EXAMPLE
a	like *a* in father	α	**κάνω** kano
e	like *e* in bed; it must always be pronounced so, even at the end of a word	ε	**βλέπω** vlepo
ee	like *ee* in see	η	**μητέρα** meetera
ee	like *ee* in see	ι	**δίνω** dheeno
o	like *o* in dog or *aw* in saw; never like *o* in so	ο	**μωρό** moro
ee	like *ee* in see	υ	**ἐσύ** esee
o	like *o* in dog or *aw* in saw; never like *o* in so	ω	**θέλω** thelo

Vowels written as two letters

SYMBOL	APPROXIMATE PRONUNCIATION	LETTER	EXAMPLE
e	like *e* in bed	αι	τραῖνο treno
ee	like *ee* in see	ει	εἶμαι eeme
ee	like *ee* in see	οι	τοῖχος teekhos
oo	like *oo* in school	ου	σούπα soopa
af	1 like *af* in raft before the consonants θ, κ, ξ, π, σ, τ, and χ	αυ	αὐτό afto
av	2 elsewhere like *av* in lava		αὔριο avreeo
ef	1 like *ef* in left before the consonants θ, κ, ξ, π, σ, τ, φ, χ and ψ	ευ	εὔκολος efkolos
	2 elsewhere like *ev* in devil		γεῦμα yevma

NOTE The vowels η, ι, υ, ει and οι are frequently pronounced like *y* in yes, when they come immediately before another vowel, e.g.

πιάνω	**py**ano	I catch	τό μυαλό	to m**ya**lo	brain
νοιώθω	**ny**otho	I feel			

The Consonants

SYMBOL	APPROXIMATE PRONUNCIATION	LETTER	EXAMPLE
v	like *v* in violin	β	βουνό voono
gh	1 like *g* in go but half-swallowed before the vowels **α, o, ω, ου** and most consonants	γ	γάλα ghala
y	2 like *y* in yes before the vowels **ε, η, ι, υ, αι, ει** and **οι**		γεῦμα yevma
dh	like *th* in this	δ	δίνω dheeno
z	like *z* in zebra	ζ	ζάχαρη zakharee
th	like *th* in thin	θ	θεία theea
k	like *k* in king	κ	καλός kalos
l	like *l* in long	λ	λόφος lofos
m	like *m* in much	μ	μήνας meenas
n	like *n* in now	ν	νύχτα neekta
ks	like *x* in mix, even at the beginning of a word	ξ	ξέρω ksero
p	like *p* in put	π	πόδι podhee

r	like *r* in rain but rolled like a Scottish *r*	ϱ	**ϱόδα** rodha
z	1 like *z* in zebra before the consonants **β, γ** and **μ**	σ, ς	**ύφασμα** eefazma
s	2 like *s* in sit		**σάλι** salee
t	like *t* in take	τ	**τιμή** teemee
f	like *f* in for	φ	**φόϱος** foros
kh	like *ch* in Scottish loch, but a softer sound before the vowels **ε, η, ι, υ, αι, ει** and **οι**	χ	**χάνω** khano
ps	like *ps* in lips, even at the beginning of a word	ψ	**ψηλός** pseelos

Consonants written as two letters

SYMBOL	APPROXIMATE PRONUNCIATION	LETTER	EXAMPLE
ngg	like *ng* in finger	γγ	**σπάγγος** spanggos
g	1 at the beginning of a word like *g* in get	γκ	**γκάζι** gazee
ngg	2 in the middle of a word like *ng* in finger		**άγκυϱα** anggeera
ngks	like *nks* in banks	γξ	**σήϱαγξ** seerangks
ngkh	like *ng* in ring followed by *ch* in Scottish loch	γχ	**ἐλέγχω** elengkho

b	1 at the beginning of a word like *b* in bar	μπ	**μπορῶ** boro
mb	2 in the middle of a word like *mb* in timber		**κολυμπῶ** koleembo
d	1 at the beginning of a word like *d* in dog	ντ	**ντομάτα** domata
nd	2 in the middle of a word like *nd* in find		**δέντρο** dhendro
dz	like *ds* in beds, even at the beginning of a word	τζ	**τζάμι** dzamee
ts	like *ts* in nets, even at the beginning of a word	τσ	**τσάϊ** tsaee

Stress

Stress is indicated in Greek spelling by an accent (´ , and sometimes `) over the stressed syllable. In the imitated pronunciation used in this book it is shown by printing the stressed syllable in bold type.

πίνω **pee**no I drink **πεινῶ** pee**no** I am hungry

Vowels at the beginning of words have 'breathing' marks over them, for example ἁ and ἐ. These make no difference to the pronunciation.

A Little Grammar in Action

Nouns and Adjectives

All nouns in Greek belong to one of three genders, that is, they are either masculine, feminine or neuter irrespective of whether they refer to living beings or inanimate objects. The word for 'the' or definite article, **ὁ,** changes its form according to the gender of the noun it precedes. It is used even before personal names.

MASCULINE	ὁ Πέτρος	o petros	Peter
FEMININE	ἡ γυναίκα	ee yeeneka	the woman
NEUTER	τό μωρό	to moro	the baby

There are three important cases in Modern Greek: nominative or subject case; accusative or object case; and genitive or possessive case. There is also a vocative case, but this is exactly the same as the nominative, except in the masculine singular (**Πέτρο! pe**tro! Peter!). The old dative or indirect object case is now used only in certain formal expressions. The ending of the noun declines, that is, it changes according to which case it is in. Similarly, the word for 'the' also varies, and any adjective accompanying the noun likewise changes its endings. There is no room here to deal with the declensions of the various categories into which Greek nouns and adjectives are divided, nor with the various ways in which they form their plurals. Instead, we have chosen examples of common declensions.

MASCULINE

SINGULAR			
Nominative	ὁ καλός ἄντρας	o kalos andras	the good man
Accusative	τόν καλόν ἄντρα	ton kalon andra	the good man
Genitive	τοῦ καλοῦ ἄντρα	too kaloo andra	of the good man

PLURAL			
Nominative	οἱ καλοί ἄντρες	ee kalee andres	the good men
Accusative	τούς καλούς ἄντρες	toos kaloos andres	the good men
Genitive	τῶν καλῶν ἀντρῶν	ton kalon andron	of the good men

FEMININE

SINGULAR

Nominative	ἡ καλή μητέρα	ee kalee meetera	the good mother
Accusative	τήν καλή μητέρα	teen kalee meetera	the good mother
Genitive	τῆς καλῆς μητέρας	tees kalees meeteras	of the good mother

PLURAL

Nominative	οἱ καλές μητέρες	ee kales meeteres	the good mothers
Accusative	τίς καλές μητέρες	tees kales meeteres	the good mothers
Genitive	τῶν καλῶν μητέρων	ton kalon meeteron	of the good mothers

NEUTER

SINGULAR

Nominative	τό καλό σπίτι	to kalo speetee	the good house
Accusative	τό καλό σπίτι	to kalo speetee	the good house
Genitive	τοῦ καλοῦ σπιτιοῦ	too kaloo speetyoo	of the good house

PLURAL

Nominative	τά καλά σπίτια	ta kala speetya	the good houses
Accusative	τά καλά σπίτια	ta kala speetya	the good houses
Genitive	τῶν καλῶν σπιτιῶν	ton kalon speetyon	of the good houses

The word for 'a' or indefinite article is **ἕνας.** It also changes its form according to the gender of the noun.

MASCULINE	ἕνας ἄντρας	enas andras	a man
FEMININE	μιά γυναίκα	mya yeeneka	a woman
NEUTER	ἕνα μωρό	ena moro	a baby

It changes as follows according to the case of the noun:

MASCULINE

Nominative	ἕνας δρόμος	enas dhromos	a road
Accusative	ἕνα δρόμο	ena dhromo	a road
Genitive	ἑνός δρόμου	enos dhromoo	of a road

FEMININE

Nominative	μιά χώρα	mya **khora**	a country
Accusative	μιά χώρα	mya **khora**	a country
Genitive	μιᾶς χώρας	myas **khoras**	of a country

NEUTER

Nominative	ἔνα παιδί	ena **pedhee**	a child
Accusative	ἔνα παιδί	ena **pedhee**	a child
Genitive	ἑνός παιδιοῦ	enos **pedhyoo**	of a child

The following are examples of the use of the cases with ὁ and ἕνας (ἕνας, μιά, etc. may often be omitted).

1 The nominative or subject case:

Ὁ ἄντρας εἶναι καλός.   The man is good.
o **andras** eene kalos

Note also: Εἶναι (μιά) καλή μητέρα.   She is a good mother.
          eene (mya) kalee **meetera**

2 The accusative or object case:

Βλέπω τόν ἄντρα καί ἕνα παιδί.   I see the man and a child.
vlepo ton **andra** ke ena **pedhee**

3 The genitive or possessive (or indirect object) case:

Τό τέλος τῆς ἡμέρας εἶναι ὡραῖο.   The end of the day is beautiful.
to **telos** tees **eemeras** eene oreo

Demonstrative Adjectives

The word for both 'this' and 'that' is usually αὐτός. It is declined like 'good'.

SINGULAR

	MASCULINE		FEMININE		NEUTER	
Nominative	αὐτός	aftos	αὐτή	aftee	αὐτό	afto
Accusative	αὐτό(v)	afto(n)	αὐτή(v)	aftee(n)	αὐτό	afto
Genitive	αὐτοῦ	aftoo	αὐτῆς	aftees	αὐτοῦ	aftoo

PLURAL

	MASCULINE		FEMININE		NEUTER	
Nominative	αὐτοί	aftee	αὐτές	aftes	αὐτά	afta
Accusative	αὐτούς	aftoos	αὐτές	aftes	αὐτά	afta
Genitive	αὐτῶν	afton	αὐτῶν	afton	αὐτῶν	afton

There is another word for 'that', **ἐκεῖνος,** which need be used only when you wish to contrast 'this' and 'that' in the same sentence. It has the same endings as **αὐτός** but the stress is always on the middle syllable.

MASCULINE		FEMININE		NEUTER	
ἐκεῖνος	ekeenos	**ἐκείνη**	ekeenee	**ἐκεῖνο**	ekeeno

Αὐτός and **ἐκεῖνος** are always followed by the word for 'the', as shown in the examples:

Προτιμῶ αὐτό τό βιβλίο.
proteemo afto to veevleeo

I prefer this book.

Δῶστε μου αὐτήν τήν τσάντα.
dhoste moo afteen teen tsanda

Give me that bag.

Αὐτά τά μῆλα εἶναι καλά ἀλλ' ἐκεῖνα τά σῦκα δέν εἶναι.

afta ta **mee**la eene ka**la** alekeena ta **see**ka dhen eene

These apples are good but those figs are not.

Possessive Adjectives

The usual words for 'my', 'your', 'his', etc. are not declined. They follow the noun and are always used in conjunction with the word for 'the' which precedes the noun.

SINGULAR			PLURAL		
μου	moo	my	μας	mas	our
σου	soo	your	σας	sas	your
του	too	his/its (masc.)	τους	toos	their
της	tees	her/its (fem.)			

NOTE: **σου** is the familiar form of 'your' used when speaking to one person. If you don't know a person well, use **σας,** which is both the plural and the polite form.

Τό σπίτι μου εἶναι μεγάλο.	My house is big.
to **speetee** moo **eene** meghalo	
Ποιός εἶναι ὁ φίλος σου;	Who is your friend?
pyos **eene** o **feelos** soo	
Ξοδεύουν τά λεφτά τους.	They spend their money.
ksodhevoon ta lefta toos	

Personal Pronouns

The words for 'I', 'you', 'he', etc., are as follows.

1 When used (for emphasis or clarity) as the subject of a verb:

ἐγώ	**τραγουδῶ**	egho	traghoodho	I	sing
ἐσύ	**τραγουδᾶς**	esee	traghoodhas	you	sing
αὐτός	**τραγουδᾶ**	aftos	traghoodha	he	sings
αὐτή	**τραγουδᾶ**	aftee	traghoodha	she	sings
αὐτό	**τραγουδᾶ**	afto	traghoodha	it	sings
ἐμεῖς	**τραγουδοῦμε**	emees	traghoodhoome	we	sing
ἐσεῖς	**τραγουδᾶτε**	esees	traghoodhate	you	sing
αὐτοί	**τραγουδοῦν**	aftee	traghoodhoon	they	sing (masc.)
αὐτές	**τραγουδοῦν**	aftes	traghoodhoon	they	sing (fem.)
αὐτά	**τραγουδοῦν**	afta	traghoodhoon	they	sing (neut.)

NOTE These pronouns are usually omitted:

τραγουδῶ	traghoodho	I sing

2 When used as the direct object of a verb:

Ὁ κύριος Φιλιππίδης (μέ) γνωρίζει	Mr Filippidis knows (me)
o **keereeos** feeleepeedhees (me) ghnoreezee	

μέ	me		me
σέ	se		you
τόν	ton		him
τήν	teen		her

τό	to	it
μᾶς	mas	us
σᾶς	sas	you
τούς	toos (masc.)	them
τίς	tees (fem.)	them
τά	ta (neut.)	them

3 When used as the indirect object of a verb:

'Ο κύριος Φιλιππίδης (μοῦ) λέει   Mr Filippidis says (to me)
o keereeos feeleepeedhees (moo) leee

μοῦ	moo	to me
σοῦ	soo	to you
τοῦ	too	to him
τῆς	tees	to her
τοῦ	too	to it
μᾶς	mas	to us
σᾶς	sas	to you
τούς	toos	to them

4 When used after a preposition:

'Ο κύριος Φιλιππίδης ἦρθε μέ (μένα)   Mr Filippidis came with (me)
o keereeos feeleepeedhees eerthe me (mena)

μένα	mena	me
σένα	sena	you
αὐτόν	afton*	him
αὐτήν	afteen*	her
αὐτό	afto*	it
μᾶς	mas	us
σᾶς	sas	you
αὐτούς	aftoos (masc.)*	them
αὐτές	aftes (fem.)*	them
αὐτά	afta (neut.)*	them

*'With him', etc., is usually μ' αὐτόν pronounced mafton, etc.

NOTE The second person plural forms of 'you', ἐσεῖς and σᾶς, should be used instead of the familiar ἐσύ, σέ, σοῦ and σένα when you speak to a person you don't know well.

Verbs

Greek verbs are too complicated for a detailed discussion in a phrase book, but for the traveller who wants a quick grasp of verbs with which he can communicate while travelling in the Greek-speaking world, the following basic rules will be helpful.

Verbs ending in -ω

Most verbs end in unstressed -ω in the first person singular of the present tense, which is conjugated as follows:

ἔχω	ekho	I have	κάνω	kano	I do, make
ἔχεις	ekhees	you have	κάνεις	kanees	you do, make
ἔχει	ekhee	he/she/it has	κάνει	kanee	he/she/it does, makes
ἔχουμε	ekhoome	we have	κάνουμε	kanoome	we do, make
ἔχετε	ekhete	you have	κάνετε	kanete	you do, make
ἔχουν	ekhoon	they have	κάνουν	kanoon	they do, make

Among useful verbs with these endings are

ἀγοράζω	aghorazo	I buy	δίνω	dheeno	I give
θέλω	thelo	I want	στέλνω	stelno	I send
λέω	leo	I say	νομίζω	nomeezo	I think
βλέπω	vlepo	I see	ἀκούω	akooo	I hear
πηγαίνω	peeyeno	I go	τρέχω	trekho	I run
τρώγω	trogho	I eat	πίνω	peeno	I drink

Verbs ending in -ῶ

These verbs are stressed differently from those listed above, and have endings such as the following:

ἀγαπῶ	aghapo	I love
ἀγαπᾶς	aghapas	you love
ἀγαπάει	aghapaee	he/she/it loves
ἀγαποῦμε	aghapoome	we love
ἀγαπᾶτε	aghapate	you love
ἀγαποῦν	aghapoon	they love

Among useful verbs with endings like **ἀγαπῶ** are

μιλῶ	meelo	I speak	**πουλῶ**	poolo	I sell

Verbs ending in -μαι

Passive verbs, i.e., those which express action done to rather than by the subject, have endings like this, but so do a number of other verbs in common use. Here are some important examples:

εἶμαι	eeme	I am	**ἔρχομαι**	erkhome	I come
εἶσαι	eese	you are	**ἔρχεσαι**	erkhese	you come
εἶναι	eene	he/she/it is	**ἔρχεται**	erkhete	he/she/it comes
εἶμαστε	eemaste	we are	**ἐρχόμαστε**	erkhomaste	we come
εἶστε	eeste	you are	**ἐρχόσαστε**	erkhosaste	you come
εἶναι	eene	they are	**ἔρχονται**	erkhonde	they come

πλένομαι	plenome	I wash myself
πλένεσαι	plenese	you wash yourself
πλένεται	plenete	he/she/it washes himself, etc.
πλενόμαστε	plenomaste	we wash ourselves
πλένεστε	pleneste	you wash yourselves
πλένονται	plenonde	they wash themselves

αἰσθάνομαι	esthanome	I feel (well, ill, etc.)
αἰσθάνεσαι	esthanese	you feel
αἰσθάνεται	esthanete	he/she/it feels
αἰσθανόμαστε	esthanomaste	we feel
αἰσθάνεστε	esthaneste	you feel
αἰσθάνονται	esthanonde	they feel

λυποῦμαι	leepoome	I am sorry
λυπᾶσαι	leepase	you are sorry
λυπᾶται	leepate	he/she/it is sorry
λυπόμαστε	leepomaste	we are sorry
λυπόσαστε	leeposaste	you are sorry
λυποῦνται	leepoonde	they are sorry

Θυμοῦμαι	theemoome	I remember
Θυμᾶσαι	theemase	you remember
Θυμᾶται	theemate	he/she/it remembers
Θυμόμαστε	theemomaste	we remember
Θυμόσαστε	theemosaste	you remember
Θυμοῦνται	theemoonde	they remember

To form the negative of a verb **δέν** (dhen) or **δέ** (dhe) is placed before it.

Δέ(ν) τό θέλω.	dhe(n) to thelo	I don't want it.
Αὐτό δέν εἶναι καλό.	afto dhen eene kalo	That's not good.

NOTE: **δέν** is clearer and is used throughout this book.

To ask a question you may use the same order of words as for a statement or you may put the verb at the beginning of the sentence, but in any case you must change the intonation. A Greek question mark looks like a semi-colon in English punctuation.

Ὁ Πέτρος εἶναι ἐδῶ.	o petros eene edho	Peter is here.
Εἶναι ὁ Πέτρος ἐδῶ;	eene o petros edho ⎫	
Εἶναι ἐδῶ ὁ Πέτρος;	eene edho o petros ⎬	Is Peter here?
Ὁ Πέτρος εἶναι ἐδῶ;	o petros eene edho ⎭	

There is no infinitive form of the verb in normal spoken Greek. It is expressed by placing the word **νά** (na) between two verbs:

Θέλω νά πηγαίνω.	thelo na peeyeno	I want to go.
Θέλω νά πηγαίνετε.	thelo na peeyenete	I want you to go.

*   *   *

NOTE Since in Greek the form of a word may change according to gender, as, for example, when the speaker is a woman, this alternative form is given in brackets in the Phrase Book.

Am I allowed to go round alone?	Ἐπιτρέπεται νά περιπλανοῦμαι μόνος (μόνη) μου;
	epeetrepete na pereeplanoome monos (monee) moo

Greek Spoken

Greek is spoken in mainland Greece, Cyprus and the many islands that are scattered across the Ionian Sea to the west and the Aegean Sea to the east. The most important of these are Corfu to the west, Crete to the south and Rhodes to the east. In all of them, especially in the tourist resorts, there are English-speaking Greeks who have worked abroad in Britain, the United States and other English-speaking countries, but there are also many with whom you will have to communicate in their own language. Signs are printed in Greek characters, which is another good reason for getting to know something about the language before visiting the land of Homer and Theseus.

ATHENS is the capital city and is situated in Attica, slightly to the east of the isthmus which joins it to the Peloponnesian Peninsula. The centre of Athens is Syntagma (Constitution) Square and the city is dominated by two hills, one of which is the Acropolis. Around the Acropolis lies the old quarter, or Plaka, which abounds in tavernas and restaurants. Apart from the monuments in the open air, Athens possesses many fine museums, chief of which are the Archaeological Museum, the Byzantine Museum and the Museum of Popular Art. The markets are along Athinas Street and the smart shops around Syntagma Square. From Athens there are excursions to many other historical spots and from its port at Piraeus you can take cruises around the islands.

CRETE is the largest Greek island and was once the centre of the Minoan civilization whose ruins can be seen at Knossos. The legendary Minotaur, half man, half bull, is supposed to have lived here. On the north coast near Knossos is Heraklion, the chief city of Crete and main tourist centre. The airport and the departure point for ferries to the mainland are situated here. Most of the buildings are modern but a few date back to the period of Venetian occupation. Amongst these are St Mark's Hall, the Loggia and the city walls. Ayios Nikolaos to the east is a popular beach resort.

RHODES is the most important of the Dodecanese Islands which include Kos, Kalymnos and Patmos. Famous as the home of the Knights of St John who conquered it in 1308, Rhodes has an old city and the Palace of the

Knights. Where the Colossus, one of the wonders of the ancient world, once stood there is now a yacht harbour. On the east side of the island lies Lindos which has an acropolis with the remains of the sanctuary of Athena.

CORFU is in the Ionian Sea and is green and fertile with olive trees, vines and tomatoes. The capital has narrow streets and fine old houses. There is also an arcade built by Napoleon in imitation of the Rue de Rivoli in Paris. The Palace of St Michael and St George is now a museum. An unusual feature of Corfu town is that it has a cricket pitch on which locals and visitors play. The main beach resorts of Corfu are Paleokastritsa and Glyfada.

THE CYCLADES are the group of islands nearest Athens and the easiest to visit on the ferry services that leave from Piraeus. TINOS is often visited by tourists and has hotels and tavernas along the pretty waterfront. MIKONOS represents the popular idea of a Greek island — gleaming white buildings in a rocky landscape, narrow streets with shops, tavernas and restaurants. DELOS was the Sacred Island of the Greeks and is today littered with the ruins of the time when it was the centre of Aegean trade. The most easterly of the islands is MILOS, where the famous statue of Venus came from, and where there are many ruins of antiquity.

CYPRUS The Greek part of Cyprus lies in the southern half of the island and its most important towns are Limassol and Paphos. The coast is often rugged and there are good sandy beaches, on one of which the legendary Aphrodite appeared from the sea. Roman and Greek remains add archaeological interest and to the west, where the Troödos mountains rise, there are wooded hills and old monasteries. In the centre of the island the capital, Nicosia, lies on the frontier with the Turkish northern part of the island.

In the much-visited areas of Greece and Cyprus you will find some people who speak English but a phrase or two in Greek will always help to establish a friendly relationship with a hospitable people.

Here to start with are some simple expressions of greeting and leave taking:

Good morning.   **Καλημέρα/Χαίρετε.**
                   kaleemera/kherete

Good afternoon.	**Χαίρετε.** kherete
Good evening.	**Καλησπέρα/Χαίρετε.** kaleespera/kherete
Good night.	**Καληνύκτα.** kaleeneekta
How are you?	**Πῶς εἶστε;** pos eeste
I'm very pleased to meet you.	**Χαίρω πολύ.** khero polee
How do you do?	**Χαίρω πολύ.** khero polee
Goodbye.	**᾿Αντίο.** adeeo

And some words of courtesy:

Please.	**Παρακαλῶ.** parakalo
Thank you.	**Εὐχαριστῶ.** efkhareesto
It's very kind of you.	**Εἶναι πολύ εὐγενικό ἐκ μέρους σας.** eene polee evyeneeko ek meroos sas
You are welcome.	**Παρακαλῶ.** parakalo
Not at all.	**Τίποτα, τίποτα.** teepota teepota
I am so sorry.	**Συγγνώμη.** seeghnomee
Excuse me.	**Μέ συγχωρεῖτε.** me seengkhoreete
It doesn't matter.	**Δέν πειράζει.** dhen peerazee

And some questions:

Do you speak English?	**Μιλᾶτε Ἀγγλικά;** meelate angleeka
Where is the hotel?	**Ποῦ εἶναι τό ξενοδοχεῖο;** poo eene to ksenodhokheeo
What did you say?	**Τί εἴπατε;** tee eepate
When does the train leave?	**Πότε φεύγει τό τραῖνο;** pote fevyee to treno
Who are you?	**Ποιός εἶστε;** pyos eeste
How much does it cost?	**Πόσο κοστίζει;** poso kosteezee
How long does it take?	**Πόση ὥρα παίρνει/κάνει;** posee ora pernee/kanee
Which is the road to . . .?	**Ποιός εἶναι ὁ δρόμος γιά . . .;** pyos eene o dhromos ya
Why are we waiting?	**Γιατί περιμένουμε;** yatee pereemenoome

Finally some useful common phrases:

Yes.	**Ναί.** ne
No.	**Ὄχι.** okhee
Why?	**Γιατί;** yatee
How?	**Πῶς;** pos
When?	**Πότε;** pote

What?	**Τί;** tee
Where?	**Ποῦ;** poo
How much?	**Πόσο;** poso
How many?	**Πόσα;** posa
Please speak slowly.	**Μπορεῖτε νά μιλήσετε πιό ἀργά;** boreete na meeleesete pyo argha
I do not understand Greek very well.	**Δέν καταλαβαίνω πολύ καλά τά Ἑλληνικά.** dhen katalaveno polee kala ta eleeneeka
Will you write it down, please?	**Μπορεῖτε νά τό γράψετε, παρακαλῶ.** boreete na to ghrapsete parakalo
How do I say . . . in Greek?	**Πῶς λέγεται στά Ἑλληνικά . . .;** pos leyete sta eleeneeka
What is the meaning of. . .?	**Τί σημαίνει . . .;** tee seemenee
Please explain how this works.	**Μοῦ ἐξηγεῖτε πῶς λειτουργεῖ αὐτό, παρακαλῶ;** moo ekseeyeete pos leetooryee afto parakalo
How far is it to . . .?	**Πόσο μακριά εἶναι . . .;** poso makreea eene˙
Where is the nearest . . .?	**Ποῦ εἶναι τό πλησιέστερο . . .;** poo eene to pleeseeestero
What time is it?	**Τί ὥρα εἶναι;** tee ora eene
Will you please help me?	**Μπορεῖτε νά μέ βοηθήσετε;** boreete na me voeetheesete
Can you point to where we are on this map?	**Μπορεῖτε νά μοῦ δείξετε στό χάρτη ποῦ εἴμαστε;** boreete na moo dheeksete sto khartee poo eemaste

Which way do I go?	**Πρός τά ποῦ πρέπει νά πάω;** pros ta poo prepee na pao
Is there an official tourist office here?	**Ὑπάρχει ἕνα ἐπίσημο τουριστικό γραφεῖο ἐδῶ;** eeparkhee ena epeeseemo tooreesteeko ghrafeeo edho
Where is	**Ποῦ εἶναι** poo eene
the station/bus terminus/bus stop?	**ὁ (σιδηροδρομικός) σταθμός/τό τέρμα/ἡ στάσις τοῦ λεωφορείου;** o (seedheerodhromeekos) stathmos/to terma/ee stasees too leoforeeoo
Where do I buy a ticket?	**Ποῦ μπορῶ νά βγάλω ἕνα εἰσιτήριο;** poo boro na vghalo ena eeseeteereeo
Am I too early?	**Ἔχω ἔρθει πολύ ἐνωρίς;** ekho erthee polee enorees
It is too late.	**Εἶναι ἀργά τώρα.** eene argha tora
We have missed the train/boat.	**Χάσαμε τό τραῖνο/τό πλοῖο.** khasame to treno/to pleeo
Do I turn	**Πρέπει νά στρίψω** prepee na streepso
right/left?	**δεξιά/ἀριστερά;** dheksya/areestera
Do I go straight ahead?	**Πρέπει νά πάω κατ' εὐθεῖαν;** prepee na pao kateftheean
What is the name of this street?	**Πῶς ὀνομάζεται αὐτή ἡ ὁδός;** pos onomazete aftee ee odhos
How do I get to . . .?	**Πῶς μπορῶ νά πάω στό (στή) . . . ;** pos boro na pao sto (stee)
How much does it cost?	**Πόσο κοστίζει;** poso kosteezee

It is too expensive. **Εἶναι πολύ ἀκριβό.**
eene polee akreevo

Please give me the **Δῶστε μου τά ρέστα παρακαλῶ.**
change. dhoste moo ta resta parakalo

I am tired. **Εἶμαι κουρασμένος/κουρασμένη.**
eeme koorazmenos/koorazmenee

I am hungry/thirsty. **Πεινῶ/διψῶ.**
peeno/dheepso

It is **Κάνει**
kanee
very hot/very cold. **πολλή ζέστη/πολύ κρύο.**
polee zestee/polee kreeo

Please take me to my **Νά μέ πᾶτε στό ξενοδοχεῖο μου, παρακαλῶ.**
hotel. na me pate sto ksenodhokheeo moo parakalo

Is the service **Περιλαμβάνεται καί τό ποσοστό σερβιτόρων;**
included? pereelamvanete ke to pososto serveetoron

Thank you very **Εὐχαριστῶ πάρα πολύ.**
much. efkhareesto para polee

And some idiomatic expressions:

Go away. **Φύγετε!**
feeyete

Leave me alone. **᾽Αφῆστε με!**
afeeste me

Shut up. **Σκασμός!**
skazmos

Oh hell! **Θεέ μου!**
thee moo

How goes it? **Πῶς πάει;**
pos paee

So so. **῎Ετσι κι ἔτσι.**
etsee kyetsi

You're joking.   **Ἀστιεύεστε;**
                        asteeeveste

Don't move.   **Μήν κινῆστε!**
                        meen keeneeste

That's it.   **Αὐτό εἶναι.**
                        afto eene

You're right.   **Ἔχετε δίκιο.**
                        ekhete dheekyo

Carry on.   **Συνεχίστε.**
                        seenekheeste

All Aboard

Getting about in Greece is easiest by self-drive car as this will enable you to visit out-of-the-way places in your own time. Failing this, use the bus services which are modern, frequent and reliable. Each region has its own bus system and information will be found at the terminal in each town. There are also organized excursions from Athens. Bus travel is not expensive.

To get from island to island there are regular ferry services from Piraeus. Each service may stop at several different islands and there are car ferries to some of the islands as well as across the Gulf of Corinth. If you are travelling in a group you may like to consider yacht hire. This is very popular and there are many firms that deal in it.

Though the Greeks are very helpful people you may well find yourself among those who do not speak English. This is where the phrases set out for every occasion will come in useful.

Arrivals and Departures

Going through Passport Control and Customs

At most of the main gateway airports and ports there will be someone with a smattering of English, but this is not the case at all frontier posts. It is useful, therefore, to know one or two basic phrases. Apart from making communication easier, they help to establish a friendly relationship with officials and often smooth the passage through frontiers.

Good morning/ afternoon/evening.	**Καλημέρα/Χαίρετε/Καλησπέρα.** kaleemera/kherete/kaleespera
I have come	**Ἔχω ἔρθει** ekho erthee
on holiday/on business.	**γιά διακοπές/γιά δουλειές.** ya dhyakopes/ya dhoolyes

I am visiting	**Ἐπισκέπτομαι**
	epees**ke**ptome
relatives/friends.	**συγγενεῖς/φίλους.**
	seengge**nees/fee**loos
Here is my passport.	**Ὁρίστε τό διαβατήριό μου.**
	o**ree**ste to dheeava**tee**reeo moo
Here is my vaccination certificate.	**Ὁρίστε τό πιστοποιητικό ἐμβολιασμοῦ μου.**
	o**ree**ste to peestopee-ee**tee**ko emvolyaz**moo** moo
The visa is stamped on page . . .	**Ἡ βίζα εἶναι στή σελίδα . . .**
	ee **vee**za **ee**ne stee se**lee**dha
They did not stamp my passport at the entry port.	**Δέν ἐσφράγισαν τό διαβατήριό μου στό λιμάνι ἀφίξεως.**
	dhen esf**ra**yeesan to dheeava**tee**reeo moo sto lee**ma**nee a**feek**seos
Will you please stamp my passport? It will be a souvenir of my holiday.	**Παρακαλῶ νά μού σφραγίσετε τό διαβατήριο; Θά εἶναι ἕνα ἐνθύμιο ἀπό τίς διακοπές μου.**
	paraka**lo** na moo sfra**yee**sete to dheeava**tee**reeo. tha **ee**ne ena en**thee**meeo apo tees dheeako**pes** moo
I will be staying	**Θά μείνω γιά**
	tha **mee**no ya
a few days/two weeks/a month.	**μερικές ἡμέρες/δύο ἑβδομάδες/ἕνα μῆνα.**
	mere**kes** ee**me**res/**dhee**o evdho**ma**dhes/ena **mee**na
I am just passing through.	**Εἶμαι ἁπλῶς περαστικός (περαστική).**
	eeme a**plos** peraste**kos** (peraste**kee**)
My wife and I have a joint passport.	**Ἡ γυναίκα μου κι ἐγώ ἔχουμε ἕνα κοινό διαβατήριο.**
	ee yee**ne**ka moo kye**gho** e**khoo**me ena kee**no** dheeava**tee**reeo
The children are on my wife's passport.	**Τά παιδιά εἶναι στό διαβατήριο τῆς γυναίκας μου.**
	ta pe**dhya ee**ne sto dheeava**tee**reeo tees yee**ne**kas moo

I didn't realize it had expired.	Δέν πρόσεξα ὅτι εἶχε λήξει.
	dhen proseksa otee eekhe leeksee
Can I telephone the British Consulate?	Μπορῶ νά τηλεφωνήσω στό Βρεταννικό Προξενεῖο;
	boro na teelefoneeso sto vretaneeko prokseneeo
I have nothing to declare.	Δέν ἔχω τίποτα νά δηλώσω.
	dhen ekho teepota na dheeloso
Do you want me to open my cases? Which one?	Θέλετε ν' ἀνοίξω τίς βαλίτσες μου; Ποιά θέλετε;
	thelete naneekso tees valeetses moo? pya thelete
They are all my personal belongings.	Ὅλα εἶναι ἀτομικά πράγματα.
	ola eene atomeeka praghmata
I have a few small gifts for my friends.	Ἔχω μερικά μικροδωράκια γιά τούς φίλους μου.
	ekho mereeka meekrodhorakya ya toos feeloos moo
I have 200 cigarettes, some wine and a bottle of spirits.	Ἔχω 200 τσιγάρα, λίγο κρασί καί ἕνα μπουκάλι οἰνοπνευματώδες ποτό.
	ekho dheeakosya tseeghara, leegho krasee ke ena bookalee eenopnevmatodhes poto
They are for my personal consumption.	Εἶναι γιά ἀτομική μου χρήση.
	eene ya atomeekee moo khreesee
Do I have to pay duty?	Πρέπει νά πληρώσω φόρο;
	prepee na pleeroso foro
I have no other luggage.	Δέν ἔχω ἄλλες ἀποσκευές.
	dhen ekho ales aposkeves
Do you want to see	Θέλετε νά κοιτάξετε
	thelete na keetaksete
my handbag/my briefcase?	στήν τσάντα μου/στό χαρτοφύλακά μου;
	steen tsanda moo/sto khartofeelaka moo
I can't find my keys.	Δέν μπορῶ νά βρῶ τά κλειδιά μου.
	dhen boro na vro ta kleedhya moo

I have 1500 drachmas in currency and £100 in traveller's cheques.	Ἔχω 1500 δραχμές μετρητά καί 100 λίρες Ἀγγλίας σέ τράβελερς τσέκ. ekho kheelyes pendakosyes dhrakhmes metreeta ke ekato leeres angleeas se travelers tsek
I can't afford to pay duty.	Δέν μπορῶ νά πληρώσω φόρο. dhen boro na pleeroso foro
Can you keep it in bond?	Μπορεῖτε νά τό κρατήσετε στήν ἀποθήκη τελωνείου; boreete na to krateesete steen apotheekee teloneeoo
Here is a list of the souvenirs I have bought.	Αὐτός εἶναι ἕνας κατάλογος ἀπό τά ἐνθύμια πού ἔχω ἀγοράσει. aftos eene enas kataloghos apo ta entheemeea poo ekho aghorasee
You haven't marked my suitcase.	Δέν ἔχετε μαρκάρει τή βαλίτσα μου. dhen ekhete markaree tee valeetsa moo
May I leave now?	Μπορῶ νά φύγω τώρα; boro na feegho tora

At Airports, Terminals and Stations

Where can I find	Ποῦ μπορῶ νά βρῶ poo boro na vro
a porter?	ἕναν ἀχθοφόρο; enan akhthoforo
a luggage trolley?	ἕνα καροτσάκι γι' ἀποσκευές; ena karotsakee yaposkeves
the left luggage office?	τήν ἀποθήκη ἀποσκευῶν; teen apotheekee aposkevon
my registered luggage?	τίς μή συνοδευόμενες ἀποσκευές; tees mee seenodhevomenes aposkeves
That's my case.	Αὐτή εἶναι ἡ βαλίτσα μου. aftee eene ee valeetsa moo

There's one piece missing.	**Λείπει μιά ἀποσκευή.** leepee mya aposkevee
That's not mine.	**Αὐτό δέν εἶναι δικό μου.** afto dhen eene dheeko moo
Have you seen the representative of my travel company?	**Ἔχετε δεῖ τόν ἀντιπρόσωπο τῆς τουριστικῆς ἑταιρείας μου;** ekhete dhee ton andeeprosopo tees tooreesteekees etereeas moo
Is there an airport bus into town?	**Ἔχει ἕνα εἰδικό λεωφορεῖο ἀπό τό ἀεροδρόμιο γιά τό κέντρο;** ekhee ena eedheeko leoforeeo apo to aerodhromeeo ya to kendro
Where does it go from?	**Ποῦ εἶναι ἡ ἀφετηρία;** poo eene ee afeteereea
Take my bag to the bus/taxi/car.	**Μοῦ φέρετε τήν τσάντα μου στό** moo ferete teen tsanda moo sto **λεωφορεῖο/ταξί/αὐτοκίνητο;** leoforeeo/taksee/aftokeeneeto
How much per case?	**Πόσο γιά κάθε βαλίτσα;** poso ya kathe valeetsa

Toilets

Is there	**Ὑπάρχει καμμία** eeparkhee kameea
a ladies' toilet/ gentlemen's toilet?	**τουαλέττα γυναικῶν/τουαλέττα ἀνδρῶν;** tooaleta yeenekon/tooaleta andhron
Have you	**Ἔχετε** ekhete
any soap?	**σαπούνι;** sapoonee
any toilet paper?	**χαρτί τουαλέττας;** khartee tooaletas

Have you	Ἔχετε
	ekhete
a clean towel?	**μιά καθαρή πετσέτα;**
	mya katharee petseta
a comb or	**μιά χτένα ἤ βούρτσα μαλλιῶν;**
hairbrush?	mya **khtena** ee **voortsa malyon**
Shall I leave a tip?	**Ν' ἀφήσω πουρμπουάρ;**
	nafeeso poorbooar

Telephone

Where are the public telephones?	**Ποῦ εἶναι τά τηλέφωνα γιά τό κοινό;**
	poo eene ta teelefona ya to keeno
I need a telephone directory.	**Χρειάζομαι ἕνα τηλεφωνικό κατάλογο.**
	khreeazome ena telefoneeko katalogho
Where can I get some change?	**Ποῦ μπορῶ νά πάρω ψιλά;**
	poo boro na paro pseela
Can I dial this number or do I ask the operator?	**Βγαίνει ὁ ἀριθμός αὐτός αὐτόματα ἤ μέσω τοῦ κέντρου;**
	vyenee o areethmos aftos aftomata ee meso too kendroo
Hullo.	**'Εμπρός.**
	embros
May I have Athens 12.345?	**Μοῦ δίνετε 'Αθήνα 12.345 παρακαλῶ;**
	moo dheenete atheena dhodheka trakosya saranda pende parakalo
Can I reverse the charges?	**Εἶναι δυνατόν νά χρεωθεῖ ὁ παραλήπτης;**
	eene dheenaton na khreothee o paraleeptees
I have been cut off.	**Μέ ἔχουν διακόψει.**
	me ekhoon dhyakopsee
You gave me the wrong number.	**Μοῦ δώσατε λάθος ἀριθμό.**
	moo dhosate lathos areethmo

May I speak to . . .?	**Μπορῶ νά μιλήσω μέ τόν (τήν) . . .;**	
	boro na meeleeso me ton (teen) . . .	
Is she not in?	**Δέν εἶναι ἐκεῖ;**	
	dhen eene ekee	
Tell her I called. My name is . . .	**Πέστε της ὅτι πῆρα τηλέφωνο. Μέ λένε . . .**	
	peste tees otee peera teelefono. me lene	

Signs

ΑΙΘΟΥΣΑ ΑΝΑΜΟΝΗΣ	ethoosa anamonees	Waiting Room
ΑΝΑΧΩΡΗΣΕΙΣ	anakhoreesees	Departures
ΑΠΟΣΚΕΥΑΙ	aposkeve	Left Luggage
ΑΠΟΧΩΡΗΤΗΡΙΟΝ	apokhoreeteereeon	W.C.
ΑΝΔΡΩΝ	andhron	Men
ΓΥΝΑΙΚΩΝ	yeenekon	Women
ΑΦΙΞΕΙΣ	afeeksees	Arrivals
ΕΙΣΙΤΗΡΙΑ	eeseeteereea	Ticket Office
ΕΙΣΟΔΟΣ	eesodhos	Entrance
ΕΛΕΓΧΟΣ ΔΙΑΒΑΤΗΡΙΩΝ	elengkhos dheeavateereeon	Passport Control
ΕΝΟΙΚΙΑΣΕΙΣ ΑΥΤΟΚΙΝΗΤΩΝ	eneekeeasees aftokeeneeton	Car Hire
ΕΞΟΔΟΣ	eksodhos	Exit
ΠΕΖΟΙ	pezee	Pedestrians
ΠΛΗΡΟΦΟΡΙΑΙ	pleeroforeee	Information
ΣΤΑΘΜΟΣ ΥΠΕΡΑΣΤΙΚΩΝ ΛΕΩΦΟΡΕΙΩΝ	stathmos eeperasteekon leoforeeon	Coach Station

ΣΤΑΣΙΣ ΛΕΩΦΟΡΕΙΩΝ	stasees leoforeeon	Bus Stop
ΤΑΞΙ	taksee	Taxis
ΤΟΥΑΛΕΤΤΕΣ	tooaletes	Toilets
ΦΥΛΑΞΙΣ ΑΠΟΣΚΕΥΩΝ	feelaksees aposkevon	Left Luggage

Taxi Rank

Where can I get a taxi?	Πού μπορῶ νά πάρω ἕνα ταξί; poo boro na paro ena taksee	
Please get me a taxi.	Μοῦ βρίσκετε ἕνα ταξί παρακαλῶ; moo vreeskete ena taksee parakalo	
Are you free?	Εἶστε ἐλεύθερος; eeste eleftheros	
Take me	Νά μέ πᾶτε na me pate	
to Omonia/to this address.	στήν Ὀμόνοια/σ' αὐτή τή διεύθυνση. steen omoneea/saftee tee dheeeftheensee	
How much will it cost?	Πόσο θά στοιχήσει; poso tha steekheesee	
That's too much.	Εἶναι πολύ ἀκριβά. eene polee akreeva	
Turn	Στρίψετε streepsete	
right at the next corner/left at the next corner.	δεξιά στήν ἐπομένη γωνία/ἀριστερά στήν ἐπομένη γωνία. dheksya steen epomenee goneea/areestera steen epomenee ghoneea	
Go straight on.	Πηγαίνετε κατ' εὐθεῖαν. peeyenete kateftheean	

I'll tell you when to stop.	**Θά σᾶς πῶ πότε νά σταματήσετε.** tha sas po pote na stamateesete
Stop.	**Σταματεῖστε.** stamateeste
I'm in a hurry.	**Βιάζομαι.** vyazome
Take it easy.	**Σιγά σιγά!** seegha seegha
Can you please carry my bags?	**Μπορεῖτε νά φέρετε τίς ἀποσκευές μου;** boreete na ferete tees aposkeves moo

Newsstand (Kiosk)

Have you got	**Ἔχετε** ekhete
an English newspaper?	**μιά 'Αγγλική ἐφημερίδα;** mya angleekee efeemereedha
an English magazine?	**ἕνα 'Αγγλικό περιοδικό;** ena angleeko pereeodheeko
any paperbacks?	**φθηνά βιβλία;** ftheena veevleea
Which is the local paper?	**Ποιά εἶναι ἡ τοπική ἐφημερίδα;** pya eene ee topeekee efeemereedha
Do you sell timetables?	**Πουλᾶτε δρομολόγια;** poolate dhromoloya
Have you got	**Ἔχετε** ekhete
a map of the city/a guide to the city?	**ἕνα χάρτη τῆς πόλεως/ἕναν ὁδηγό τῆς πόλεως;** ena khartee tees poleos/enan odheegho tees poleos
Have you any	**Ἔχετε** ekhete
writing paper and envelopes?	**χαρτί ἀλληλογραφίας καί φάκελλα;** khartee aleeloghrafeeas ke fakela

Have you any	Ἔχετε
	ekhete
sellotape?	σελοτέϊπ;
	seloteeep
matches?	σπίρτα;
	speerta
stamps?	γραμματόσημα;
	ghramatoseema
a ball-point pen?	ἕνα μπίκ;
	ena beek
some string?	σπάγγο;
	spanggo

Information Bureau

Is there an information bureau here?	Ἔχει ἕνα γραφεῖο πληροφοριῶν ἐδῶ;
	ekhee ena ghrafeeo pleeroforeeon edho
Have you any leaflets?	Ἔχετε πληροφοριακά φυλλάδια;
	ekhete pleeroforeeaka feeladheea
Have you a guide to	Ἔχετε ἕναν ὁδηγό γιά
	ekhete enan odheegho ya
the hotels?	τά ξενοδοχεῖα;
	ta ksenodhokheea
the pensions?	τίς πανσιόν;
	tees pansyon
the youth hostels?	τούς ξενώνες νεότητος;
	toos ksenones neoteetos
the camp sites?	τούς χώρους γιά κάμπινγκ;
	toos khoroos ya kampeengg
Do you find accommodation for visitors?	Βρίσκετε δωμάτια γιά ἐπισκέπτες;
	vreeskete dhomateea ya epeeskeptes

I want	**Θέλω**
	thelo
a first-class hotel.	**ἕνα ξενοδοχεῖο πρώτης κατηγορίας.**
	ena ksenodhokheeo protees kateeghoreeas
a second-class hotel.	**ἕνα ξενοδοχεῖο δευτέρας κατηγορίας.**
	ena ksenodhokheeo dhefteras kateeghoreeas
a pension.	**μιά πανσιόν.**
	mya pansyon
a double room.	**ἕνα δίκλινο δωμάτιο.**
	ena dheekleeno dhomateeo
a single room.	**ἕνα μονόκλινο δωμάτιο.**
	ena monokleeno dhomateeo
We'll go right away.	**Θά πᾶμε ἀμέσως.**
	tha pame amesos
How do I get there?	**Πῶς μπορῶ νά πάω ἐκεῖ;**
	pos boro na pao ekee

At Airports

Where is	**Ποῦ εἶναι**
	poo eene
the check-in/ transfer desk?	**ὁ ἔλεγχος εἰσιτηρίων καί ἀποσκευῶν/τό γραφεῖο μεταβιβάσεων;**
	o elengkhos eeseeteereeon ke aposkevon/to ghrafeeo metaveevaseon
Can I take this on board as hand luggage?	**Μπορῶ νά πάρω αὐτό μές στό ἀεροπλάνο;**
	boro na paro afto mes sto aeroplano
Do I have to pay excess?	**Πρέπει νά πληρώσω ἔξτρα;**
	preepee na pleeroso ekstra

You haven't given me a luggage claim tag.	Δέν μοῦ ἔχετε δώσει μιά ἀπόδειξη ἀποσκευῶν. **dhen** moo ekhete **dhosee** mya apodheeksee aposke**von**
I've missed my flight. Can you give me another flight?	Ἔχασα τήν πτήση μου. Μπορεῖτε νά μοῦ δώσετε μιά ἄλλη πτήση; ekhasa teen ptee**see** moo. bo**reete** na moo **dhosete** mya alee ptee**see**
When is the next flight to . . .?	Πότε εἶναι ἡ ἑπομένη πτήση γιά . . .; pote eene ee epomenee ptee**see** ya . . .
Is there a bar on the other side of the customs barrier?	Ἔχει ἕνα μπάρ πέρα ἀπό τό τελωνεῖο; ekhee ena **bar** pera apo to telo**neeo**
Where is the flight indicator?	Ποῦ εἶναι ὁ πίναξ πτήσεων; poo eene o peenaks ptee**seon**
Is there a duty-free shop?	Ὑπάρχει κατάστημα ἀφορολογήτων εἰδῶν; ee**parkhee** katasteema aforoloyeeton ee**dhon**
Where can I get some flight insurance?	Ποῦ μπορῶ νά βγάλω ἀσφάλεια πτήσεως; poo boro na vghalo asfalya ptee**seos**
Is there a wheelchair available?	Ἔχει διαθέσιμη μιά ἀναπηρική πολυθρόνα; ekhee dhee**atheseemee** mya anapeeree**kee** polee**throna**

At Railway Stations

Where is the ticket office?	Ποῦ εἶναι τό ἐκδοτήριο εἰσιτηρίων; poo eene to ekdho**teereeo** eesee**teereeon**
One first class ticket to . . .	Ἔνα εἰσιτήριο πρώτης τάξεως γιά . . . ena eesee**teereeo** protees takseos ya
One second class ticket to . . .	Ἔνα εἰσιτήριο δευτέρας τάξεως γιά . . . ena eesee**teereeo** dhefteras takseos ya

A return ticket to . . .	Ἕνα εἰσιτήριο μετ᾽ ἐπιστροφῆς γιά . . . ena eeseeteereeo metepeestrofees ya
How much is a child's fare?	Πόσο ἔχει ἕνα εἰσιτήριο γιά παιδί; poso ekhee ena eeseeteereeo ya pedhee
Can I reserve	Μπορῶ νά κρατήσω boro na krateeso
a seat/a couchette/a sleeping berth?	μιά θέση/μιά κουκέτα/ἕνα κρεββάτι σέ βαγκόν-λί; mya thesee/mya kooketa/ena krevatee se vagonlee
Is there a supplement to pay?	Χρειάζεται νά πληρώσω ἔξτρα; khreeazete na pleeroso ekstra
Do I have to change?	Πρέπει ν᾽ ἀλλάξω τραῖνο; prepee nalakso treno
Is there	Ὑπάρχει eeparkhee
a restaurant/ buffet car?	ἐστιατόριο/μπουφές; esteeatoreeo/boofes
Where is the platform for the train to Olympia?	Ποῦ εἶναι ἡ πλατφόρμα γιά τά Ὀλύμπια; poo eene ee platforma ya ta oleembeea
Does my friend need a platform ticket?	Χρειάζεται ὁ φίλος μου ἕνα εἰσιτήριο γιά νά μπεῖ στήν πλατφόρμα; khreeazete o feelos moo ena eeseeteereeo ya na bee steen platforma
At what time does the train leave?	Τί ὥρα φεύγει τό τραῖνο; tee ora fevyee to treno

At a Port

Which is quay number six?	Ποιά εἶναι ἡ ἀποβάθρα νούμερο ἕξη; pya eene ee apovathra noomero eksee

Where is the car ferry terminal?	**Ποῦ εἶναι ἡ ἀποβάθρα γιά τό φέρρυ μπώτ;** poo eene ee apovathra ya to feree bot
At what time can I go on board?	**Τί ὥρα μπορῶ νά ἐπιβιβαστῶ;** tee ora boro na epeeveevasto
Will there be an announcement when visitors must disembark?	**Θά τό ἀναγγείλουν στό μεγάφωνο πότε πρέπει νά ἀποβιβαστοῦν οἱ ἐπισκέπτες;** tha to ananggeeloon sto meghafono pote prepee na apoveevastoon ee epeeskeptes
When does the boat leave?	**Πότε φεύγει τό πλοῖο;** pote fevyee to pleeo

VOCABULARY

bench	τό παγκάκι	to panggakee
bus driver	ὁ ὁδηγός λεωφορείου	o odheeghos leoforeeoo
clock	τό ρολόϊ	to roloee
gate	ἡ πόρτα/ἡ εἴσοδος	ee porta/ee eesodhos
left luggage office	ἡ ἀποθήκη ἀποσκευῶν	ee apotheekee aposkevon
locker	τό αὐτόματο ντουλάπι ἀποσκευῶν	to aftomato doolapee aposkevon
porter	ὁ ἀχθοφόρος	o akthoforos
security officer	ὁ ὑπεύθυνος ἀσφαλείας	o eepeftheenos asfaleeas
station buffet	τό κυλικεῖον τοῦ σταθμοῦ	to keeleekeeon too stathmoo
station master	ὁ σταθμάρχης	o stathmarkhees
tannoy	τό σύστημα μεγαφώνων	to seesteema meghafonon
ticket collector	ὁ ἐλεγκτής εἰσιτηρίων	o elengktees eeseeteereeon
vending machine for . . .	ἡ αὐτόματη μηχανή γιά . . .	ee aftomatee meekhanee ya . . .
waiting room	ἡ αἴθουσα ἀναμονῆς	ee ethoosa anamonees

En Route

General Expressions

At what time	**Τί ὥρα θά** tee ora tha
do we start/take off?	**ξεκινήσουμε/ἀπογειωθοῦμε;** ksekee**nee**soome/apoyeeo**thoo**me
Why is there a delay?	**Γιατί ἔχει καθυστέρηση;** yatee ekhee katheestereesee
Have I got time to go to the toilet?	**Ἔχω ὥρα νά πάω στήν τουαλέττα;** ekho ora na **pa**o steen tooaleta
I have mislaid my ticket.	**Δέν ξέρω ποῦ ἔχω βάλει τό εἰσιτήριό μου.** dhen ksero poo ekho valee to eesee**tee**reeo moo
Take my address and passport number.	**Νά πάρετε τή διεύθυνσή μου καί τόν ἀριθμό τοῦ διαβατηρίου.** na **pa**rete tee dheeef**theen**see moo ke ton areethmo too dheeavatee**ree**oo
Is this seat reserved?	**Εἶναι πιασμένη αὐτή ἡ θέση;** eene pyaz**me**nee af**tee** ee **the**see

Travelling by Air

Are you the Chief Steward (Stewardess)?	**Εἶστε ὁ (ἡ) ἐπί κεφαλῆς ἀεροσυνοδός;** eeste o (ee) epee kefa**lees** aeroseeno**dhos**
Which button do I press to call you?	**Ποιό κουμπί πατῶ γιά νά σᾶς καλέσω;** pyo koom**bee** pato ya na sas kaleso
Can you help me to adjust my seat?	**Μπορεῖτε νά μέ βοηθήσετε νά ρυθμίσω τή θέση μου;** bo**ree**te na me voee**thee**sete na reeth**mee**so tee **the**see moo

I haven't got a sick bag.	Δέν ἔχω μιά χαρτοσακκούλα ἐμετοῦ; dhen ekho mya khartosakoola emetoo
How high are we flying?	Πόσο ψηλά εἴμαστε; poso pseela eemaste
What speed are we doing?	Τί ταχύτητα κάνουμε; tee takheeteeta kanoome
What is that down there?	Ποιά πόλη εἶναι ἐκεῖ κάτω; pya polee eene ekee kato
Is there a map of the route?	Ὑπάρχει χάρτης διαδρομῆς; eeparkhee khartees dheeadhromees
Are there any duty-free goods available?	Ὑπάρχουν ἀφορολόγητα εἴδη; eeparkhoon aforoloyeeta eedhee
Can I pay you in foreign currency/English money?	Μπορῶ νά πληρώσω μέ boro na pleeroso me ξένο νόμισμα/Ἀγγλικά χρήματα; kseno nomeesma/angleeka khreemata
The airvent is stuck.	Ὁ ἀνεμιστήρας ἔχει κολλήσει. o anemeesteeras ekhee koleesee
May I change my seat?	Μπορῶ ν' ἀλλάξω θέση; boro nalakso thesee

VOCABULARY

aircraft	τό ἀεροπλάνο	to aeroplano
arrival gate	ἡ εἴσοδος ἀφίξεων	ee eesodhos afeekseon
ashtray	τό σταχτοδοχεῖο	to stakhtodhokheeo
flight deck	ὁ θάλαμος χειρισμοῦ	o thalamos kheereezmoo
fuselage	τό σκάφος	to skafos
jet engine	ἡ μηχανή τζέτ	ee meekhanee dzet
light	τό φῶς	to fos
luggage shelf	τό ράφι ἀποσκευῶν	to rafee aposkevon

propeller	ὁ ἕλικας	o eleekas
tail	ἡ οὐρά	ee oora
tray meal	τό προπαρασκευασμένο γεῦμα	to proparaskevazmeno yevma
window	τό παράθυρο	to paratheero
wing	τό φτερό	to ftero

SIGNS

ΠΡΟΣΔΕΘΗΤΕ	prozdhetheete	Fasten your seat belt
ΕΞΟΔΟΣ ΚΙΝΔΥΝΟΥ	eksodhos keendheenoo	Emergency Exit
ΜΗ ΚΑΠΝΙΖΕΤΕ	mee kapneezete	No Smoking

Travelling by Rail

Is this the train for . . .?	Εἶναι αὐτό τό τραῖνο γιά . . . ; eene afto to treno ya
Can you tell me where carriage 5 is?	Μπορεῖτε νά μοῦ πεῖτε ποῦ εἶναι τό βαγόνι No. 5; boreete na moo peete poo eene to vaghonee noomero pende
I have a couchette reservation.	Ἔχω κρατήσει μιά κουκέτα. ekho krateesee mya kooketa
This is my seat reservation.	Ὁρίστε τήν ἀπόδειξη γιά τή θέση μου. oreeste teen apodheeksee ya tee thesee moo
Is this seat taken?	Εἶναι κατειλημμένη αὐτή ἡ θέση; eene kateeleemenee aftee ee thesee
Is the dining car at the front or back?	Εἶναι τό ἐστιατόριο μπροστά ἤ πίσω; eene to esteeatoreeo brosta ee peeso

Two tickets for the first service, please.	**Δύο εἰσιτήρια γιά τό πρῶτο σερβίρισμα, παρακαλῶ.** dheeo eeseeteereea ya to proto serveereezma parakalo
Is the buffet car open throughout the journey?	**Εἶναι ὁ μπουφές ἀνοικτός γιά ὅλο τό ταξίδι;** eene o boofes aneektos ya olo to takseedhee
Can I leave my big case in the baggage car?	**Μπορῶ ν' ἀφήσω τή μεγάλη βαλίτσα μου στό βαγόνι ἀποσκευῶν;** boro nafeeso tee meghalee valeetsa moo sto vaghonee **dhen boro**
What station is this?	**Ποιός σταθμός εἶναι αὐτός;** **pyos** stathmos **eene** aftos
The heating is	**Ἡ θέρμανση εἶναι** ee thermanse **eene**
on/off/too high/too low.	**ἀνοικτή/κλειστή/πολύ ὑψηλή/πολύ χαμηλή.** aneektee/kleestee/polee eepseelee/polee khameelee
I can't	**Δέν μπορῶ** dhen boro
open the window/close the window.	**ν' ἀνοίξω τό παράθυρο/νά κλείσω τό παράθυρο.** naneekso to paratheero/na **kleeso** to paratheero
Where do I have to change?	**Ποῦ πρέπει ν' ἀλλάξουμε τραῖνο;** poo **prepee** nalaksoome treno
Is this where I get my connection for Patras?	**Εἶναι ἐδῶ ποῦ παίρνω τήν ἀνταπόκριση γιά τήν Πάτρα;** eene **edho** poo **perno** teen andapokreesee ya teen patra

Vocabulary

blanket	**ἡ κουβέρτα**	ee kooverta
compartment	**τό κουπέ**	to koope

corridor	ὁ διάδρομος	o dheeadromos
cushion	τό μαξιλλάρι	to makseelaree
luggage rack	τό ράφι ἀποσκευῶν	to rafee aposkevon
non smoking	μή καπνίζοντες	mee kapneezondes
sleeping berth	τό κρεββάτι	to krevatee
sleeping car	τό βαγκόν-λί	to vagonlee
sliding door	ἡ ὀλισθαίνουσα πόρτα	ee oleesthenoosa **porta**

Signs

ΜΗ ΚΥΠΤΕΤΕ ΠΡΟΣ ΤΑ ΕΞΩ	mee **keeptete** pros ta ekso	Do not lean out of the window
ΜΗ ΧΡΗΣΙΜΟΠΟΙΗΤΕ ΤΟ W.C. ΚΑΤΑ ΤΗΝ ΔΙΑΡΚΕΙΑΝ ΣΤΑΘΜΕΥΣΕΩΣ	mee **khreeseemopeeeete** to W.C. **kata** teen dheearkeean **stathmefseos**	Do not use the toilet while the train is stationary

Travelling on a Steamer

Where is the purser's office?	Ποῦ εἶναι τό γραφεῖο τοῦ στιούαρντ; poo eene to ghrafeeo too styooard
Can you show me my cabin?	Μπορεῖτε νά μοῦ δείξετε τήν καμπίνα μου; boreete na moo **dheeksete** teen kambeena moo
Are you the steward?	Εἶστε ὁ καμαρότος; eeste o kamarotos
Is there	Ὑπάρχει eeparkhee
a children's nursery/a shop/a gymnasium?	ἕνας παιδικός σταθμός/ἕνα μαγαζί/ἕνα γυμναστήριο; enas pedheekos stathmos/ena maghazee/ena yeemnasteereeo
Where can I get seasick tablets?	Ποῦ μπορῶ νά πάρω χάπια γιά τή ναυτία; poo boro na paro khapya ya tee nafteea

On which side do we disembark?	Ἀπό ποιά πλευρά θά ἀποβιβαστοῦμε; apo pya plevra tha apoveevastoome
The sea is	Ἡ θάλασσα ee thalasa
calm/rough.	εἶναι ἥσυχη/ἔχει κύματα. eene eeseekhee/ekhee keemata
Is there a duty-free shop?	Ἔχει ἕνα κατάστημα ἀφορολογήτων εἰδῶν; ekhee ena katasteema aforoloyeeton eedhon

VOCABULARY

aft	στήν πρύμνη	steen preemnee
anchor	ἡ ἄγκυρα	ee anggeera
bridge	ἡ γέφυρα	ee yefeera
captain	ὁ πλοίαρχος	o pleearkhos
crew	τό πλήρωμα	to pleeroma
deck	τό κατάστρωμα	to katastroma
funnel	τό φουγάρο	to foogharo
lifebelt	τό σωσίβιο	to soseeveeo
mast	τό κατάρτι	to katartee
port (harbour)	τό λιμάνι	to leemanee
port (left)	ἀριστερά	areestera
propeller	ἡ προπέλα	ee propela
radar	τό ραντάρ	to radar
raft	ἡ σχεδία	ee skhedheea
rail	ἡ κουπαστή	ee koopastee
starboard (right)	δεξιά	dheksya

Travelling by Coach

| Is this the coach for Sounion? | Εἶναι αὐτό τό πούλμαν γιά τό Σούνιο;
eene afto to poolman ya to sooneeo |
| Can I sit near the driver? | Μπορῶ νά καθήσω κοντά στόν ὁδηγό;
boro na katheeso konda ston odheegho |

Are the seats numbered?	**Εἶναι ἀριθμισμένες οἱ θέσεις;** eene areethmeezmenes ee thesees
Do I pay on the coach?	**Πληρώνω μές στό αὐτοκίνητο;** pleerono mes sto aftokeeneeto
Is there a stop en route?	**Κάνει στάση πρίν ἀπό τό τέρμα;** kanee stasee preen apo to terma
Would you mind closing the window? It's draughty.	**Σᾶς πειράζει ἄν κλείσετε τό παράθυρο; Κάνει ρεῦμα.** sas peerazee an kleesete to paratheero? kanee revma
Can you help me with my luggage?	**Μπορεῖτε νά μέ βοηθήσετε μέ τίς ἀποσκευές μου;** boreete na me voeetheesete me tees aposkeves moo

VOCABULARY

back seat	**ἡ πισινή θέση**	ee peeseenee thesee
driver	**ὁ ὁδηγός**	o odheeghos
foot rest	**τό ἀκουμπιστήρι γιά τά πόδια**	to akoombeesteeree ya ta podhya
front seat	**ἡ μπροστινή θέση**	ee brosteenee thesee
guide	**ὁ (ἡ) ξεναγός**	o (ee) ksenaghos
luggage compartment	**τό ντουλάπι ἀποσκευῶν**	to doolapee aposkevon

Buses and Metro

Where is the bus stop?	**Ποῦ εἶναι ἡ στάσις τοῦ λεωφορείου;** poo eene ee stasees too leoforeeoo
Does one have to queue?	**Πρέπει νά κάνουμε σειρά;** prepee na kanoome seera
Can I buy a book of tickets?	**Μπορῶ νά ἀγοράσω ἕνα καρνέ;** boro naghoraso ena karne

Do you go by the Acropolis?	**Περνᾶτε ἀπό τήν 'Ακρόπολη;** pernate apo teen akropolee
Will you tell me when we reach Omonia?	**Μπορεῖτε νά μοῦ πεῖτε ὅταν θά φτάσουμε στήν 'Ομόνοια;** boreete na moo peete otan tha ftasoome steen omoneea
I want to get off at the next stop.	**Θέλω νά κατεβῶ στήν ἄλλη στάση.** thelo na katevo steen alee stasee
Will you ring the bell please?	**Νά κτυπήσετε τό κουδούνι παρακαλῶ;** na kteepeesete to koodhoonee parakalo
I want to go to Plaka.	**Θέλω νά πάω στήν Πλάκα.** thelo na pao steen plaka
When is the	**Πότε εἶναι τό** pote eene to
first bus/next bus/last bus?	**πρῶτο λεωφορεῖο/ἐπόμενο λεωφορεῖο/τελευταῖο λεωφορεῖο;** proto leoforeeo/epomeno leoforeeo/telefteo leoforeeo
Which line do I take?	**Ποιά γραμμή πρέπει νά πάρω;** pya ghramee prepee na paro
Do I have to change?	**Πρέπει ν' ἀλλάξω;** prepee nalakso
At what time is the last metro?	**Τί ὥρα εἶναι τό τελευταῖο τραῖνο;** tee ora eene to telefteo treno

VOCABULARY

automatic door	**ἡ αὐτόματη πόρτα**	ee aftomatee porta
barrier	**ἡ εἴσοδος**	ee eesodhos
escalator	**οἱ κινητές σκάλες**	ee keeneetes skales

Other Vehicles

Where can I hire a bicycle?	**Ποῦ μπορῶ νά νοικιάσω ἕνα ποδήλατο;** poo boro na neekyaso ena podheelato
Please put some air in this tyre.	**Παρακαλῶ νά γεμίσετε αὐτό τό λάστιχο.** parakalo na yemeesete afto to lasteekho
One of the spokes is broken.	**Μία ἀκτίνα εἶναι σπασμένη.** meea akteena eene spazmenee
The brake is not working.	**Τό φρένο δέν λειτουργεῖ.** to freno dhen leetooryee
Do you have a bicycle with . . . gears?	**Ἔχετε ἕνα ποδήλατο μέ . . . ταχύτητες;** ekhete ena podheelato me . . . takheeteetes
The saddle needs	**Ἡ σέλλα θέλει** ee sela thelee
lowering/ raising.	**χαμήλωση/ἀνύψωση.** khameelosee/aneepsosee
Are there any horse-drawn vehicles at this resort?	**Ἔχει ὀχήματα συρόμενα ἀπό ἄλογα σ' αὐτό τό μέρος;** ekhee okheemata seeromena apo alogha safto to meros
Will you put the roof down please?	**Μπορεῖτε νά χαμηλώσετε τή σκεπή παρακαλῶ;** boreete na khameelosete tee skepee parakalo
Will you take the children on the driver's box?	**Παίρνετε τά παιδιά στή θέση τοῦ ὁδηγοῦ παρακαλῶ;** pernete ta pedhya stee thesee too odheeghoo parakalo

---

VOCABULARY

bicycle pump	**ἡ τρόμπα ποδηλάτου**	ee tromba podheelatoo
carrier	**ἡ σχάρα**	ee skhara
chain	**ἡ ἁλυσίδα**	ee aleeseedha

crossbar	ἡ ἀμπάρα	ee ambara
donkey	τό γαϊδούρι	to ghaeedhooree
handlebars	τό τιμόνι	to teemonee
harness	ἡ ἱπποσκευή	ee eeposkevee
lamp	τό φῶς	to fos
mudguard	τό φτερό	to ftero
pedal	τό πεντάλι	to pedalee
rear lights	τά πισινά φῶτα	ta peeseena fota
whip	τό μαστίγιο	to masteeyeeo

Walking About

IN TOWN

Is this the main shopping street?	Εἶναι αὐτός ὁ κύριος δρόμος γιά τά μαγαζιά; eene aftos o keereeos dhromos ya ta maghazya
Where is	Πού εἶναι poo eene
the town hall/the police station?	τό δημαρχεῖο/ἡ ἀστυνομία; to deemarkheeo/ee asteenomeea
Can you direct me to the Tourist Office?	Μπορεῖτε νά μέ κατευθύνετε στό Τουριστικό Γραφεῖο; boreete na me kateftheenete sto tooreesteeko ghrafeeo
In what part of the town are the theatres/the nightclubs?	Σέ ποιό μέρος τῆς πόλης εἶναι se pyo meros tees polees eene τά θέατρα/τά νυκτερινά κέντρα; ta theatra/ta neektereena kendra
Can I get there by bus/by metro/on foot?	Μπορῶ νά πάω ἐκεῖ μέ boro na pao ekee me τό λεωφορεῖο/τόν ἠλεκτρικό/τά πόδια; to leoforeeo/ton eelektreeko/ta podhya
Where is	Πού εἶναι poo eene

the nearest station/the nearest bus stop?	ὁ πλησιέστερος σταθμός/ἡ πλησιέστερη στάσις (λεωφορείων); o pleeseeesteros stathmos/ee pleeseeesteree stasees (leoforeeon)	
Is there a market in the town?	Ὑπάρχει μιά ἀγορά στήν πόλη; eeparkhee mya aghora steen polee	
What day is market day?	Ποιά εἶναι ἡ ἡμέρα τῆς ἀγορᾶς; pya eene ee eemera tees aghoras	
Is the business centre near?	Εἶναι κοντά τό ἐμπορικό κέντρο; eene konda to emboreeko kendro	
Must one cross at the traffic lights?	Εἶναι ἀπαραίτητη ἡ διασταύρωση τοῦ δρόμου στά φανάρια; eene apareeteetee ee deeastavrosee too dhromoo sta fanareea	
Do pedestrians have right of way here?	Ἔχουν προτεραιότητα ἐδῶ οἱ πεζοί; ekhoon protereoteeta edho ee pezee	
Is there a public toilet near?	Ἔχει τουαλέττες ἐδῶ κοντά; ekhee tooaletes edho konda	

VOCABULARY

castle	τό κάστρο	to kastro
cathedral	ὁ καθεδρικός ναός	o kathedhreekos naos
cemetery	τό νεκροταφεῖο	to nekrotafeeo
church	ἡ ἐκκλησία	ee ekleeseea
city centre	τό κέντρο τῆς πόλης	to kendro tees polees
concert hall	ἡ αἴθουσα συναυλιῶν	ee ethoosa seenavleeon
convent	ἡ μονή	ee monee
courts	τά δικαστήρια	ta dheekasteereea
docks	τό λιμάνι	to leemanee
exhibition	ἡ ἔκθεση	ee ekthesee
factory	τό ἐργοστάσιο	to erghostaseeo
fortress	τό φρούριο	to frooreeo
fountain	τό συντριβάνι	to seendreevanee

gardens	ὁ κῆπος	o keepos
harbour	τό λιμάνι	to leemanee
lake	ἡ λίμνη	ee leemnee
monastery	τό μοναστήρι	to monasteeree
monument	τό μνημεῖο	to mneemeeo
museum	τό μουσεῖο	to mooseeo
old town	ἡ παλιά πόλη	ee palya polee
opera house	ἡ ὄπερα	ee opera
palace	τό παλάτι	to palatee
park	τό πάρκο	to parko
Parliament	ἡ Βουλή	ee voolee
ruins	τά ἐρείπια	ta ereepeea
shopping centre	τό ἐμπορικό κέντρο	to emboreeko kendro
stadium	τό στάδιο	to stadheeo
statue	τό ἄγαλμα	to aghalma
stock exchange	τό χρηματιστήριο	to khreemateesteereeo
subway (subterranean passage)	ἡ ὑπόγεια διάβαση	ee eepoyeea dheeavasee
tower	ὁ πύργος	o peerghos
traffic lights	τά φανάρια	ta fanareea
university	τό πανεπιστήμιο	to penepeesteemeeo
zoo	ὁ ζωολογικός κῆπος	o zo-oloyeekos keepos

IN THE COUNTRY

May we walk through here?	Μπορούμε νά περάσουμε ἀπό ἐδῶ; boroome na perasoome apo edho
Is this a public footpath?	Εἶναι αὐτό ἕνα μονοπάτι γιά τό κοινό; eene afto ena monopatee ya to keeno
Do I need permission to fish?	Χρειάζομαι ἄδεια γιά τό ψάρεμα; khreeazoome adheea ya to psarema
Which way is	Πρός τά ποῦ εἶναι pros ta poo eene
north/south/ east/west?	ὁ βορρᾶς/ὁ νότος/ἡ ἀνατολή/ἡ δύση; o voras/o notos/ee anatolee/ee dheesee

Is there a bridge or ford across this stream?	Ἔχει μιά γέφυρα ἤ ἕνα πέρασμα σ' αὐτό τό ποταμάκι;	
	ekhee mya **ye**feera ee **e**na **pe**razma saf**to** to potamak**ee**	
How far is the nearest village?	Πόσο μακριά εἶναι τό πλησιέστερο χωριό;	
	poso makr**ee**a **ee**ne to pleesee**e**stero khor**yo**	
I am lost. Can you please direct me to . . . ?	Ἔχω χαθεῖ. Μπορεῖτε νά μέ κατευθύνετε πρός . . . ;	
	ekho khath**ee**. bor**ee**te na me katefth**ee**nete pros	
Will you please show me the route on this map?	Μπορεῖτε νά μοῦ δείξετε τή διαδρομή σ' αὐτό τό χάρτη;	
	bor**ee**te na moo **dhee**ksete tee dheeadhrom**ee** saf**to** to khart**ee**	

VOCABULARY

barn	ὁ ἀχερώνας	o akheronas
bird	τό πουλί	to poolee
brook	τό ρυάκι	to reeakee
canal	τό κανάλι	to kanalee
cat	ἡ γάτα	ee ghata
cliff	ὁ γκρεμός	o gremos
cottage	τό σπιτάκι	to speetakee
cow	ἡ ἀγελάδα	ee ayeladha
dog	τό σκυλί	to skeelee
farm	τό ἀγρόκτημα	to aghrokteema
field	τό χωράφι	to khorafee
footpath	τό μονοπάτι	to monopatee
forest	τό δάσος	to **dh**asos
goat	ἡ γίδα	ee yeedha
heath	ὁ χερσότοπος	o khersotopos
hill	ὁ λόφος	o lofos
horse	τό ἄλογο	to alogho
inn	τό πανδοχεῖο	to pandhokheeo
lake	ἡ λίμνη	ee leemnee

marsh	ὁ βάλτος	o valtos
moorland	ὁ χερσότοπος	o khersotopos
mountain	τό βουνό	to voono
orchard	τό περιβόλι	to pereevolee
peak	ἡ κορυφή	ee koreefee
pig	τό γουρούνι	to ghooroonee
pond	ἡ λιμνούλα	ee leemnoola
river	ὁ ποταμός	o potamos
sea	ἡ θάλασσα	ee thalasa
sheep	τό πρόβατο	to provato
spring	ἡ βρύση	ee vreesee
stream	τό ποταμάκι	to potamakee
swamp	ὁ βάλτος	o valtos
tree	τό δέντρο	to dhendro
valley	ἡ κοιλάδα	ee keeladha
village	τό χωριό	to khoreeo
vineyard	τό ἀμπέλι	to ambelee
waterfall	ὁ καταρράκτης	o kataraktees
well	τό πηγάδι	to peeghadhee
wood	τό δασάκι	to dhasakee

Motoring

At the Frontier

Here is
'Ορίστε
oreeste

my registration
book/green card
insurance/driving
licence.
τό πιστοποιητικό ἰδιοκτησίας/τήν πράσινη
κάρτα/τό δίπλωμα ὁδηγοῦ.
to peestopee-eeteeko eedhyokteeseeas/teen
praseene karta/to dheeploma odheeghoo

I have an
international
licence.
Ἔχω διεθνές δίπλωμα ὁδηγοῦ.
ekho dhee-ethnes dheeploma odheeghoo

This is a translation of my British licence.	Ὁρίστε μιά μετάφραση τοῦ ᾿Αγγλικοῦ διπλώματός μου.
	oreeste mya metafrasee too anggleekoo dheeplomatos moo
This is a self-drive car. Here are the documents.	Αὐτό τό αὐτοκίνητο τό ἔχω νοικιάσει. Ὁρίστε τά χαρτιά.
	afto to aftokeeneeto to ekho neekyasee. oreeste ta khartya
Do you want to open the boot?	Θέλετε ν᾿ ἀνοίξετε τό πόρτ-μπαγκάζ;
	thelete naneeksete to port bagaz
I arrived today.	᾿Ηρθα σήμερα.
	eertha seemera
I am staying for two weeks.	Θά μείνω γιά δύο ἑβδομάδες.
	tha meeno ya dheeo evdhomadhes
Does this customs post close at night?	Κλείνει τή νύχτα αὐτό τό τελωνεῖο;
	kleenee tee neekta afto to teloneeo
At what time does it close?	Τί ὥρα κλείνει;
	tee ora kleenee
Do you sell petrol coupons?	Πουλᾶτε κουπόνια βενζίνης;
	poolate kooponya venzeenees
Do you want me to stop the engine?	Θέλετε νά κλείσω τή μηχανή;
	thelete na kleeso tee meekhanee

On the Road

Greek roads are classified either as National Roads or as 'other roads'. The limited National Road system is good but you have to pay to drive on certain sections, which can be expensive. On the main highways there are good service areas and excellent restaurants which are licensed. Other roads go through towns and villages which you would miss on the main highway. Country roads are narrow and picturesque — perfect if you are not in a hurry and want to absorb the atmosphere of the region.

Can you tell me how to get to Patras?	Μπορεῖτε νά μοῦ πεῖτε πῶς πάω στήν Πάτρα; boreete na moo peete pos pao steen patra
How many kilometres is it?	Πόσα χιλιόμετρα εἶναι; posa kheelyometra eene
Is it a good road?	Εἶναι καλός ὁ δρόμος; eene kalos o dhromos
Is it hilly — or flat?	Ἔχει ἀνηφοριές – ἤ εἶναι ἐπίπεδος; ekhee aneeforees — ee eene epeepedhos
Is it straight — or winding?	Εἶναι εὐθύς – ἤ ἔχει στροφές; eene efthees — ee ekhee strofes
What is the speed limit on this section?	Τί εἶναι τό ὅριο ταχύτητος σ' αὐτό τό τμῆμα τοῦ δρόμου; tee eene to oreeo takheeteetos safto to tmeema too dhromoo
Will you point out the route on this map please?	Μπορεῖτε νά μοῦ δείξετε τή διαδρομή σ' αὐτό τόν χάρτη παρακαλῶ; boreete na moo dheeksete tee dheeadhromee safto ton khartee parakalo
How much does this section of motorway cost?	Πόσο κοστίζει αὐτό τό τμῆμα τῆς ἐθνικῆς ὁδοῦ; poso kosteezee afto to tmeema tees ethneekees odhoo
Do I pay at the exit?	Πρέπει νά πληρώσω στήν ἔξοδο; prepee na pleeroso steen eksodho
I am sorry I have no change.	Δυστυχῶς δέν ἔχω ψιλά. dheesteekhos dhen ekho pseela
How far is it to the next petrol station?	Πόσο μακριά εἶναι τό ἐπόμενο βενζινάδικο; poso makreea eene to epomeno venzeenadheeko
I want twenty-five litres, please.	Θέλω εἴκοσι πέντε λίτρα, παρακαλῶ. thelo eekosee pende leetra parakalo
Give me 400 drachmas worth.	Δῶστε μου βενζίνη γιά 400 δραχμές. dhoste moo venzeenee ya tetrakosyes drahkhmes

Fill her up, please.	**Γεμίστε το, παρακαλῶ.** yemeeste to parakalo
Please check the oil and water.	**᾿Ελέγξετε τό λάδι καί τό νερό, παρακαλῶ.** elengksete to ladhee ke to nero parakalo
I need some air in the tyres.	**Χρειάζομαι ἀέρα στά λάστιχα.** khreeazome aera sta lasteekha
I think the windscreen fluid needs topping up.	**Νομίζω ὅτι τό σπρέϋ θέλει συμπλήρωση.** nomeezo otee to **spree** thelee seembleerosee
Have you any distilled water for the battery?	**῎Εχετε ἀποσταγμένο νερό γιά τή μπαταρία;** ekhete apostaghmeno nero ya tee batareea
Please clean the windscreen.	**Μπορεῖτε νά καθαρίσετε τό πάρ-μπρίζ παρακαλῶ;** boreete na kathareesete to **parbreez** parakalo
Have you any paper towels?	**Μήπως ἔχετε χαρτοπετσέτες;** meepos ekhete khartopetsetes
Have you got a carwash?	**῎Εχετε πλυντήριο αὐτοκινήτων;** ekhete pleendeereeo aftokeeneeton
Can I park here?	**Μπορῶ νά παρκάρω ἐδῶ;** boro na parkaro **edho**
Where is the nearest car park?	**Ποῦ εἶναι τό πλησιέστερο πάρκινγκ;** poo **eene** to pleeseeestero **parkeengg**

Trouble with the Police

Usually the police are polite and helpful to visitors, but they are more likely to be so if you appear friendly and co-operative. A few phrases in their language can sometimes work miracles.

I'm sorry, I did not see you signal.	**Μέ συγχωρεῖτε, δέν πρόσεξα ὅτι κάνατε σινιάλο.** me seengkhoreete, **dhen** proseksa otee kanate see**nya**lo

I thought I had right of way.	**Νόμισα ὅτι εἶχα προτεραιότητα.** nomeesa otee eekha proteroteeta
I apologize. I won't do it again.	**Ζητῶ συγγνώμη. Δέν θά τό ξανακάνω.** zeeto seeghnomee. **dhen** tha to ksanakano
Here is my name and address.	**Ὁρίστε τό ὄνομα καί ἡ διεύθυνσή μου.** oreeste to onoma ke ee dheeeftheensee moo
This is my passport.	**Ὁρίστε τό διαβατήριό μου.** oreeste to dheeavateereeo moo
Do I have to pay a fine?	**Πρέπει νά πληρώσω πρόστιμο;** prepee na pleeroso prosteemo
How much?	**Πόσο;** poso
I haven't got any cash on me. Can I settle up at a police station?	**Δέν ἔχω μετρητά μαζί μου. Μπορῶ νά πληρώσω σ' ἕνα τμῆμα ἀστυνομίας;** **dhen** ekho metreeta mazee moo. boro na pleeroso sena **tmeema** asteenomeeas
Thank you for your courtesy.	**Εὐχαριστῶ γιά τήν εὐγενικότητά σας.** efkhareesto ya teen evyeneekoteeta sas

Car Rental

I want to hire	**Θέλω νά νοικιάσω** thelo na neekyaso
a car	**ἕνα αὐτοκίνητο.** ena aftokeeneeto
a small car.	**ἕνα μικρό αὐτοκίνητο.** ena meekro aftokeeneeto
a family saloon.	**ἕνα οἰκογενειακό αὐτοκίνητο.** ena eekoyenyako aftokeeneeto
a large car.	**ἕνα μεγάλο αὐτοκίνητο.** ena meghalo aftokeeneeto
a sports car.	**ἕνα αὐτοκίνητο σπόρ.** ena aftokeeneeto spor

a van.	**ἕνα φορτηγό.** ena forteegho
I shall need it for . . . days.	**Θά τό χρειαστῶ γιά . . . ἡμέρες.** tha to khreeasto ya . . . eemeres
How much is the daily charge?	**Τί εἶναι ἡ ἡμερήσια τιμή;** tee eene ee eemereesya teemee
Is it cheaper by the week?	**Εἶναι πιό φθηνά γιά τήν ἑβδομάδα;** eene pyo ftheena ya teen evdhomadha
Does that include mileage and insurance?	**Περιλαμβάνονται καί τά χιλιόμετρα καί ἡ ἀσφάλεια;** pereelamvanonde ke ta kheelyometra ke ee asfalya
Does it include	**Περιλαμβάνεται καί ἡ** pereelamvanete ke ee
third party insurance/ comprehensive insurance?	**κοινή ἀσφάλεια/μιχτή ἀσφάλεια;** keenee asfaleea/meektee asfaleea
What is the mileage charge?	**Πόσο κοστίζει γιά κάθε χιλιόμετρο;** poso kosteezee ya kathe kheelyometro
Is the insurance for car and passengers?	**Εἶναι ἡ ἀσφάλεια γιά τό αὐτοκίνητο καί τούς ἐπιβάτες;** eene ee asfalya ya to aftokeeneeto ke toos epeevates
Where do I pick up the car?	**᾽Από ποῦ τό παίρνω;** apo poo to perno
Can you bring it to my hotel?	**Μπορεῖτε νά τό φέρετε στό ξενοδοχεῖο μου;** boreete na to ferete sto ksenodhokheeo moo
Can I leave it at another town or at the airport?	**Μπορῶ νά τό ἀφήσω σέ μιά ἄλλη πόλη ἤ στό ἀεροδρόμιο;** boro na to afeeso se mya alee polee ee sto aerodhromeeo
Is there a deposit to pay?	**Πρέπει νά πληρώσω προκαταβολή;** prepee na pleeroso prokatavolee

May I pay with my credit card?	**Μπορῶ νά πληρώσω μέ τό πιστωτικό δελτίο μου;** boro na pleeroso me to peestoteeko dhelteeo moo	
Will you please check the documents with me?	**Μπορεῖτε νά ἐξετάσετε τά χαρτιά μέ μένα;** boreete na eksetasete ta khartya me mena	
Will you show me the gears and instrument panel?	**Μπορεῖτε νά μοῦ δείξετε τίς ταχύτητες καί τό ταμπλώ;** boreete na moo **dhee**ksete tees ta**khee**teetes ke to tab**lo**	
Is the tank full of petrol?	**Εἶναι γεμάτη βενζίνη ἡ δεξαμενή;** eene ye**matee** ven**zee**nee ee dheksame**nee**	

Road Signs

ΑΛΤ	alt	Halt
ΑΠΑΓΟΡΕΥΕΤΑΙ Η ΣΤΑΘΜΕΥΣΙΣ	apaghorevete ee stathmefsees	No Parking
ΑΡΓΑ	argha	Slow
ΑΣΤΥΝΟΜΙΑ	asteenomeea	Police
ΔΙΟΔΙΑ	dheeodheea	Toll Post
ΕΘΝΙΚΗ ΟΔΟΣ	ethneekee odhos	National Road
ΕΙΣΟΔΟΣ	eesodhos	Entrance
ΕΙΣΟΔΟΣ ΠΡΑΤΗΡΙΟΥ	eesodhos prateereeoo	Service Station Entrance
ΕΛΑΤΤΩΣΑΤΕ ΤΑΧΥΤΗΤΑ	elatosate takheeteeta	Reduce Speed
ΕΞΟΔΟΣ	eksodhos	Exit
ΕΞΟΔΟΣ ΕΡΓΟΣΤΑΣΙΟΥ	eksodhos erghostaseeoo	Factory Exit

ΕΞΟΔΟΣ ΟΧΗΜΑΤΩΝ	eksodhos okheematon	Vehicles Coming Out
ΕΡΓΑ ΕΚΤΕΛΟΥΝΤΑΙ	ergha ekteloonde	Roadworks
ΗΣΥΧΙΑ ΝΟΣΟΚΟΜΕΙΟΝ	eeseekheea nosokomeeon	Quiet - Hospital
Η ΤΑΧΥΤΗΤΑ ΕΛΕΓΧΕΤΑΙ ΑΠΟ ΡΑΝΤΑΡ	ee takheeteeta elengkhete apo radar	Radar Speed Checks
ΚΙΝΔΥΝΟΣ	keendheenos	Danger
ΚΙΝΔΥΝΟΣ ΠΥΡΚΑΙΑΣ ΣΤΟ ΔΑΣΟΣ	keendheenos peerkayas sto dhasos	Danger of Forest Fire
ΜΕΓΙΣΤΗ ΤΑΧΥΤΗΣ	meyeeste takheetees	Maximum Speed
ΜΟΝΟΔΡΟΜΟΣ	monodhromos	One Way
ΟΔΟΣ ΚΛΕΙΣΤΗ	odhos kleestee	Road Closed
ΠΡΟΣΟΧΗ	prosokhee	Caution
ΠΡΟΣΟΧΗ ΣΤΑ ΤΡΑΙΝΑ	prosokhee sta trena	Caution Trains (Level Crossing)
ΣΤΑΣΙΣ ΛΕΩΦΟΡΕΙΩΝ	stasees leoforeeon	Bus Stop
ΣΤΑΥΡΟΔΡΟΜΙΟΝ	stavrodhromeeon	Crossroads
ΣΥΝΕΧΕΙΣ (under Ζ bend sign)	seenekhees	Continuous (Bends)
ΤΕΛΩΝΕΙΟΝ	teloneeon	Customs
ΧΩΡΟΣ ΣΤΑΘΜΕΥΣΕΩΣ	khoros stathmefseos	Car Park

66 Motoring

Trouble on the Road

OTHER PEOPLE'S

There has been an accident three miles back.	Ἔχει γίνει ἕνα ἀτύχημα πέντε χιλιόμετρα πίσω. ekhee yeenee ena ateekheema pende kheelyometra peeso
Will you phone the police please?	Μπορεῖτε νά τηλεφωνήσετε τήν ἀστυνομία παρακαλῶ; boreete na teelefoneesete teen asteenomeea parakalo
No, I did not see it happen.	Ὄχι, δέν τό εἶδα. okhee dhen to eedha
The car registration number was . . .	Ὁ ἀριθμός κυκλοφορίας τοῦ αὐτοκινήτου ἦταν . . . o areethmos keekloforeeas too aftokeeneetoo eetan
I do not think anyone is hurt.	Δέν νομίζω ὅτι κάποιος ἔχει τραυματιστεῖ. dhen nomeezo otee kapyos ekhee travmateestee
Someone is badly hurt.	Κάποιος ἔχει τραυματιστεῖ σοβαρά. kapyos ekhee travmateestee sovara

YOURS

Are you all right?	Εἶστε ἐντάξει; eeste endaksee
My passengers are not hurt.	Οἱ ἐπιβάτες μου δέν ἔπαθαν τίποτα. ee epeevates moo dhen epathan teepota
The car is damaged.	Τό αὐτοκίνητο ἔχει πάθει ζημιές. to aftokeeneeto ekhee pathee zeemyes
May I have your insurance details?	Μπορῶ νά ἔχω τά στοιχεῖα τῆς ἀσφαλείας σας; boro na ekho ta steekheea tees asfaleeas sas

Your name and address, please?	Τό ὄνομα καί τή διεύθυνσή σας παρακαλῶ; to onoma ke tee dheeeftheensee sas parakalo
Will you please fill out this form?	Συμπληρώνετε αὐτό τό ἔντυπο παρακαλῶ; seembleeronete afto to endeepo parakalo
I think we shall have to call the police.	Νομίζω πώς πρέπει νά καλέσουμε τήν ἀστυνομία. nomeezo pos prepee na kalesoome teen asteenomeea
Excuse me, would you mind being a witness?	Μέ συγχωρεῖτε, θά σᾶς πείραζε νά γίνετε μάρτυρας; me seengkhoreete tha sas peeraze na yeenete marteeras
It happened because he put his brakes on suddenly.	Ἔγινε γιατί πάτησε ἀπότομα τό φρένο. eyeene yatee pateese apotoma to freno
He came out of a side road without signalling.	Βγῆκε ἀπό μία πάροδο χωρίς νά κάνει σινιάλο. vyeeke apo meea parodho khorees na kanee seenyalo
He tried to overtake on a narrow stretch of road.	Προσπάθησε νά προσπεράσει σ' ἕνα στενό τμῆμα τοῦ δρόμου. prospatheese na prosperasee sena steno tmeema too dhromoo
He turned off without signalling.	Ἔστριψε χωρίς νά κάνει σινιάλο. estreepse khorees na kanee seenyalo
May I explain to someone who understands English?	Μπορῶ νά δώσω ἐξήγηση σέ κάποιον πού μιλάει Ἀγγλικά; boro na dhoso ekseeyeesee se kapyon poo meelaee anggleeka

If you are unfortunate enough to have an accident be sure to get all the details from the other driver involved. Your insurance company will have provided you with an accident report form. Fill it up on the spot and include the required details from the other driver. Above all, keep cool.

Breakdown

If you have a breakdown put the red triangle behind your car at once or you may be penalized. Get the car off the road if possible.

Thank you for stopping. I am in trouble. Will you help me?	Εὐχαριστῶ πού σταματήσατε. Ἔχω δυσκολίες. Μπορεῖτε νά μέ βοηθήσετε; efkhareesto poo stamateesate. ekho dheeskoleees. boreete na me voeetheesete
My car has broken down.	Τό αὐτοκίνητό μου ἔχει χαλάσει. to aftokeeneeto moo ekhee khalasee
I have locked myself out of the car.	Ἔχω κλειδώσει τό ἁμάξι μου μέ τά κλειδιά μέσα. ekho kleedhosee to amaksee moo me takleedhya mesa
Will you tell the next garage that you pass?	Μπορεῖτε νά εἰδοποιήσετε τό πρῶτο γκαράζι πού θά περάσετε; boreete na eedhopeeeesete to proto garazee poo tha perasete
Will you please telephone a garage for me?	Μπορεῖτε νά τηλεφωνήσετε ἕνα γκαράζι γιά μένα; boreete na teelefoneesete ena garazee ya mena
Can you give me a lift to the next telephone?	Μπορεῖτε νά μέ πᾶτε στό ἑπόμενο τηλέφωνο; boreete na me pate sto epomeno teelefono
Can you send a breakdown truck?	Μπορεῖτε νά στείλετε ἕνα γερανό; boreete na steelete ena yerano
I am fourteen kilometres from Athens on the National Road.	Εἶμαι δεκατέσσερα χιλιόμετρα ἀπ' τήν 'Αθήνα στήν 'Εθνική 'Οδό. eeme dhekatesera kheelyometra apteen atheena steen ethneekee odho
How long will you be?	Πόση ὥρα θά κάνετε; posee ora tha kanete

Repairs

There's something wrong with the engine.	'Η μηχανή ἔχει βλάβη. ee meekhanee ekhee vlavee
The clutch is slipping.	Τό ἀμπραγιάζ δέν πιάνει καλά. to abrayaz dhen pyanee kala
There is a noise from the . . .	Ἔχει θόρυβο ἀπό τό (τήν) . . . ekhee thoreevo apo to (teen) . . .
The brakes are not working.	Τά φρένα δέν λειτουργοῦν. ta frena dhen leetoorghoon
The cooling system is leaking.	Τό σύστημα ψύξεως στάζει. to seesteema pseekseos stazee
My fan belt is broken.	Τό λουρί τοῦ βαντιλατέρ μου ἔχει σπάσει. to looree too vandeelater moo ekhee spasee
I've got a flat tyre.	Ἔνα λάστιχο ἔχει σπάσει. ena lasteekho ekhee spasee
Would you please mend this puncture?	Μπορεῖτε νά ἐπισκευάσετε αὐτό τό σπασμένο λάστιχο; boreete na epeeskevasete afto to spazmeno lasteekho
The electrical system has failed.	Τό ἡλεκτρικό σύστημα ἔχει χαλάσει. to eelektreeko seesteema ekhee khalasee
The engine is overheating.	'Η μηχανή ὑπερθερμαίνεται. ee meekhanee eeperthermenete
The car won't start.	Τό αὐτοκίνητο δέν παίρνει ἐμπρός. to aftokeeneeto dhen pernee embros
What is the matter?	Τί βλάβη ἔχει; tee vlavee ekhee

Is it	**Εἶναι**
	eene
broken?	**σπασμένο;**
	spazmeno
burnt out?	**καμμένο;**
	kameno
disconnected?	**ἀποσυνδεδεμένο;**
	aposeendhedhemeno
jammed?	**μπλοκαρισμένο;**
	blokareezmeno

| Is it leaking? | **Στάζει;** |
| | stazee |

| Is there a short circuit? | **Ἔχει βραχυκύκλωμα;** |
| | ekhee vrakheekeekloma |

| Do I need a new part? | **Χρειάζομαι ἀνταλλακτικό;** |
| | khreeazome andalakteeko |

| Is there a Ford agent in town? | **Ἔχει μία ἀντιπροσωπεία τῆς Φόρντ στήν πόλη;** |
| | ekhee meea andeeprosopeea tees ford steen polee |

| Can you send for the part? | **Μπορεῖτε νά παραγγείλετε τό ἀνταλλακτικό;** |
| | boreete na paranggeelete to andalakteeko |

| Is it serious? | **Εἶναι σοβαρό;** |
| | eene sovaro |

| How long will it take to repair? | **Πόση ὥρα θά χρειαστεῖ ἡ ἐπισκευή.** |
| | posee ora tha khreeastee ee epeeskevee |

| Can I hire another car? | **Μπορῶ νά νοικιάσω ἄλλο αὐτοκίνητο;** |
| | boro na neekyaso alo aftokeeneeto |

| What will it cost? | **Πόσο θά στοιχίσει;** |
| | poso tha steekheesee |

| I will get the part flown from Britain. | **Θά κανονίσω νά στείλουν τό ἀνταλλακτικό ἀεροπορικῶς ἀπ' τή Βρεταννία.** |
| | tha kanoneeso na steeloon to andalakteeko aeroporeekos aptee vretaneea |

Your mechanic has been very kind. I would like to tip him.	Ὁ μηχανικός σας ἦταν πολύ βοηθητικός. Θά ἤθελα νά τόν φιλοδωρήσω.	o meekhaneekos sas eetan polee voeetheeteekos. tha eethela na ton feelodhoreeso

Vocabulary

alternator	ὁ ἐναλλακτήρας	o enalakteeras
battery	ἡ μπαταρία	ee batareea
bearings	τά κουζινέτα	ta koozeeneta
brakes	τά φρένα	ta frena
brake lining	ἡ ἐπένδυση τῶν φρένων	ee ependheese ton frenon
bulbs	οἱ λάμπες	ee lambes
carburettor	τό καρμπυρατέρ	to karbeerater
clutch	τό ντεμπραγιάζ	to debrayaz
cooling system	τό σύστημα ψύξεως	to seesteema pseekseos
dip switch	ὁ διακόπτης ἀλλαγῆς φώτων	o dheeakoptees alayees foton
distributor	τό ντιστριμπυτέρ	to deestreebeeter
dynamo	τό δυναμό	to dheenamo
electrical system	τό ἡλεκτρικό σύστημα	to eelektreeko seesteema
engine	ἡ μηχανή	ee mekhanee
exhaust pipe	ἡ ἐξάτμιση	ee eksatmeesee
fan	ὁ ἀνεμιστήρας	o anemeesteeras
filter	τό φίλτρο	to feeltro
fuel pump	ἡ ἀντλία βενζίνης/καυσίμου	ee andleea venzeenees/kafseemoo
fuel tank	ἡ δεξαμενή καυσίμου	ee dheksamenee kafseemoo
gears	οἱ ταχύτητες	ee takheeteetes
generator	ἡ γεννήτρια	ee yeneetreea
hand brake	τό χειρόφρενο	to kheerofreno
headlights	τά μεγάλα φῶτα	ta meghala fota
heating system	ἡ θέρμανση	ee thermansee
horn	τό κλάξον	to klakson
ignition	ἡ ἀνάφλεξη	ee anafleksee

indicator	τό φλάς	to **flas**
lubrication system	τό σύστημα λιπάνσεως	to **see**steema lee**pan**seos
points	οἱ πλατίνες	ee plateenes
radiator	τό ψυγεῖο	to pseeyeeo
seat	ἡ θέση	ee thesee
sidelights	τά μικρά φῶτα	ta mee**kra fo**ta
silencer	ὁ σιγαστήρας	o seeghasteeras
sparking plug	τό μπουζί	to boozee
speedometer	τό κοντέρ	to konder
starter motor	ἡ μίζα	ee **mee**za
suspension	ἡ συσπανσιόν	ee seespansyon
transmission	ἡ μετάδοση κινήσεως	ee metadhosee kee**nee**seos
wheels	οἱ ῥόδες	ee **rod**hes
windscreen	τό πάρ-μπρίζ	to par**breez**
windscreen wiper	ὁ ὑαλοκαθαριστήρας	o eealokathar**ee**steeras

A Place to Stay

There are places to stay to suit every budget level in Greece from the great luxury palaces of the beach resorts to modest boarding houses. If you have not booked a hotel in advance, ask at the tourist office of each town. They will help you find a place within your price range. If you don't want to stay at a hotel there are villas and country cottages, camping sites and rooms in private houses. Standards of comfort vary, but hotel prices are controlled.

Hotels and Pensions

Finding a Room

I am travelling with the ... travel agency.	Ταξιδεύω μέ τήν τουριστική έταιρεία ... takseedhevo me teen tooreesteekee etereea
Here is my hotel coupon.	Ὁρίστε τό κουπόνι γιά τό ξενοδοχεῖο μου. oreeste to kooponee ya to ksenodhokheeo moo
My room is already reserved.	Ἔχω κιόλας κλείσει δωμάτιο. ekho kyolas kleesee dhomateeo
I am travelling independently.	ταξιδεύω ἰδιωτικῶς. takseedhevo eedheeoteekos
Will a porter bring my luggage in?	Μπορεῖ ἕνας βοηθός νά φέρει μέσα τίς ἀποσκευές μου; boree enas voeethos na feree mesa tees aposkeves moo
Can I leave my car here?	Μπορῶ ν' ἀφήσω τό αὐτοκίνητό μου ἐδῶ; boro nafeeso to aftokeeneetoo moo edho
Is there a car park?	Ἔχει χῶρο σταθμεύσεως αὐτοκινήτων; ekhee khoro stathmefseos aftokeeneeton

Are you   Εἶστε ἐσεῖς
         eeste esees

     the receptionist/   ὁ (ἡ) ρεσεψιονίστ/θυρωρός/διευθυντής
     concierge/manager?   (διευθύντρια)
         o (ee) resepsyoneest/theeroros/
         dhee-eftheendees (dhee-eftheendreea)

Have you a   Ἔχετε ἕνα
         ekhete ena

     single room/   μονόκλινο δωμάτιο/δίκλινο δωμάτιο/δωμάτιο
     double   μέ τρία κρεββάτια;
     room/three-   monokleeno dhomateeo/**dheek**leeno
     bedded room?   dhomateeo/dhomateeo me **tree**a krevatya

Have you a room   Ἔχετε δωμάτιο
         ekhete dhomateeo

     with two beds?   μέ δύο κρεββάτια;
         με **dhee**o krevatya

     with a double bed?   μέ διπλό κρεββάτι;
         me dhee**plo** krevatee

     with a full-size   μέ μεγάλη μπανιέρα καί χωριστή τουαλέττα;
     bath and separate   me meghalee ban**yera** ke khoree**stee** tooaleta
     toilet?

     with bath or   μέ μπάνιο ἤ ντούς;
     shower?   me banyo ee **doos**

     looking over the   πού βλέπει μπροστά;
     front?   poo vlepee brosta

How much is it   Πόσο κοστίζει
         poso kosteezee

     per day?   τήν ἡμέρα;
         teen eemera

     per week?   τήν ἑβδομάδα;
         teen evdhomadha

     for bed and   γιά δωμάτιο καί πρωϊνό;
     breakfast?   ya dhomateeo ke proee**no**

     for full board?   γιά πλήρη πανσιόν;
         ya pleeree pansy**on**

Is there a reduction   Ἔχει ἔκπτωση
         ekhee ekptosee

for a longer stay/for children?	γιά μακρόχρονη διαμονή/γιά παιδιά; ya makrokhronee dheeamonee/ya pedhya
Are there special mealtimes for children?	Ἔχει εἰδικές ὧρες γιά γεύματα γιά παιδιά; ekhee eedheekes ores ya yevmata ya pedhya
I don't want to pay more than . . . drachmas per day.	Δέν θέλω νά πληρώσω περισσότερο ἀπό . . . δραχμές τήν ἡμέρα. dhen thelo na pleeroso pereesotero apo . . . dhrakhmes teen eemera
Have you anything cheaper?	Ἔχετε τίποτα πιό φθηνό; ekhete teepota pyo ftheeno
Do I have to fill in a visitor's card?	Πρέπει νά συμπληρώσω κάρτα γιά ἐπισκέπτες; prepee na seembleeroso karta ya epeeskeptes
Here is my passport.	Ὁρίστε τό διαβατήριό μου. oreeste to dheeavateereeo moo
How long will you keep it?	Πόσον καιρό θά τό κρατήσετε; poson kero tha to krateesete
I'd like to go up to my room right away.	Θά ἤθελα νά πάω πάνω στό δωμάτιό μου ἀμέσως. tha eethela na pao pano sto dhomateeo moo amesos
Will you send up the luggage?	Μπορεῖτε νά στείλετε πάνω τίς ἀποσκευές μου; boreete na steelete pano tees aposkeves moo
This case is for Room 3 and that one for Number 12.	Αὐτή ἡ βαλίτσα εἶναι γιά τό δωμάτιο Νο 3 καί ἐκείνη γιά τό Νο 12. aftee ee valeetsa eene ya to dhomateeo noomero treea ke ekeenee ya to noomero dhodheka
May I have the room key?	Μπορῶ νά ἔχω τό κλειδί τοῦ δωματίου μου; boro na ekho to kleedhee too dhomateeoo moo
Is the key in the door?	Εἶναι τό κλειδί στήν πόρτα; eene to kleedhee steen porta

Where is the lift? Do I work it myself?	**Ποῦ εἶναι τό ἀσανσέρ; Τό χρησιμοποιῶ μόνος μου;** poo eene to asanser? to khreeseemopeeo monos moo
Is breakfast included?	**Περιλαμβάνεται καί τό πρωϊνό;** pereelamvanete ke to proeeno
Do you do demi pension?	**Κάνετε ντεμί πανσιόν;** kanete demee pansyon
Can I put all extras on my bill?	**Μπορῶ νά βάλω ὅλα τά ἔξτρα στό λογαριασμό;** boro na valo ola ta ekstra sto loghareeazmo
Is there a post box in the hotel?	**Ὑπάρχει γραμματοκιβώτιο στό ξενοδοχεῖο;** eparkhee ghramatokeevoteeo sto ksenodhokheeo
Can you get the daily papers for me?	**Μπορεῖτε νά μοῦ παίρνετε τίς καθημερινές ἐφημερίδες;** boreete na moo pernete tees katheemereenes efeemereedhes

Moving In

This room is too	**Αὐτό τό δωμάτιο εἶναι πολύ** afto to dhomateeo eene polee
small/large/ dark/high up.	**μικρό/μεγάλο/σκοτεινό/ψηλά.** meekro/meghalo/skoteeno/pseela
It is too noisy.	**Ἔχει πολύ θόρυβο.** ekhee polee thoreevo
Haven't you got a double bed?	**Δέν ἔχετε ἕνα διπλό κρεββάτι;** dhen ekhete ena dheeplo krevatee
Please make the twin beds into one double.	**Μπορεῖτε νά βάλετε τά δύο μονά κρεββάτια μαζί;** boreete na valete ta dheeo mona krevatya mazee
I need a child's cot.	**Χρειάζομαι ἕνα κρεββατάκι γιά τό μωρό.** khreeazome ena krevatakee ya to moro

I shall need	**Θά χρειαστῶ**
	tha khreeasto
another pillow/	**καί ἕνα ἄλλο μαξιλλάρι/καί μιά ἄλλη**
another blanket.	**κουβέρτα.**
	ke ena alo makseelaree/ke mya alee kooverta
clothes hangers.	**κρεμάστρες.**
	kremastres
some writing	**χαρτί ἀλληλογραφίας.**
paper.	khartee aleeloghrafeeas

The bedside light is	**Τό πορτατίφ δέν λειτουργεῖ. Ἡ λάμπα κάηκε.**
not working. The	to portateef dhen leetooryee. ee lamba kaeeke
bulb is broken.	

Which is	**Ποιά εἶναι**
	pya eene
the hot tap/cold	**ἡ ζεστή βρύση/κρύα βρύση;**
tap?	ee zestee vreesee/ee kreea vreesee

| Is this the electric | **Εἶναι αὐτή ἡ πρίζα γιά ξυριστική μηχανή;** |
| razor socket? | eene aftee ee preeza ya kseereesteekee meekhanee |

| What is the voltage? | **Πόσα βόλτ εἶναι;** |
| | posa volt eene |

My plug won't fit.	**Ἡ πρίζα μου δέν ταιριάζει. Ἔχετε ἕνα σταυρό;**
Have you an	ee preeza moo dhen tereeazee. ekhete ena stavro
adaptor?	

Is there an	**Ὑπάρχει ἡλεκτρολόγος στό χωριό;**
electrician in the	eeparkhee eelektrologhos sto khoreeo
village?	

| Is there a hotel | **Ὑπάρχει πλυντήριο στό ξενοδοχεῖο;** |
| laundry? | eeparkhee pleendeereeo sto ksenodhokheeo |

Are there facilities	**Ὑπάρχουν εὐκολίες γιά πλύσιμο καί σιδέρωμα**
for washing and	**ρούχων;**
ironing clothes?	eeparkhoon efkoleees ya pleeseemo ke seedheroma rookhon

| The blind is stuck. | **Τό ρολό ἔχει κολλήσει.** |
| | to rolo ekhee koleesee |

Will you bring some drinking water?	**Μπορεῖτε νά μοῦ φέρετε νερό γιά πιόσιμο;** boreete na moo ferete nero ya pyoseemo
Can I leave valuables in the hotel safe?	**Μπορῶ ν' ἀφήσω εἴδη ἀξίας στό χρηματοκιβώτιο τοῦ ξενοδοχείου;** boro nafeeso eedhee akseeas sto khreematokeevoteeo too ksenodhokheeoo
What time is breakfast/ lunch/dinner?	**Τί ὥρα σερβίρεται τό** tee ora serveerete to **πρωϊνό/μεσημερινό/δεῖπνο;** proeeno/meseemereeno/dheepno
Do you serve breakfast in bed?	**Σερβίρετε πρωϊνό στό δωμάτιο;** serveerete proeeno sto dhomateeo
Does the hotel do packed lunches?	**Προετοιμάζετε φαγητό γιά πικνίκ;** proeteemazete fayeeto ya peekneek

Small Hotels and Pensions

Do you have set times for meals?	**Ἔχετε καθορισμένες ὧρες γιά τά γεύματα;** ekhete kathoreezmenes ores ya ta yevmata
May I have a towel and soap?	**Μπορῶ νά ἔχω μία πετσέτα καί σαπούνι;** boro na ekho meea petseta ke sapoonee
At what time do you lock the front door at night?	**Τί ὥρα κλειδώνετε τήν ἐξώπορτα τήν νύχτα;** tee ora kleedhonete teen eksoporta teen neekta
May I have a key?	**Μπορῶ νά ἔχω ἕνα κλειδί;** boro na ekho ena kleedhee
Is it all right to leave the car in the street?	**Εἶναι ἐντάξει ν' ἀφήσω τό αὐτοκίνητο στό δρόμο;** eene endaksee nafeeso to aftokeeneeto sto dhromo
Will our things be safe?	**Θά εἶναι σίγουρα τά πράγματά μας;** tha eene seeghoora ta praghmata mas
Where is the nearest garage?	**Ποῦ εἶναι τό πλησιέστερο γκαράζι;** poo eene to pleeseeestero garazee

Rooms in Private Houses

Do you have a room free?	Ἔχετε ἐλεύθερο δωμάτιο; ekhete elefthero dhomateeo
Do you do breakfast?	Κάνετε πρωϊνό; kanete proeeno
Is there a café nearby?	Ἔχει ἕνα καφέ-μπάρ κοντά; ekhee ena kafebar konda
Would you like me to pay now?	Θέλετε νά πληρώσω τώρα; thelete na pleeroso tora
At what time will it be convenient to use the bathroom?	Τί ὥρα θά εἶναι εὐνοϊκό γιά νά χρησιμοποιήσω τό λουτρό; tee ora tha eene evnoeeko ya na khreeseemopeeeeso to lootro
Do I need to tell you if I have a bath?	Πρέπει νά σᾶς πῶ ἄν θά κάνω μπάνιο; prepee na sas po an tha kano banyo
Could you wake us in the morning?	Μπορεῖτε νά μᾶς ξυπνήσετε τό πρωΐ; boreete na mas kseepneesete to proee
Is there a lounge?	Ὑπάρχει σαλόνι; eeparkhee salonee
Shall I lock my room?	Πρέπει νά κλειδώσω τό δωμάτιό μου; prepee na kleedhoso to dhomateeo moo

Paying the Bill

May I have my bill, please?	Μπορῶ νά ἔχω τό λογαριασμό παρακαλῶ; boro na ekho to loghareeazmo parakalo
Will you prepare my bill for first thing tomorrow?	Μπορεῖτε νά ἔχετε ἕτοιμο τό λογαριασμό μου πρωΐ-πρωΐ αὔριο; boreete na ekhete eteemo to loghareeazmo moo proee proee avreeo
I think there is a mistake.	Νομίζω ὅτι ἔχει γίνει λάθος. nomeezo otee ekhee yeenee lathos

I don't understand this item.	**Δέν καταλαβαίνω τί εἶναι αὐτό ἐδῶ;** **dhen** katalaveno **tee eene** afto edho	
May I pay by cheque?	**Μπορῶ νά πληρώσω μέ τσέκ;** boro na pleeroso me tsek	
I have a Eurocheque card.	**Ἔχω μία κάρτα Eurocheque.** ekho **meea** karta Eurocheque	
Do you accept credit cards?	**Δέχεστε πιστωτικές κάρτες;** **dhe**kheste peestotee**kes** kartes	
Is service included?	**Περιλαμβάνεται τό ποσοστό ὑπηρεσίας;** pereelamvanete to pososto eepeereseeas	
Is VAT (tax) included?	**Περιλαμβάνεται καί ὁ ΦΚΕ (ὁ φόρος);** pereelamvanete ke o **fee** kapa epseelon (o foros)	
May I have a receipt please?	**Μπορῶ νά ἔχω μιά ἀπόδειξη παρακαλῶ;** boro na ekho mya apodheeksee parakalo	
Please forward my mail to this address.	**Μπορεῖτε νά στείλετε τά γράμματά μου σ' αὐτή τή διεύθυνση.** boreete na **stee**lete ta **ghra**mata moo saftee tee dheeeeftheensee	
We have enjoyed ourselves very much.	**Περάσαμε πολύ εὐχάριστα.** perasame polee efkhareesta	
May I have one of your leaflets?	**Μπορῶ νά ἔχω ἕνα φυλλάδιό σας;** boro na ekho ena feeladheeo sas	

VOCABULARY

bar	**τό μπάρ**	to bar
barman	**τό γκαρσόνι**	to garsonee
bed	**τό κρεββάτι**	to krevatee
chair	**ἡ καρέκλα**	ee karekla
chambermaid	**ἡ καμαριέρα**	ee kamareeera
children's playground	**ἡ παιδική χαρά**	ee pedheekee khara
discotheque	**τό ντισκοτέκ**	to deeskotek

door	ἡ πόρτα	ee porta
hall	τό χώλ	to khol
lift	τό ἀσανσέρ	to asanser
light switch	ὁ διακόπτης	o dheeakoptees
lounge	τό σαλόνι	to salonee
luggage porter	ὁ θυρωρός	o theeoros
manager	ὁ διευθυντής	o dhee-eftheendees
mirror	ὁ καθρέπτης	o kathreptees
night club	τό νυκτερινό κέντρο	to neektereeno kendro
playroom	ἡ αἴθουσα	ee ethoosa
	διασκεδάσεως	dheeaskedhaseos
radio	τό ραδιόφωνο	to radheeofono
restaurant	τό ἑστιατόριο	to esteeatoreeo
stairs	ἡ σκάλα	ee skala
swimming pool	ἡ πισίνα	ee peeseena
telephone operator		
(man)	ὁ τηλεφωνητής	o teelefoneetees
(woman)	ἡ τηλεφωνήτρια	ee teelefoneetreea
waiter	ὁ σερβιτόρος	o serveetoros
waitress	ἡ σερβιτόρα	ee serveetora
wardrobe	ἡ ντουλάπα	ee doolapa
window	τό παράθυρο	to paratheero

Catering for Yourself

Villas and Apartments

I have booked	Ἔχω κρατήσει
	ekho krateesee
a villa/an	μιά βίλλα/ἕνα διαμέρισμα.
apartment.	mya veela/ena dheeamereezma
Will you please show me round it?	Μπορεῖτε νά μοῦ δείξετε ποῦ εἶναι ὅλα τά πράγματα;
	boreete na moo dheeksete poo eene ola ta praghmata

Here is my voucher.	Ὁρίστε τήν ἀπόδειξή μου.
	oreeste teen apodheeksee moo
Where is the	Ποῦ εἶναι
	poo eene
light switch/the power point/the fuse box?	ὁ διακόπτης (φωτός)/ἡ πρίζα/τό κιβώτιο ἀσφαλειῶν;
	o dheeakoptees (fotos)/ee preeza/to keevoteeo asfaleeon
Do all the outside doors lock?	Κλειδώνουν ὅλες οἱ ἐξώπορτες;
	kleedhonoon oles ee eksoportes
How do the shutters work?	Πῶς λειτουργοῦν τά παραθυρόφυλλα;
	pos leetoorghoon ta paratheerofeela
How does the hot water system work?	Πῶς λειτουργεῖ τό σύστημα ζεστοῦ νεροῦ;
	pos leetooryee to seesteema zestoo neroo
Where is the mains valve?	Ποῦ εἶναι ὁ κρουνός διακοπῆς;
	poo eene o kroonos dheeakopees
Is there mains gas?	Ὑπάρχει κεντρική παροχή γκαζιοῦ;
	eeparkhee kendreekee parokhee gazyoo
Are gas cylinders delivered?	Διανέμονται μπουκάλες γκαζιοῦ;
	dheeanemonde bookales gazyoo
Is there any domestic help?	Ἔχει οἰκιακή βοήθεια;
	ekhee eekeeakee voeethya
At what time does the house help come?	Τί ὥρα ἔρχεται ἡ οἰκιακή βοηθός;
	tee ora erkhete ee eekeeakee voeethos
Can we have three sets of house keys?	Μπορούμε νά ἔχουμε τρεῖς σειρές κλειδιῶν γιά τό σπίτι;
	boroome na ekhoome trees seeres kleedhyon ya to speetee
When is the rubbish collected?	Πότε παίρνουν τά σκουπίδια;
	pote pernoon ta skoopeedhya
Are the shops near by?	Εἶναι κοντά τά μαγαζιά;
	eene konda ta maghazya

Where is	Πού εἶναι
	poo eene
the bus stop/the station?	ἡ στάσις λεωφορείων/ὁ σταθμός;
	ee stasees leoforeeon/o stathmos

| Have you a map of the area? | Ἔχετε ἕνα χάρτη τῆς περιοχῆς; |
| | ekhete ena khartee tees pereeokhees |

Camping

| Where can we camp for the night? | Πού μπορούμε νά κατασκηνώσουμε ἀπόψε; |
| | poo boroome na kataskeenosoome apopse |

| Have you a site free? | Ἔχετε ἐλεύθερο χῶρο; |
| | ekhete elefthero khoro |

Do you rent	Νοικιάζετε
	neekyazete
bungalows?	μπάνγκαλοου;
	banggalo-oo
tents?	σκηνές;
	skeenes
cooking equipment?	μέσα μαγειρεύματος;
	mesa mayeerevmatos

Are there	Ὑπάρχουν
	eeparkhoon
toilets?	τουαλέττες;
	tooaletes
washing facilities?	εὐκολίες πλυσίματος;
	efkoleees pleeseematos
cooking facilities?	εὐκολίες μαγειρεύματος;
	efkoleees mayeerevmatos

| How much does it cost per night? | Πόσο κοστίζει τή νύχτα; |
| | poso kosteezee tee neekta |

| Can I put my tent here? | Μπορῶ νά στήσω τή σκηνή μου ἐδῶ; |
| | boro na steeso tee skeenee moo edho |

May we put our caravan here?	Μπορούμε νά βάλουμε τό τροχόσπιτό μας ἐδῶ;	boroome na valoome to trokhospeeto mas edho
Is there room for a trailer?	Ἔχει χῶρο γιά μιά ρεμούλκα;	ekhee khoro ya mya remoolka
Is there a night guard?	Ὑπάρχει νυκτοφύλακας;	eeparkhee neektofeelakas
Where is	Ποῦ εἶναι	poo eene
the camp shop?	τό μαγαζί τῆς κατασκηνώσεως;	to maghazee tees kataskeenoseos
the restaurant?	τό ἐστιατόριο;	to esteeatoreeo
the nearest shopping centre?	τά πλησιέστερα καταστήματα;	ta pleeseeestera katasteemata
At what time do I have to vacate the site?	Τί ὥρα πρέπει νά φύγω ἀπ' τόν χῶρο κατασκηνώσεως;	tee ora prepee na feegho apton khoro kataskeenoseos
Where is the drinking tap?	Ποῦ εἶναι ἡ βρύση ποσίμου ὕδατος;	poo eene ee vreesee poseemoo eedhatos

VOCABULARY

barbecue	ἡ ψησταριά	ee pseestareea
basin	ἡ λεκάνη	ee lekanee
bucket	ὁ κουβᾶς	o koovas
camping gas	τό ἐμφιαλωμένο γκάζι	to emfeealomeno gazee
frame tent	ἡ σκηνή μέ σκελετό	ee skeenee me skeleto
grill	ἡ σχάρα	ee skhara
guy ropes	τά σχοινιά στερεώσεως	ta skheenya stereoseos
ice-bucket	τό παγοδοχεῖο	to paghodhokheeo
insecticide	τό ἐντομοκτόνο	to endomoktono
knife	τό μαχαίρι	to makheree

mosquito repellant	ἡ κρέμα γιά τά κουνούπια	ee krema ya ta koonoopya
sleeping bag	τό σλίπινγκ-μπάγκ	to sleepeengg bag
spade	τό φτυάρι	to ftyaree
stove	ἡ γκαζιέρα	ee gazyera
tent	ἡ σκηνή	ee skeenee
tent pegs	οἱ πάσσαλοι σκηνῆς	ee pasalee skeenees
waterproof sheet	ὁ μουσαμᾶς	o moosamas

Youth Hostelling

Is there a youth hostel in this town?	Ἔχει ἕνα ξενώνα νεότητος σ' αὐτή τήν πόλη; ekhee ena ksenona neoteetos saftee teen polee
Have you room for tonight?	Ἔχετε ἄδειο κρεββάτι γιά ἀπόψε; ekhete adhyo krevatee ya apopse
We are members of the Youth Hostels Association.	Εἴμαστε μέλη τοῦ Ὀργανισμοῦ Ξενώνων Νεότητος. eemaste melee too orghaneezmoo ksenonon neoteetos
What are the house rules?	Τί εἶναι οἱ κανόνες τοῦ ξενώνα; tee eene ee kanones too ksenona
How long can we stay?	Πόσον καιρό μποροῦμε νά μείνουμε; poson kero boroome na meenoome
Is there a youth hostel at . . .?	Ὑπάρχει ἕνας ξενώνας νεότητος εἰς . . . ; eeparkhee enas ksenonas neoteetos ees

Eating and Drinking

Though Greece is not a gourmet's paradise, the food is nevertheless very enjoyable – this is evident by the success of Greek restaurants in the cities of Europe. Most dishes are simple but the quality of the ingredients is good, especially the fish and lamb, and the use of fresh herbs gives Greek cooking an aromatic flavour that lingers long in the memory. A Greek meal often consists of a variety of dishes which are all served at the same time and the people round the table will select portions from those dishes which appeal to them.

As in most Mediterranean countries, a meal is a great social occasion with much conversation and gesticulation and restaurants provide an attractive setting in which to get to know something of the Greek people and their way of life.

A restaurant is called an **estiatorio (ἐστιατόριο)** and a simpler eating house goes under the name of **taverna (ταβέρνα).** The frequently encountered oriental type of coffee house is known as a **kaffeneion (καφενεῖο(ν))** and it serves spirits and liqueurs as well as coffee. A pastry shop or tea room is called a **zaharoplasteion (ζαχαροπλαστεῖο(ν))** and here you will find cakes, ice creams, traditional Greek sweetmeats and coffee or other non-alcoholic beverages and even liqueurs and beer. Many of the cafés in tourist resorts serve the usual mineral drinks, tea, coffee, snacks and other items that are international.

Can you recommend	**Μπορεῖτε νά συστήσετε**
	boreete na seesteesete
a good restaurant?	**ἕνα καλό ἐστιατόριο;**
	ena kalo esteeatoreeo
a restaurant that is not too expensive?	**ἕνα ἐστιατόριο πού νά μήν εἶναι πολύ ἀκριβό;**
	ena esteeatoreeo poo na **meen eene** polee akreevo

a typical restaurant of the region?	ἕνα χαρακτηριστικό ἑστιατόριο τῆς περιοχῆς; ena kharakteereesteeko esteeatoreeo tees pereeokhees
a restaurant which serves European (non-Greek) food?	ἕνα ἑστιατόριο πού νά σερβίρει Εὐρωπαϊκό φαγητό; ena esteeatoreeo poo na serveeree evropaeeko fayeeto
Is there a good snack bar nearby?	Ἔχει ἕνα καλό καφέ-μπάρ ἐδῶ κοντά; ekhee ena kalo kafebar edho konda
Where can I find a self-service restaurant?	Ποῦ μπορῶ νά βρῶ ἕνα ἑστιατόριο αὐτοεξυπηρετήσεως; poo boro na vro ena esteeatoreeo aftoekseepeereeteeseos
Do I need to reserve a table?	Πρέπει νά κλείσω ἕνα τραπέζι ἀπό μπροστά; prepee na kleeso ena trapezee apo brosta
I'd like a table for two	Θά ἤθελα ἕνα τραπέζι γιά δύο tha eethela ena trapezee ya dheeo
at nine o'clock.	γιά τίς ἐννέα. ya tees enea
not too near the door.	ὄχι πολύ κοντά στήν πόρτα okhee polee konda steen porta
in the corner.	στή γωνία. stee ghoneea
away from the kitchen.	μακριά ἀπό τήν κουζίνα. makreea apo teen koozeena

At the Restaurant

A table for four, please.	Ἕνα τραπέζι γιά τέσσερα ἄτομα, παρακαλῶ. ena trapezee ya tesera atoma parakalo
Is this our table?	Εἶναι αὐτό τό τραπέζι μας; eene afto to trapezee mas
This table will do fine.	Αὐτό τό τραπέζι εἶναι ἐντάξει. afto to trapezee eene endaksee

The tablecloth is dirty.	**Τό τραπεζομάντηλο εἶναι λερωμένο.** to trapezomandeelo eene leromeno
The table is unsteady.	**Τό τραπέζι δέν εἶναι σταθερό.** to trapezee **dhen** eene stathero
The ashtray is missing.	**Λείπει τό σταχτοδοχεῖο.** leepee to stakhtodhokheeo
May I see the menu?	**Μπορῶ νά δῶ τό τιμολόγιο;** boro na **dho** to teemoloyeeo
We will have an aperitif while we look at it.	**Θά ἔχουμε ἕνα ἀπεριτίφ ἐνῶ κοιτάζουμε στό τιμολόγιο.** tha ekhoome ena apereeteef eno keetazoome sto teemoloyeeo
Please bring the wine list.	**Μπορεῖτε νά μᾶς φέρετε τόν κατάλογο ποτῶν παρακαλῶ;** boreete na mas ferete ton katalogho poton parakalo
Have you a set menu?	**Ἔχετε ἕνα μενού τῆς ἡμέρας;** ekhete ena menoo tees eemeras
What do you recommend today?	**Τί θά συνιστούσατε γιά σήμερα;** tee tha seeneestoosate ya seemera
What does it consist of?	**Ἀπό τί ἀποτελεῖται;** apo tee apoteleete
It sounds good. I'll try it.	**Φαίνεται καλό. Θά τό δοκιμάσω.** fenete kalo. tha to dhokeemaso
The soup is cold. Please warm it up.	**Ἡ σούπα εἶναι κρύα. Μπορεῖτε νά τήν ζεστάνετε παρακαλῶ;** ee soopa eene kreea. boreete na teen zestanete parakalo
This fork is dirty. May I have another one?	**Αὐτό τό πηρούνι δέν εἶναι καθαρό. Μπορῶ νά ἔχω ἕνα ἄλλο;** afto to peeroonee **dhen** eene katharo. boro na ekho ena alo

Will you call our waiter?	**Μπορεῖτε νά καλέσετε τό σερβιτόρο μας;** boreete na kalesete to serveetoro mas
We did not order this.	**Δέν παραγγείλαμε αὐτό.** dhen paranggeelame afto
I'd like to speak to the head waiter.	**Θά ἤθελα νά μιλήσω στόν ἐπί κεφαλῆς σερβιτόρο.** tha eethela na meeleeso ston epee kefalees serveetoro
My compliments to the chef.	**Συγχαρητήρια στό μάγερα.** seengkhareeteereea sto mayera
It's very good.	**Εἶναι πολύ καλό.** eene polee kalo
Have you any house wine?	**Ἔχετε ἕνα συνηθισμένο κρασί εἰδικό γιά τό ἐστιατόριο;** ekhete ena seeneetheezmeno krasee eedheeko ya to esteeatoreeo
I'd like	**Θά ἤθελα** tha eethela
a half bottle/a carafe.	**ἕνα μισό μπουκάλι/μία καράφα.** ena meeso bookalee/meea karafa
Which is the local wine?	**Ποιό εἶναι τό τοπικό κρασί;** pyo eene to topeeko krasee
This wine is corked.	**Αὐτό τό κρασί ἔχει τή γεύση τοῦ φελλοῦ.** afto to krasee ekhee tee yefsee too feloo
The children will share a portion.	**Τά παιδιά θά μοιραστοῦν μία μερίδα.** ta pedhya tha meerastoon meea mereedha
May we have some water?	**Μπορούμε νά ἔχουμε λίγο νερό;** boroome na ekhoome leegho nero
Have you any mineral water?	**Ἔχετε μεταλλικό νερό;** ekhete metaleeko nero
Have you a high chair for the child?	**Ἔχετε ἕνα ψηλό καρεκλάκι γιά τό μικρό;** ekhete ena pseelo kareklakee ya to meekro

Will you please bring some cushions.	**Μπορεῖτε νά μᾶς φέρετε μερικά μαξιλλάρια;** boreete na mas ferete mereeka makseelareea
May I have the bill, please?	**Μοῦ δίνετε τό λογαριασμό παρακαλῶ;** moo dheenete to loghareeazmo parakalo
Is service included?	**Περιλαμβάνεται καί τό ποσοστό ὑπηρεσίας;** pereelamvanete ke to pososto eepeereseeas
Where are the toilets?	**Ποῦ εἶναι οἱ τουαλέττες;** poo eene ee tooaletes

Vᴏᴄᴀʙᴜʟᴀʀʏ

bill	ὁ λογαριασμός	o loghareeazmos
boiled	βραστός	vrastos
cheese	τό τυρί	to teeree
dessert	τό ἐπιδόρπιο, τό γλυκό	to epeedhorpeeo, to ghleeko
fish	τό ψάρι	to psaree
fork	τό πηρούνι	to peeroonee
fried	τηγανητός	teeghaneetos
fruit	τό φροῦτο	to frooto
glass	τό ποτήρι	to poteeree
grilled	τῆς σχάρας	tees skharas
knife	τό μαχαίρι	to makheree
meat	τό κρέας	to kreas
medium	μετρίως ψημένος	metreeos pseemenos
menu	τό τιμολόγιο	to teemoloyeeo
mustard	ἡ μουστάρδα	ee moostardha
napkin	ἡ πετσέτα	ee petseta
oil	τό λάδι	to ladhee
omelette	ἡ ὀμελέττα	ee omeleta
pepper	τό πιπέρι	to peeperee
plate	τό πιάτο	to pyato
rare	μισοψημένος	meesopseemenos
roast	ψητός	pseetos
salad	ἡ σαλάτα	ee salata

salt	τό ἁλάτι	to alatee
soft drink	τό ἀναψυκτικό	to anapseekteeko
soup	ἡ σούπα	ee soopa
spoon	τό κουτάλι	to kootalee
starter	τό ὀρεκτικό, ὁ μεζές	to orekteeko, o mezes
stuffed	γεμιστός	yemeestos
sweet	τό γλυκό	to ghleeko
table	τό τραπέζι	to trapezee
vegetables	τά λαχανικά	ta lakhaneeka
vinegar	τό ξύδι	to kseedhee
water	τό νερό	to nero
well done	καλοψημένος	kalopseemenos
wine	τό κρασί	to krasee
wine list	ὁ κατάλογος ποτῶν	o kataloghos poton

The Menu

Starters

Greek starters are called **Mezedes** (μεζέδες) and they are one of the most delightful items in the Greek meal. Usually at least an hour, if not more, is devoted to the business of eating starters accompanied by wine or Ouzo (οὖζο), an aniseed-tasting drink. Traditionally, the Mezedes are separate from dinner and are eaten at cocktail parties or in tavernas during the early part of the evening and dinner is eaten much later. However, many Greeks eat their Mezedes as starters at home and visitors will find that restaurants serve Mezedes as a kind of hors d'œuvres.

The Mezedes are very varied, consisting of fish, meat, olives or cheese, all in small morsels which can be picked up by hand.

Here are some of them:

Ἀγκινάρες	angeenares	artichokes
Ἀχινοί	akheenee	sea urchins
Ἐλιές	elyes	olives

Καλαμαράκια	kalamarakya	baby squid
Καλαμάρια γεμιστά	kalamareea yemeesta	stuffed squid
Κάστανα μέ κότα	kastana me kota	chestnut and chicken spread
Λουκάνικα	lookaneeka	sausage (generally spiced)
Μελιτζάνα πουρές	meleedzana poores	aubergine purée
Ντολμάδες	dolmadhes	stuffed vine leaves
Σαγανάκι	saghanakee	fried cheese and egg
Σπανακόπιττες	spanakopeetes	spinach puffs
Συκωτάκια	seekotakya	lamb's liver and lemon
Συκωτάκια μέ κρασί	seekotakya me krasee	lamb's liver in wine
Ταραμοσαλάτα	taramosalata	fish roe pâté
Τυρόπιττες	teeropeetes	cheese puffs
Φύλλο	feelo	pastry wafers
Χαβιάρι	khavyaree	caviar

Soups

Greeks enjoy soup and it often forms the main meal in modest households. Meat, chicken or fish is used to make the stock and rice gives the soup body. A typically Greek ingredient is lemon juice, which is put in at the last moment to provide a sharp contrast in flavour to the other ingredients.

Κακαβιά	kakavya	fish soup
Κοτόζουμο	kotozoomo	chicken stock
Κοτόσουπα αὐγολέμονο	kotosoopa avgholemono	chicken and lemon soup
Κρεατόσουπα	kreatosoopa	beef broth
Μαγειρίτσα	mayeereetsa	an Easter soup made with lamb entrails
Τζατζίκι σούπα	dzadzeekee soopa	cucumber soup
Φακή	fakee	lentil soup
Χυλός	kheelos	wheat stock (sometimes with fruit and spices)
Ψαρόζουμο	psarozoomo	fish stock

Fish

The coasts of Greece are rich in fish and in the villages nestling in rocky coves and on the islands you will find plenty of fresh fish which are cooked simply over a charcoal fire and sprinkled with herbs. Among the varieties of fish there are bass, halibut, mackerel, red mullet, sardines, tuna fish and swordfish as well as plenty of shellfish which thrive among the rocks.

Γαρίδες γκρατέν	ghareedhes graten	prawns au gratin
Γαρίδες μέ σπανάκι	ghareedhes me spanakee	prawns and spinach
Καλαμαράκια τηγανητά	kalamarakya teeghaneeta	fried squid
'Οκταπόδι κρασάτο	oktapodhee krasato	octopus in wine
Ταραμοκεφτέδες	taramokeftedhes	fish roe cakes
Ψάρια τηγανητά	psareea teeghaneeta	fried fish
Ψάρι πλακί	psaree plakee	baked fish
Ψάρι τῆς σχάρας	psaree tees skharas	grilled fish

Meat

'Αρνί μέ κριθαράκι γιουβέτσι	arnee me kreetharakee yoovetsee	lamb with small pasta
'Αρνί μπούτι τοῦ φούρνου	arnee bootee too foornoo	roast leg of lamb
Γιαπράκια μέ γιαούρτι	yaprakya me yaoortee	stuffed vine leaves with yoghourt
Γιουβαρλάκια	yoovarlakya	rice meatballs
Κεφτέδες	keftedhes	meatballs
Κρέας μέ ρύζι	kreas me reezee	meat and rice mould
Κρεατόπιττες	kreatopeetes	meat pasties
Μοσχάρι κρασί	moskharee krasee	veal and wine casserole
Μοσχάρι ψητό	moskharee pseeto	roast veal
Μουσακᾶς	moosakas	moussaka (meat and aubergine pie)
Παστίτσιο	pasteetsyo	macaroni and meat
Πιπεριές καί ντομάτες γεμιστές	peeperyes ke domates yemeestes	stuffed peppers and tomatoes

Σουβλάκια	soovlakya	kebabs
Στιφάδο	steefadho	meat stew
Χοιρινό ψητό	kheereeno pseeto	roast pork

Vegetables

Αγκινάρες βραστές	angeenares vrastes	boiled artichokes
Κουνουπίδι αλά Μακεδονικά	koonoopeedhee ala makedhoneeka	cauliflower Macedonian style
Μελιτζάνα τηγανητή	meleedzana teeghaneetee	fried aubergine
Ντοματοσαλάτα	domatosalata	tomato salad
Πιπεριές ορεκτικά	peepereees orekteeka	marinated pepper salad
Σπανακόρυζο	spanakoreezo	spinach with rice
Φασολάκια	fasolakya	french beans

Sauces

Αυγολέμονο	avgholemono	The most famous of all Greek sauces made with egg and lemon
Καυτερό βούτυρο	kaftero vooteero	brown butter sauce
Κοπανιστή γιά σαλάτα	kopaneestee ya salata	cheese salad dressing
Λαδόξυδο	ladhokseedho	French dressing
Σκορδαλιά	skordhalya	garlic sauce

Chicken

Κότα καπαμά	kota kapama	spiced chicken
Κότα μεθυσμένη	kota meetheezmenee	chicken with brandy and cream sauce
Κότα πιλάφι	kota peelafee	chicken pilaf
Κότα σουσάμι	kota soosamee	chicken with sesame seeds
Κοτόπιττα	kotopeeta	chicken pie
Κοτόπουλο ψητό	kotopoolo pseeto	roast chicken

Sweets

Γαλατομπούρεκα	ghalatobooreka	custard pastries
Κάστανα πουρέ	kastana poore	chestnut purée
Κουραμπιέδες	koorambyedhes	castor-sugared shortcakes with nuts
Κρέμα σοκολάτα	krema sokolata	chocolate mousse
Λουκουμάδες	lookoomadhes	honey fritters
Μελομακάρουνα	melomakaroona	nut and honey shortcakes
Μπακλαβάς	baklavas	nut and syrup pastry
Χαλβάς	khalvas	almond or pine nut slice

Drinks

Wine

The wines of Greece have a very distinctive flavour, especially the Retsina (ρετσίνα) wines whose resin flavour takes some getting used to.

There is only one really Greek aperitif and this is Ouzo, an aniseed-tasting liquor which, when diluted with water, turns cloudy, not unlike the French Pernod.

The Greeks also make liqueurs. These are similar to the world-famous types such as crème de menthe, Cointreau, etc., and they make a pleasant ending to a meal. There are also brandies called Metaxa and Cambas.

In Cyprus there are several local dinner wines, similar in type to Greek wines but lighter in character. One of these is named Otello, perhaps to commemorate the fact that the Moor of Venice resided on the island.

I'd like a glass of	**Θά ἤθελα ἕνα ποτήρι** tha eethela ena poteeree
red wine/white wine.	**κόκκινο κρασί/ἄσπρο κρασί.** kokeeno krasee/aspro krasee

Is there a local wine?	Ὑπάρχει κανένα τοπικό κρασί;	
	eeparkhee kanena topeeko krasee	
Two beers, please.	Δύο μπύρες παρακαλῶ.	
	dheeo beeres parakalo	
I would like to try an Ouzo.	Θά ἤθελα νά δοκιμάσω ἕνα οὖζο.	
	tha eethela na dhokeemaso ena oozo	
Will you bring a Dubonnet, please?	Δῶστε μου ἕνα Ντυμπονέ, παρακαλῶ.	
	dhoste moo ena deebone parakalo	
with ice and lemon.	μέ παγάκια καί λεμόνι.	
	me paghakya ke lemonee	
I'd like a Scotch	Θά ἤθελα ἕνα οὐΐσκυ	
	tha eethela ena ooeeskee	
with ice.	μέ παγάκια.	
	me paghakya	
with soda water.	μέ σόδα.	
	me sodha	
with plain water.	μέ νερό.	
	me nero	
Have you any non-alcoholic drinks?	Ἔχετε μή οἰνοπνευματώδη ποτά;	
	ekhete **mee** eenopnevmatodhee pota	

VOCABULARY

beer	ἡ μπύρα	ee beera
bottle	τό μπουκάλι	to bookalee
brandy	τό κονιάκ	to konyak
cider	ὁ μηλίτης	o meeleetees
gin	τό τζίν	to tzeen
glass	τό ποτήρι	to peteeree
lager	τό λάγκερ	to lager
lemon	τό λεμόνι	to lemonee
lime	τό μοσχολέμονο	to moskholemono
orange	τό πορτοκάλι	to portokalee

rum	τό ρούμι	to roomee
sherry	τό σέρρυ	to seree
dry/medium/	ὄχι γλυκό/	okhee ghleeko/
sweet	μέτριο/γλυκό	metreeo/ghleeko
soda	ἡ σόδα	ee sodha
vermouth	τό βερμούτ	to vermoot
vodka	ἡ βότκα	ee votka
whisky	τό οὐΐσκυ	to ooeeskee

Soft Drinks

May we have	Μπορούμε νά ἔχουμε	boroome na ekhoome
a pot of tea?	μία τσαγιέρα τσάϊ,	meea tsayera tsaee
a lemon tea?	ἕνα τσάϊ μέ λεμόνι;	ena tsaee me lemonee
a coffee with a drop of milk?	ἕνα καφέ μέ λίγο γάλα;	ena kafe me leegho ghala
a coffee with milk?	ἕνα καφέ μέ γάλα;	ena kafe me ghala
a coffee with cream?	ἕνα καφέ μέ κρέμα;	ena kafe me krema
a black coffee?	ἕνα καφέ χωρίς γάλα;	ena kafe khorees ghala
an iced coffee?	παγωμένο καφέ;	paghomeno kafe
a Greek (Turkish) coffee?	ἕνα Ἑλληνικό (Τουρκικό) καφέ;	ena eleeneeko (toorkeeko) kafe
sweet/medium/ without sugar?	γλυκό/μέτριο/σκέτο (χωρίς ζάχαρη);	ghleeko/metreeo/sketo (khorees zakharee)
Have you	Ἔχετε	ekhete
any lemonade?	λεμονάδα;	lemonadha

Have you	Ἔχετε
	ekhete
a long, cool drink with plenty of ice?	ἕνα μεγάλο παγωμένο ἀναψυκτικό μέ πολλά παγάκια;
	ena meghalo paghomeno anapseekteeko me pola paghakya
an orange juice with soda water?	ἕνα χυμό πορτοκαλιοῦ μέ σόδα;
	ena kheemo portokalyoo me sodha
a glass of cold milk?	ἕνα ποτήρι κρύο γάλα;
	ena poteeree kreeo ghala
Have you a straw?	Ἔχετε ἕνα καλαμάκι;
	ekhete ena kalamakee
Do you make milk shakes?	Κάνετε φραπέ γάλακτος;
	kanete frape ghalaktos
Have you a bottle with a screw top?	Ἔχετε ἕνα μπουκάλι μέ βιδωτό βούλωμα;
	ekhete ena bookalee me veedhoto vooloma

Vocabulary

chocolate	ἡ σοκολάτα	ee sokolata
cup	τό φλυτζάνι	to fleedzanee
fruit juice	ὁ χυμός φρούτων	o kheemos frooton
ginger ale	ἡ τζιτζιμπύρα	ee dzeedzeebeera
mineral water	τό μεταλλικό νερό	to metaleeko nero
syphon	τό σιφόνι	to seefonee
tonic	τό τόνικ	to toneek
tumbler	τό μεγάλο ποτήρι	to meghalo poteeree

Shopping

Buying Food

Eating out is fun but so is buying food in the various types of food shops and markets. Greeks set great store by freshness and quality, and buying food is an important operation involving much discussion about the product.

At the Butcher's

What kind of meat is that?	**Τί εἶδος κρέατος εἶναι αὐτό;** tee eedhos kreatos eene afto
What do you call that cut?	**Πῶς λέγεται αὐτό τό κομμάτι τό κρέας;** pos leyete afto to komatee to kreas
I'd like some steaks please.	**Θά ἤθελα μερικά μπιφτέκια παρακαλῶ.** tha eethela mereeka beeftekya parakalo
How much does that weigh?	**Τί βάρος ἔχει αὐτό;** tee varos ekhee afto
Will you please trim off the fat?	**Μπορεῖτε νά κόψετε τό λίπος παρακαλῶ;** boreete na kopsete to leepos parakalo
Will you take the meat off the bone?	**Μπορεῖτε νά βγάλετε τά κόκκαλα παρακαλῶ;** boreete na vghalete ta kokala parakalo
Will you mince it?	**Μοῦ τό κάνετε κιμά παρακαλῶ;** moo to kanete keema parakalo
Please slice it	**Παρακαλῶ νά τό κόψετε σέ** parakalo na to kopsete se
very fine/thick.	**πολύ λεπτές φέτες/χοντρές φέτες.** polee leptes fetes/khondres fetes
Will you chine the cutlets?	**Βγάζετε τά κόκκαλα ἀπ' τίς μπριζόλες παρακαλῶ;** vghazete ta kokala aptees breezoles parakalo

I'll have a little more.	**Θά ἔχω λίγο περισσότερο.**	
	tha ekho leegho pereesotero	
That's too much.	**Αὐτό εἶναι πάρα πολύ.**	
	afto eene para polee	
Put it in a plastic bag, please.	**Νά τό βάλετε σέ μιά πλαστική σακκούλα, παρακαλῶ.**	
	na to valete se mya plasteekee sakoola parakalo	
Cut it in cubes.	**Νά τό κόψετε σέ τετραγωνικά κομμάτια.**	
	na to kopsete se tetraghoneeka komatya	

Vocabulary

bacon	**τό μπέϊκον**	to beeekon
beef	**τό βοδινό**	to vodheeno
steak	**τό μπιφτέκι**	to beeftekee
fillet	**τό φιλέτο**	to feeleto
brains	**τά μυαλά**	ta myala
butcher	**ὁ χασάπης**	o khasapees
cooking fat	**ἡ λάρδα**	ee lardha
cutlet	**ἡ μπριζόλα**	ee breezola
escalope	**ἡ κοτολέττα**	ee kotoleta
kidneys	**τά νεφρά**	ta nefra
lamb — shoulder/leg	**τό ἀρνίσιο — ἡ ὠμοπλάτη/τό μπούτι**	to arneesyo — ee omoplatee/to bootee
liver	**τό συκώτι**	to seekotee
pig's trotters	**τά χοιρινά ποδαράκια**	ta kheereena podharakya
pork chops	**οἱ χοιρινές μπριζόλες**	ee kheereenes breezoles
pork, leg of	**τό χοιρινό — τό μπούτι**	to kheereeno — to bootee
sausages	**τά λουκάνικα**	ta lookaneeka
stewing beef	**τό βοδινό κατσαρόλας**	to vodheeno katsarolas
sweetbreads	**τά ἀχαμνά**	ta akhamna
tongue	**ἡ γλῶσσα**	ee ghlosa
veal	**τό μοσχαρίσιο**	to moskhareesyo

At the Fishmonger's

Will you clean the fish?	**Μπορεῖτε νά καθαρίσετε τό ψάρι;** boreete na kathareesete to psaree
Leave/take off	**᾽Αφῆοστε/κόψετε** afeeste/kopsete
the head/tail/fins.	**τό κεφάλι/τήν οὐρά/τά πτερύγια.** to kefalee/teen oora/ta ptereeyeea
Have you any shellfish?	**Ἔχετε θαλασσινά;** ekhete thalaseena
What is the name of that fish?	**Πῶς λέγεται αὐτό τό ψάρι;** pos leyete afto to psaree

VOCABULARY

anchovies	οἱ ἀντσούγιες	ee andzooyes
bass	τό λαβράκι	to lavrakee
carp	ὁ κυπρῖνος	o keepreenos
cod	ὁ βακαλάος	o vakalaos
crab	τό καβούρι	to kavooree
crayfish	ἡ καραβίδα	ee karaveedha
eel	τό χέλι	to khelee
fishmonger	ὁ ψαροπώλης	o psaropolees
herring	ἡ ρέγγα	ee rengga
lobster	ὁ ἀστακός	o astakos
mullet (grey)	ὁ κέφαλος	o kefalos
mullet (red)	τό μπαρμπούνι	to barboonee
mussels	τά μύδια	ta meedhya
octopus	τό χταπόδι	to khtapodhee
oysters	τά στρείδια	ta streedhya
perch	ἡ πέρκη	ee perkee
plaice	ἡ γλῶσσα	ee ghlosa
prawns	οἱ γαρίδες	ee ghareedhes
salmon	ὁ σολομός	o solomos
sardines	οἱ σαρδέλλες	ee sardheles

sole	ἡ γλῶσσα	ee ghlosa
squid	τό καλαμάρι	to kalamaree
trout	ἡ πέστροφα	ee pestrofa
tuna fish	ὁ τόννος	o tonos
turbot	τό καλκάνι	to kalkanee
whitebait	οἱ μαρίδες	ee mareedhes

At the Delicatessen/Grocer's

What kind of sausages have you got?	Τί εἴδους λουκάνικα ἔχετε; tee eedhoos lookaneeka ekhete
I'd like	Θά ἤθελα tha eethela
a mild one/a peppery one/one without garlic.	ἕνα ὄχι πολύ πιπεράτο/ἕνα πιπεράτο/ἕνα χωρίς σκόρδο. ena okhee polee peeperato/ena peeperato/ena khorees skordho
May I see your selection of pâtés?	Μπορῶ νά δῶ τή συλλογή σας ἀπό πατέ παρακαλῶ; boro na dho tee seeloyee sas apo pate parakalo
I prefer	Προτιμῶ proteemo
a coarse pâté/smooth pâté/game pâté.	ἕνα χοντροκομμένο/ἕνα λεπτό/ἕνα ἀπό θήραμα. ena khondrokhomeno/ena lepto/ena apo theerama
What is the name of that cheese?	Πῶς λέγεται αὐτό τό τυρί; pos leyete afto to teeree
Have you any goat's cheese?	Ἔχετε γιδίσιο τυρί; ekhete yeedheesyo teeree
Do I have to take the whole cheese or will you cut it?	Πρέπει νά τό πάρω ἀκέραιο ἤ μπορεῖτε νά τό κόψετε; prepee na to paro akereo ee boreete na to kopsete

May I test it for ripeness?	Ἐπιτρέπεται νά δῶ ἄν εἶναι ὥριμο;	epeetrepete na **dho** an **eene** oreemo
Have you any	Ἔχετε	ekhete
sweet biscuits/plain biscuits?	γλυκά μπισκότα/γαλέτες;	**ghleeka** bee**skota**/gha**letes**
Do you sell breakfast cereals?	Πουλᾶτε δημητριακά προϊόντα γιά πρόγευμα;	poo**late** dheemeetree**aka** pro**eeonda** ya pro**yevma**
I'll take a little of each salad.	Θά ἔχω λίγο ἀπό κάθε σαλάτα.	tha **ekho leegho** apo **kathe** sa**lata**
Have you a tube of tomato purée?	Ἔχετε ἕνα σωληνάκι ντοματοπολτό;	**ekhete ena** solee**nakee** domato**polto**
Have you a jar of olives?	Ἔχετε ἕνα βαζάκι ἐλιές;	**ekhete ena** va**zakee** el**yes**

VOCABULARY

biscuits	τά μπισκότα	ta bee**skota**
bread	τό ψωμί	to pso**mee**
brush	ἡ βούρτσα	ee **voortsa**
butter	τό βούτυρο	to **vooteero**
cereals	τά δημητριακά προϊόντα γιά πρόγευμα	ta dheemeetree**aka** pro**eeonda** ya pro**yevma**
cheese	τό τυρί	to tee**ree**
chitterlings	τά ἐντόσθια	ta en**dostheea**
chocolate	ἡ σοκολάτα	ee soko**lata**
cleaning fluid	τό ὑγρό γιά καθάρισμα	to **eeghro** ya katha**reezma**
coffee	ὁ καφές	o ka**fes**
crisps	τά πατατάκια	ta pata**takya**
detergent	τό ἀπορρυπαντικό	to aporeepan**deeko**
disinfectant	τό ἀπολυμαντικό	to apoleeman**deeko**

dried fruit	οἱ ξηροί καρποί	ee kseeree karpee
duster	τό ξεσκονόπανο	to kseskonopano
eggs	τά αὐγά	ta avgha
flour	τό ἀλεύρι	to alevree
garlic sausage	τό σαλάμι μέ σκόρδο	to salamee me skordho
grocer	ὁ παντοπώλης	o pandopolees
ham	τό ζαμπόν	to zambon
herbs	τά μπαχαρικά	ta bakhareeka
jam	ἡ μαρμελάδα	ee marmeladha
macaroni	τά μακαρόνια	ta makaronya
margarine	ἡ μαργαρίνη	ee marghareenee
matches	τά σπίρτα	ta speerta
milk	τό γάλα	to ghala
mustard	ἡ μουστάρδα	ee moostardha
oil	τό λάδι	to ladhee
olives	οἱ ἐλιές	ee elyes
paper napkins	οἱ χαρτοπετσέτες	ee khartopetsetes
pepper	τό πιπέρι	to peeperee
pickles	τά τουρσιά	ta toorsya
salt	τό ἀλάτι	to alatee
smoked fish	τό καπνιστό ψάρι	to kapneesto psaree
spaghetti	τό σπαγέτο	to spayeto
sugar	ἡ ζάχαρη	ee zakharee
tea	τό τσάι	to tsaee
tinned food	ἡ κονσέρβα	ee konserva
vinegar	τό ξύδι	to kseedhee
washing powder	ἡ σκόνη πλυσίματος	ee skonee pleeseematos

CHEESES

τό κασέρι	to kaseree	a firm, golden cheese
ἡ κεφαλογραβιέρα	ee kefaloghravyera	a Cretan cheese, something like gruyère
τό κεφαλοτύρι	to kefaloteeree	a hard cheese used for grating
ἡ κοπανιστή	ee kopaneestee	peppery-flavoured blue mould cheese

ἡ φέτα	ee feta	a salted, white, soft crumbly cheese made from ewe's or cow's milk. The best-known Greek cheese.

At the Greengrocer and Fruiterer's

Is the melon ripe?
Εἶναι ὥριμο τό πεπόνι;
eene oreemo to peponee

How many will make a kilo?
Πόσα θά κάνουν ἕνα κιλό;
posa tha kanoon ena keelo

It's for eating
today/
tomorrow.
Εἶναι γιά νά τό φᾶμε
eene ya na to fame
σήμερα/αὔριο.
seemera/avreeo

Will you please weigh this bunch?
Ζυγίζετε αὐτό τό μάτσο παρακαλῶ;
zeeyeezete afto to matso parakalo

This lettuce is rather limp.
Αὐτό τό μαρούλι εἶναι μαραμένο.
afto to maroolee eene marameno

Are these apples crisp?
Εἶναι αὐτά τά μῆλα κριτσανιστά;
eene afta ta meela kreetsaneesta

Have you got a stronger bag?
Ἔχετε μιά τσάντα πιό γερή;
ekhete mya tsanda pyo yeree

I will put it in my carrier.
Θά τό βάλω στή δική μου τσάντα.
tha to valo stee dheekee moo tsanda

Have you got a box?
Ἔχετε ἕνα χαρτοκούτι;
ekhete ena khartokootee

Vocabulary

almonds	τά ἀμύγδαλα	ta ameeghdhala
apples	τά μῆλα	ta meela
apricots	τά βερίκοκα	ta vereekoka
artichokes	οἱ ἀγκινάρες	ee anggeenares
asparagus	τά σπαράγγια	ta sparanggya
aubergines	οἱ μελιτζάνες	ee meleetzanes
avocado	τό ἀβοκάντο	to avokado
banana	ἡ μπανάνα	ee banana
beetroot	τό κοκκινογοῦλι	to kokeenoghoolee
blackberries	τά βατόμουρα	ta vatomoora
cabbage	ἡ μάπα	ee mapa
cauliflower	τό κουνουπίδι	to koonoopeedhee
celery	τό σέλινο	to seleeno
cherries	τά κεράσια	ta kerasya
chestnuts	τά κάστανα	ta kastana
courgettes	τά κολοκυθάκια	ta kolokeethakya
cress	τό νεροκάρδαμο	to nerokardhamo
cucumber	τό ἀγγούρι	to anggooree
dates	οἱ χουρμάδες	ee khoormadhes
figs	τά σῦκα	ta seeka
garlic	τό σκόρδο	to skordho
grapefruit	ἡ φράπα	ee frapa
grapes	τά σταφύλια	ta stafeelya
greengages	οἱ πράσινες μπουρνέλλες	ee praseenes boorneles
hazel nuts	τά φουντούκια	ta foondookya
leeks	τά πράσα	ta prasa
lemons	τά λεμόνια	ta lemonya
lettuce	τό μαρούλι	to maroolee
melon	τό πεπόνι	to peponee
mushrooms	τά μανιτάρια	ta maneetareea
nuts	οἱ ξηροί καρποί	ee kseeree karpee
onions	τά κρεμμύδια	ta kremeedhya
oranges	τά πορτοκάλια	ta portokalya
peaches	τά ροδάκινα	ta rodhakeena
pears	τά ἀχλάδια	ta akhladhya

peppers		ee peepereees
pineapple		o ananas
plums	τά δαμάσκηνα	ta dhamaskeena
potatoes	οἱ πατάτες	ee patates
radishes	τά ρεπανάκια	ta repanakya
raspberries	τά σμέουρα	ta zmeoora
spinach	τό σπανάκι	to spanakee
strawberries	οἱ φράουλες	ee fraooles
sweet corn	ἡ κούκλα, τό καλαμπόκι	ee kookla, to kalambokee
tangerines	τά μανταρίνια	ta mandareenya
tomatoes	οἱ ντομάτες	ee domates
turnip	τό γογγύλι	to ghonggeelee

Other Shops

Although you will not find high fashion in Greece, there are many traditional craftsmen producing attractive goods. In clothes look out for leather coats and jackets, also furs. In jewellery you will find the echoes of ancient designs and for something really inexpensive but original buy the Greek worry beads found in most shops. Handwoven bags, skirts and waistcoats abound and so do pottery and copper coffee pots.

I want to go shopping.	Θέλω νά πάω γιά ψώνια.	thelo na pao ya psonya
Where are the best shops?	Ποῦ εἶναι τά καλύτερα μαγαζιά;	poo eene ta kaleetera maghazya
the shops where everyone goes?	τά μαγαζιά ὅπου ψωνίζουν ὅλοι;	ta maghazya opoo psoneezoon olee
the cheaper shops?	τά φθηνότερα μαγαζιά;	ta ftheenotera maghazya
Where is the market?	Ποῦ εἶναι ἡ ἀγορά;	poo eene ee aghora

What time do you
close?

Τί ὥρα κλείνετε;
tee ora kleenete

Is there a grocer near
here?

Ἔχει ἕνα παντοπωλείο ἐδῶ κοντά;
ekhee ena pandopoleeo edho konda

VOCABULARY

antique shop	τό μαγαζί γιά ἀντίκες	to maghazee ya antekes
art gallery	ἡ πινακοθήκη	ee peenakotheekee
baker's	τό ἀρτοπωλείο	to artopoleeo
bank	ἡ τράπεζα	ee trapeza
beauty salon	τό ἰνστιτοῦτο καλλονῆς	to eenstectooto kalonees
bookshop	τό βιβλιοπωλείο	to veevleeopoleeo
butcher's	τό κρεοπωλείο	to kreopoleeo
chemist's	τό φαρμακείο	to farmakeeo
confectionery	τό ζαχαροπλαστείο	to zakharoplasteeo
dairy	τό γαλακτοπωλείο	to ghalaktopoleeo
delicatessen	τό μαγαζί γιά σπεσιαλιτέ	to maghazee ya speseealeetee
department store	τό κατάστημα μέ διάφορα τμήματα πωλήσεως	to katasteema me dheeafora tmeemata poleesees
dry cleaner's	τό στεγνοκαθαριστήριο	to steghnokatharesteereeo
fishmonger's	τό ἰχθυοπωλείο	to eekhtheeopoleeo
greengrocer's	τό μανάβικο	to manaveeko
grocer's	τό παντοπωλείο	to pandopoleeo
hairdresser's (men's)	τό κουρείο	to kooreeo
hairdresser's (women's)	τό κομμωτήριο	to komoteereeo
hardware store	τό μαγαζί μέ σιδερικά εἴδη	to maghazee me seedhereeka eedhee
jeweller's	τό κοσμηματοπωλείο	to kozmeematopoleeo
newsagent	ὁ ἐφημεριδοπώλης	o efeemereedhopolees
optician	ὁ ὀπτικός	o opteekos

photographer	ὁ φωτογράφος	o fotohrafos
shoemaker	ὁ ὑποδηματοποιός	o eepodheematopeeos
shoe repairer	ὁ τσαγκάρης	o tsagarees
shoe shop	τό κατάστημα	to katasteema
	ὑποδημάτων	eepodhoeematon
stationer's	τό χαρτοπωλεῖο	to khartopoleeo
supermarket	τό σουπερμάρκετ	to soopermarket
tailor	ὁ ράφτης	o raftees
tobacconist	ὁ καπνοπώλης	o kapnopolees
toy shop	τό κατάστημα	to katasteema
	παιχνιδιῶν	pekhneedhyon
travel agent's	τό γραφεῖο ταξιδίων	to ghrafeeo takseedheeon
watchmaker	ὁ ὡρολογοποιός	o orologhopeeos
wine merchant's	τό οἰνοπωλεῖο	to eenopoleeo

Buying Clothes

I am just looking, thank you.	Ἁπλῶς κοιτάζω, εὐχαριστῶ. aplos keetazo, efkhareesto
I would like to look at some shirts	Θά ἤθελα νά δῶ μερικά πουκάμισα. tha eethela na **dho** mereeka pookameesa
plain/coloured/ striped.	μονόχρωμα/χρωματιστά/ριγέ. monokhroma/khromateesta/reeye
with long sleeves/short sleeves.	μέ μακριά μανίκια/μέ κοντά μανίκια. me makreea maneekya/me konda maneekya
in cotton.	βαμβακερά. vamvakera
My size is . . .	Τό νούμερό μου εἶναι . . . to **noo**mero moo **ee**ne
My collar/ waist/chest/hip size is . . .	Ὁ λαιμός/ἡ μέση/τό στῆθος/οἱ γοφοί μου εἶναι . . . πόντοι. o lemos/ee mesee/to steethos/ee ghofee moo eene . . . pondee

This colour does not suit me.	**Αὐτό τό χρῶμα δέν μοῦ πάει.**
	afto to **khroma dhen** moo paee
Have you something	**Ἔχετε κάτι**
	ekhete **katee**
in red/in wool?	**σέ κόκκινο/μάλλινο;**
	se **kokeeno/maleeno**
It is not my style.	**Δέν εἶναι τοῦ γούστου μου.**
	dhen eene too ghoostoo moo
I want something more casual.	**Θέλω κάτι πιό πρόχειρο.**
	thelo katee pyo prokheero
Is there a fitting room where I can try it on?	**Ἔχει μία αἴθουσα ὅπου νά τό προβάρω;**
	ekhee **meea** ethoosa opoo boro na to provaro
Can I return it if it is unsuitable?	**Μπορῶ νά τό ἐπιστρέψω ἅμα δέν μοῦ ταιριάζει;**
	boro na to epeestrepso ama **dhen** moo tereeazee
May I have a receipt?	**Μπορῶ νά ἔχω μιά ἀπόδειξη;**
	boro na ekho mya **apodheeksee**
It does not fit. It is too	**Δέν μοῦ ἔρχεται. Εἶναι πολύ**
	dhen moo erkhete. eene polee
large/small/narrow/wide.	**μεγάλο/μικρό/στενό/φαρδύ.**
	meghalo/meekro/steno/fardhee
Can you show me something else?	**Μπορεῖτε νά μοῦ δείξετε κανένα ἄλλο;**
	boreete na moo **dheeksete** kanena alo
The zip is	**Τό φερμουάρ εἶναι**
	to fermooar eene
stuck/broken.	**κολλημένο/χαλασμένο.**
	koleemeno/khalazmeno

VOCABULARY

MATERIALS

camel hair	τό καμηλόμαλλο	to kameelomalo
chiffon	τό σιφφόν	to seefon
cotton	τό βαμβάκι	to vamvakee
crepe	τό κρέπ	to krep
denim	τό ντενίμ, τό χοντρό βαμβακερό	to deneem, to khondro vamvakero
felt	ή τσόχα	ee tsokha
flannel	ή φανέλλα	ee fanela
gabardine	ή γκαμπαρντίνα	ee gabardeena
lace	ή δαντέλλα	ee dhandela
leather	τό δέρμα	to dherma
linen	τό λινό	to leeno
nylon	τό νάϋλον	to naeelon
pique	ὁ πικές	o peekes
poplin	ή ποπλίνα	ee popleena
rayon	τό ραιγιόν	to reyon
satin	τό σατέν	to saten
silk	τό μετάξι	to metaksee
suede	τό καστόρι	to kastoree
taffeta	ὁ ταφτᾶς	o taftas
tweed	τό τουήντ	to tooeed
velour	τό μάλλινο βελοῦδο	to maleeno veloodho
velvet	τό βελοῦδο	to veloodho
wool	τό μαλλί	to malee
worsted	τό μάλλινο ὕφασμα πενιέ	to maleeno eefazma penye

MEASUREMENTS

arm	τό μανίκι	to maneekee
chest	τό στῆθος	to steethos
hips	οἱ γοφοί	ee ghofee
leg	τό σκέλος	to skelos
length	τό μάκρος	to makros

| neck | ὁ λαιμός | o lemos |
| waist | ἡ μέση | ee mesee |

COLOURS

beige	μπέζ	bez
biscuit	ἀνοικτό καφέ	aneekto kafe
black	μαῦρο	mavro
blue	μπλέ	ble
brown	καφέ	kafe
green	πράσινο	praseeno
grey	γκρί	gree
mauve	μώβ	mov
pastel colours	τά ἀπαλά χρώματα	ta apala khromata
orange	πορτοκαλί	portokalee
red	κόκκινο	kokeeno
rose	ρός	roz
strong colours	τά ζωηρά χρώματα	ta zoeera khromata
violet	βιολεττί	vyoletee
white	ἄσπρο, λευκό	aspro, lefko
yellow	κίτρινο	keetreeno

ITEMS OF CLOTHING

anorak	τό ἀδιάβροχο μέ κουκούλα	to adhyavrokho me kookoola
bathing hat	τό σκουφί γιά τό κολύμπι	to skoofee ya to koleembee
bathrobe	τό μπουρνούζι	to boornoozee
belt	ἡ ζώνη	ee zonee
blazer	τό σακκάκι σπόρ	to sakakee spor
blouse	ἡ μπλούζα	ee blooza
boots	οἱ μπότες	ee botes
bra	τό σουτιέν	to sootyen
briefs	ἡ κυλότα	ee keelota
buckle	ἡ ἀγκράφα	ee agrafa
button	τό κουμπί	to koombee
cap	ὁ σκοῦφος	o skoofos

cardigan	ἡ πλεκτή ζακέτα	ee plektee zaketa
coat (top)	τό παλτό	to palto
dinner jacket	τό σμόκιν	to zmokeen
dress	τό φόρεμα	to forema
dressing gown	ἡ ρόμπα	ee roba
elastic	τό λάστιχο	to lasteekho
girdle	ὁ κορσές	o korses
gloves	τά γάντια	ta ghandya
gym shoes	τά παπούτσια ἀπό καουτσούκ	ta papootsya apo kaootsook
handkerchief	τό μαντήλι	to mandeelee
hat	τό καπέλλο	to kapelo
hook and eye	ἡ κόπιτσα	ee kopeetsa
jacket (men's)	τό σακκάκι	to sakakee
jacket (women's)	ἡ ζακέτα	ee zaketa
jeans	τό.παντελόνι ἀπό δίμητο, τζίνς	to pandelonee apo dheemeeto, jeans
jumper	ἡ πλεκτή μπλούζα	ee plektee blooza
negligé	ἡ ρόμπα μέ δαντέλλες	ee roba me danteles
nightdress	τό νυχτικό	to neekhteeko
overcoat	τό παλτό	to palto
panties	ἡ κυλότα	ee keelota
pants suit	τό γυναικεῖο κοστούμι	to yeenekeeo kostoomee
pocket	ἡ τσέπη	ee tsepee
press stud	ἡ σούστα	ee soosta
pullover	τό πουλόβερ	too poolover
pyjamas	ἡ πυτζάμα	ee peetzama
raincoat	τό ἀδιάβροχο	to adhyavrokho
sandals	τά σανδάλια	ta sandhalya
scarf	τό κασκόλ	to kaskol
shirt	τό πουκάμισο	to pookameeso
shoelaces	τά κορδόνια	ta kordhonya
shoes	τά παπούτσια	ta papootsya
shorts	τό σόρτς	to sorts
skirt	ἡ φούστα	ee foosta
slip	τό κομπιναιζόν	to kombeenezon
slippers	οἱ παντόφλες	ee pandofles

socks	οἱ κάλτσες	ee kaltses
stockings	οἱ κάλτσες	ee kaltses
suit (men's)	τό κοστούμι	to kostoomee
suit (women's)	τό ταγιέρι	to tayeree
suspenders	οἱ ζαρτιέρες	ee zartyeres
sweater	τό πουλόβερ	to poolover
swimsuit	τό μαγιό	to mayo
thread	ἡ κλωστή	ee klostee
tie	ἡ γραβάτα	ee ghravata
tights	τό καλτσόν	to kaltson
trousers	τό παντελόνι	to pandelonee
T-shirt	τό φανελλάκι	to fanelakee
underpants	τό σώβρακο	to sovrako
vest	ἡ φανέλλα	ee fanela
waistcoat	τό γελέκο	to yeleko
zip	τό φερμουάρ	to fermooar

At the Shoe Shop

I want a pair of	Θέλω ἕνα ζευγάρι
	thelo ena zevgharee
walking shoes.	παπούτσια περιπάτου.
	papootsya pereepatoo
evening shoes.	παπούτσια τουαλέτας.
	papootsya tooaletas
moccasins.	μοκκασίνια.
	mokaseenya
boots.	μπότες.
	botes
suede shoes.	καστόρινα παπούτσια.
	kastoreena papootsya
slippers.	παντόφλες.
	pandofles
sandals.	σανδάλια.
	sandhalya
canvas shoes.	λινά παπούτσια
	leena papootsya

My size is .' . . 　　Τό νούμερό μου εἶναι . . .
　　　　　　　　　to noomero moo eene

I like a 　　　　　Τά θέλω νά εἶναι
　　　　　　　　　ta thelo na eene
　broad/narrow 　　εὐρύχωρα/ἐφαρμοστά.
　fitting. 　　　　evreekhora/efarmosta

I want shoes with 　Θέλω παπούτσια μέ
　　　　　　　　　thelo papootsya me
　high heels. 　　ψηλά τακούνια.
　　　　　　　　　pseela takoonya
　low heels. 　　χαμηλά τακούνια.
　　　　　　　　　khameela takoonya
　flat heels. 　　χωρίς τακούνια.
　　　　　　　　　khorees takoonya
　leather soles. 　δερμάτινες σόλες.
　　　　　　　　　dhermateenes soles
　rubber soles. 　λαστιχένιες σόλες.
　　　　　　　　　lasteekhenyes soles
　cork soles. 　　σόλες ἀπό φελλό.
　　　　　　　　　soles apo felo

These are not 　　Αὐτά δέν εἶναι ἀναπαυτικά.
comfortable. 　　afta dhen eene anapafteeka

May I try the other 　Μπορῶ νά δοκιμάσω καί τό ἄλλο παπούτσι;
shoe? 　　　　　boro na dhokeemaso ke to alo papootsee

Have you got a shoe 　Ἔχετε ἕνα κόκκαλο ὑποδημάτων;
horn? 　　　　　ekhete eena kokalo eepodheematon

They are not my 　　Αὐτά δέν εἶναι τοῦ γούστου μου.
style. 　　　　　afta dhen eene too ghoostoo moo

What other colours 　Τί ἄλλα χρώματα ἔχετε;
have you got? 　　tee ala khromata ekhete

How much are they? 　Πόσο κοστίζουν;
　　　　　　　　　poso kosteezoon

| That is more than I want to pay. | Αὐτό εἶναι περισσότερο ἀπ' ὅτι θέλω νά πληρώσω. |
| | afto eene pereesotero apotee thelo na pleeroso |

| I will wear them. Will you please wrap up my own shoes? | Θά τά φορέσω. Μπορεῖτε νά διπλώσετε τά δικά μου παπούτσια παρακαλῶ; |
| | tha ta foreso. boreete na dheeplosete ta dheeka moo papootsya parakalo |

Do you sell	Πουλᾶτε
	poolate
shoe polish/ shoe cleaner/ shoe brushes?	βερνίκι/κρέμα στιλβώσεως/βούρτσες ὑποδημάτων;
	verneekee/krema steelvoseos/voortses eepodheematon

Tobacconist's

Stamps can also be purchased at a street kiosk.

| A packet/carton of . . . cigarettes, please. | Ἕνα πακέτο/μιά κούτα . . . ena paketo/mya koota . . . τσιγάρα παρακαλῶ. tseeghara parakalo |

| A box of matches, please. | Ἕνα κουτί σπίρτα παρακαλῶ. ena kootee speerta parakalo |

| Do you sell English cigarettes? | Πουλᾶτε 'Αγγλικά τσιγάρα; poolate anggleeka tseeghara |

| What is the local brand? | Ποιά εἶναι ἡ τοπική μάρκα; pya eene ee topeekee marka |

Are they	Εἶναι
	eene
Virginian/French/ Egyptian/Turkish/ American?	τῆς Βιργινίας/Γαλλικά/Αἰγυπτιακά/ Τούρκικα/ 'Αμερικανικά; tees veeryeeneeas/ghaleeka/ eyeepteeaka/ toorkeeka/ amereekaneeka

Have you any	Ἔχετε τσιγάρα ekhete tseeghara
filter tip/ king-sized/ menthol-cooled cigarettes?	μέ φίλτρο/μεγάλου μεγέθους/ἄρωμα μέντας; me feeltro/meghaloo meyethoos/aroma mentas;
Do you sell pipe tobacco?	Πουλᾶτε καπνό πίπας; poolate kapno peepas
May I see your selection of pipes?	Μπορῶ νά δῶ τή συλλογή πίπων πού ἔχετε; boro na dho tee seeloyee peepon poo ekhete
I'd like a cigar.	Θά ἤθελα ἕνα πούρο. tha eethela ena pooro
Have you a cigar cutter?	Ἔχετε ἕνα ψαλλιδάκι γιά πούρα; ekhete ena psaleedhakee ya poora
Have you anything for cleaning a pipe?	Ἔχετε κάτι πού καθαρίζει πίπες; ekhete katee poo kathareezee peepes
I'd like some snuff.	Θά ἤθελα λίγη πρέζα. tha eethela leeyee preza
Have you got any stamps?	Ἔχετε γραμματόσημα; ekhete ghramatoseema

VOCABULARY

box	τό κουτί	to kootee
carton	ἡ κούτα	ee koota
cigarette case	ἡ τσιγαροθήκη	ee tseegarotheekee
cigarette lighter	ὁ ἀναπτήρας	o anapteeras
flint	ἡ τσακμακόπετρα	ee tsakmakopetra
gas	τό γκάζι	to ghazee
lighter fluid	ἡ βενζίνη ἀναπτῆρος	ee venzeenee anapteeros
matches	τά σπίρτα	ta speerta
packet	τό πακέτο	to paketo
pipe	ἡ πίπα	ee peepa

pipe cleaners	οἱ καθαριστές πίπας	ee kathareestes peepas
pouch	τό σακκουλάκι γιά καπνό	to sakoolakee ya kapno
stamps	τά γραμματόσημα	ta ghramatoseema

Hardware Stores and Electrical Goods

I'd like	Θά ἤθελα tha eethela	
a heavy-duty saucepan.	μιά κατσαρόλα μεγάλης ἀντοχῆς. mya katsarola meghalees andokhees	
a non-stick frying pan.	ἕνα τηγάνι μέ ἀντικολλητικό πάτο. ena teeghanee me andeekoleeteeko pato	
Have you	Ἔχετε ekhete	
a grill/charcoal?	μιά σχάρα/κάρβουνα; mya skhara/karvoona	
I need a	Χρειάζομαι ἕνα khreeazome ena	
plastic bucket/ metal bucket.	πλαστικό κουβᾶ/μετάλλινο κουβᾶ. plasteeko koova/metaleeno koova	
Give me a ball of strong twine.	Δῶστε μου ἕνα κουβάρι γερό σπάγγο. dhoste moo ena koovaree yero spanggo	
I need a tow rope and a hook.	Χρειάζομαι ἕνα σχοινί ρυμουλκήσεως καί ἕνα γάντζο. khreeazome ena skheenee reemoolkeeseos ke ena ghandzo	
I need a battery for	Χρειάζομαι μιά μπαταρία γιά khreeazome mya batareea ya	
my torch/my radio.	τό φακό μου/τό ραδιόφωνό μου. to fako moo/to radheeofono moo	
Can you repair this?	Μπορεῖτε νά ἐπισκευάσετε αὐτό παρακαλῶ; boreete na epeeskevasete afto parakalo	

VOCABULARY

adaptor	ὁ σταυρός	o stavros
basket	τό καλάθι	to kalathee
battery	ἡ μπαταρία	ee batareea
brush	ἡ βούρτσα	ee voortsa
bulb	ἡ λάμπα	ee lamba
car radio	τό ραδιόφωνο αὐτοκινήτου	to radheeofono aftokeeneetoo
chamois leather	τό σαμουά	to samooa
distilled water	τό ἀποσταγμένο νερό	to apostaghmeno nero
duster	τό ξεσκονόπανο	to kseskonopano
fork	τό πηρούνι	to peeroonee
hammer	τό σφυρί	to sfeeree
insulating tape	ἡ ἀπομονωτική ταινία	ee apomonoteekee teneea
iron	τό σίδερο	to seedhero
kettle	τό τσαγιερό	to tsayero
knife	τό μαχαίρι	to makheree
mallet	τό ξύλινο σφυρί	to kseeleeno sfeeree
penknife	ὁ σουγιάς	o sooyas
percolator	ἡ συσκευή πού βράζει καφέ	ee seeskeevee poo vrazee kafe
plug	ἡ πρίζα	ee preeza
saw	τό πριόνι	to preeonee
scissors	τό ψαλίδι	to psaleedhee
screwdriver	τό κατσαβίδι	to katsaveedhee
shaver	ἡ ξυριστική μηχανή	ee kseereesteekee meekhanee
spoon	τό κουτάλι	to kootalee
string	ὁ σπάγγος	o spanggos
tweezers	ἡ ντανάλια	ee danalya
wire	τό σύρμα	to seerma
wrench	τό Γαλλικό κλειδί	to ghaleeko kleedhee

Chemist's

Do I need a doctor's prescription?	Χρειάζομαι μιά συνταγή γιατρού; khreeazome mya seendayee yatroo
Is there an all-night chemist open?	Ὑπάρχει διανυκτερεῦον φαρμακεῖο; eeparkhee dheeaneekterevon farmakeeo
Can you make up this prescription?	Μπορεῖτε νά μοῦ ἑτοιμάσετε αὐτή τή συνταγή παρακαλῶ; boreete na moo eteemasete aftee tee seendayee parakalo
When will it be ready?	Πότε θά εἶναι ἕτοιμη; pote tha eene eteemee
Will you write down the instructions, in English if possible?	Μπορεῖτε νά γράψετε τίς ὁδηγίες, στά Ἀγγλικά ἂν εἶναι δυνατόν; boreete na ghrapsete tees odheeyeees, sta anggleeka an eene dheenaton
Is this safe for children?	Εἶναι ἀσφαλές γιά τά παιδιά; eene asfales ya ta pedhya
Have you anything	Ἔχετε κάτι ekhete katee
for a cold/for a sore throat/for a cough.	γιά τό κρυολόγημα/γιά τή λαρυγγίτιδα/γιά τό βήχα; ya to kreeoloyeema/ya tee lareenggeeteedha/ya to veekha
I'd like to buy a thermometer.	Θά ἤθελα ν' ἀγοράσω ἕνα θερμόμετρο. tha eethela naghoraso ena thermometro
Would you please have a look at	Μπορεῖτε νά ἐξετάσετε παρακαλῶ boreete na eksetasete parakalo
this cut/this bruise?	αὐτό τό κόψιμο/αὐτή τή μελανιά; afto to kopseemo/aftee tee melanya
What kind of bandage would be best?	Τί εἶδος ἐπιδέσμου θά ἦταν τό πιό καλό; tee eedhos epeedhezmoo tha eetan to pyo kalo

I've got	Ἔχω	
	ekho	
diarrhoea.	**διάρροια.**	
	dhyareea	
an upset stomach.	**ἀνακατωσούρα στό στομάχι.**	
	anakatosoora sto stomakhee	
indigestion.	**δυσπεψία.**	
	dheespepseea	
a headache.	**πονοκέφαλο.**	
	ponokefalo	
sunburns.	**ἡλιοκαύματα.**	
	eelyokavmata	
I am constipated.	**Εἶμαι δυσκοίλιος (δυσκοίλια).**	
	eeme dheeskeeleeos (dheeskeeleea)	

VOCABULARY

antibiotics	τά ἀντιβιοτικά	ta andeeveeoteeka
aspirin	ἡ ἀσπιρίνη	ee aspeereenee
bandage	ὁ ἐπίδεσμος	o epeedhezmos
band-aids	οἱ λευκοπλάστες	ee lefkoplastes
contraceptive	τό ἀντισυλληπτικό	to andeeseeleepteeko
corn plaster	τά ἔμπλαστρα γιά κάλους	ta emblastra ya kaloos
cotton wool	τό βαμβάκι	to vamvakee
cough lozenges	οἱ παστίλιες γιά τό βήχα	ee pasteelyes ya to veekha
cough mixture	τό φάρμακο γιά τό βήχα	to farmako ya to veekha
disinfectant	τό ἀπολυμαντικό	to apoleemandeeko
ear drops	οἱ σταγόνες γιά τά αὐτιά	ee staghones ya ta aftya
gargle	τό φάρμακο γιά γαργάρα	to farmako ya gharghara
gauze	ἡ γάζα	ee ghaza
insect repellant	ἡ κρέμα γιά τά κουνούπια	ee krema ya ta koonoopya

iodine	τό ἰώδιο	to eeodheeo
iron pills	τά χάπια μέ σίδερο	ta khapya me seedhero
laxative	τό καθαρτικό	to katharteeko
lip salve	ἡ βαζελίνη γιά τά χείλια	ee vazeleene ya ta kheelya
sanitary towels	οἱ πετσέτες περιόδου	ee petsetes pereeodhoo
sedative	τό καταπραϋντικό φάρμακο	to katapraeendeeko farmako
sleeping pill	τά ὑπνωτικά χάπια	ta eepnoteeka khapya
thermometer	τό θερμόμετρο	to thermometro
tranquillizers	τά καταπραϋντικά χάπια	ta katapraeendeeka khapya
vitamins	οἱ βιταμίνες	ee veetameenes

TOILET ARTICLES

after shave	ἡ κολώνια ξυρίσματος	ee kolonya kseereezmatos
astringent	ἡ στυπτική λοσιόν	ee steepteekee losyon
bath oil	τό λάδι γιά μπάνιο	to ladhee ya banyo
bath salts	τά ἅλατα γιά μπάνιο	to alata ya banyo
cologne	ἡ κολόνια	ee kolonya
cream:	ἡ κρέμα	ee krema
cleansing	τό γαλάκτωμα	to ghalaktoma
cuticle	ἡ τονωτική κρέμα νυχιῶν	ee tonoteekee krema neekhyon
foundation	ἡ κρέμα "βάσεως"	ee krema vaseos
moisturizing	ἡ κρέμα ὑδατική	ee krema eedhateekee
deodorant	τό ἀποσμητικό	to apozmeeteeko
emery boards	οἱ χάρτινες λίμες (νυχιῶν)	ee kharteenes leemes (neekhyon)
eye pencil	τό μολύβι φρυδιῶν	to moleevee freedhyon
eye shadow	ἡ σκιά γιά τά μάτια	ee skya ya ta matya
face pack	ἡ μάσκα ὀμορφιᾶς	ee maska omorfyas
face powder	ἡ πούδρα	ee poodhra
hairbrush	ἡ βούρτσα μαλλιῶν	ee voortsa malyon
hair spray	τό λάκερ	to laker

lipstick	τό κραγιόν	to krayon
mascara	ἡ μάσκαρα	ee maskara
nailbrush	ἡ βούρτσα νυχιῶν	ee voortsa neekhyon
nailfile	ἡ λίμα νυχιῶν	ee leema neekhyon
nail polish	τό βερνίκι νυχιῶν	to verneekee neekhyon
nail polish remover	τό ἀσετόν	to aseton
nail scissors	τό ψαλλιδάκι	to psaleedhakee
nappies	οἱ πάνες	ee panes
nappy pins	οἱ παραμάνες γιά πάνες	ee paramanes ya panes
perfume	τό ἄρωμα	to aroma
plastic pants	τό πλαστικό κυλοτάκι	to plasteeko keelotakee
rouge	τό ρούζ	to rooz
safety pin	ἡ παραμάνα	ee paramana
shampoo	τό σαμπουάν	to sambooan
shaving brush	τό πινέλο ξυρίσματος	to peenelo kseereezmatos
shaving cream	ἡ κρέμα ξυρίσματος	ee krema kseereezmatos
soap	τό σαπούνι	to sapoonee
sponge	τό σφουγγάρι	to sfoonggaree
suntan oil	τό λάδι γιά ἡλιοθεραπεία	to ladhee ya eelyotherapeea
tissues	τά χαρτομάντηλα	ta khartomandeela
toilet paper	τό χαρτί ὑγείας	to khartee eeyeeas
toothbrush	ἡ ὀδοντόβουρτσα	ee odhondovoortsa
toothpaste	ἡ ὀδοντόκρεμα	ee odhondokrema
tweezers	τό τσιμπιδάκι	to tseembeedhakee

At the Photographer's

I'd like to buy a camera.	**Θά ἤθελα ν' ἀγοράσω μία φωτογραφική μηχανή.** tha eethela naghoraso meea fotoghrafeekee meekhanee
One that is cheap and easy to use.	**Μία πού εἶναι φθηνή καί πού χρησιμοποιεῖται εὔκολα.** meea poo eene ftheenee ke poo khreeseemopeeeete efkola

Will you please check my camera?	**Μπορεῖτε νά ἐξετάσετε τή φωτογραφική μου μηχανή παρακαλῶ;** boreete na eksetasete tee fotoghrafeekee moo meekhanee parakalo
The film gets stuck.	**Τό φίλμ πιάνει.** to feelm pyanee
The exposure meter is not working.	**Τό φωτόμετρο δέν λειτουργεῖ.** to fotometro **dhen** leetooryee
The flash does not light up.	**Τό φλάς δέν ἀνάβει.** to **flas dhen** anavee
The film winder is jammed.	**τό φίλμ δέν κουρδίζει.** to feelm **dhen** koordheezee
Can you do it soon?	**Μπορεῖτε νά τό κάνετε γρήγορα;** boreete na to **kanete** ghreeghora
Will you please process this film?	**᾽Εμφανίζετε αὐτό τό φίλμ παρακαλῶ;** emfaneezete afto to feelm parakalo
I would like	**Θά ἤθελα** tha eethela
prints with a matt finish/prints with a glossy finish.	**μάτ φωτογραφίες/γυαλιστερές φωτογραφίες.** **mat** fotoghrafeees/yaleesteres fotoghrafeees
I want some	**Θέλω ἔνα** **the**lo ena
black-and-white/colour/polaroid film.	**ἀσπρόμαυρο/ἔγχρωμο/πολαρόϊντ φίλμ.** aspromavro/**engk**hromo/polaroeed feelm
Is this film for use in daylight or artificial light?	**Εἶναι αὐτό τό φίλμ γιά τό φῶς τῆς ἡμέρας ἤ γιά τεχνητό φῶς;** eene afto to feelm ya to fos tees eemeras ee ya tekhneeto fos
I need a light meter.	**Χρειάζομαι ἔνα φωτόμετρο.** khreeazome ena fotometro

How much is an
electronic flash?

Πόσο κοστίζει ἕνα ἠλεκτρονικό φλάς;
poso kosteezee ena eelektroneeko flas

Vocabulary

120 film	φίλμ 120	feelm ekaton eekosee
127 film	φίλμ 127	feelm ekaton eekosee epta
135 film	φίλμ 135	feelm ekaton treeanda pende
620 film	φίλμ 620	feelm eksakosya eekosee
24 exposures	24 στάσεις	eekosee tesera stasees
36 exposures	36 στάσεις	treeanda eksee stasees
a fast film	ἕνα φίλμ μεγάλης ταχύτητος	ena feelm meghalees takheeteetos
a fine-grain film	ἕνα λεπτόκοκκο φίλμ	ena leptokoko feelm
camera case	ἡ θήκη τῆς φωτογραφικῆς μηχανῆς	ee theekee tees fotoghrafeekees meekhanees
cartridge	ἡ κασέτα	ee kaseta
cine film 8mm/16mm	ἕνα κινηματογραφικό φίλμ 8/16 χιλιοστῶν	ena keeneematoghrafeeko feelm okto/dhekaeksee kheelyoston
colour slides	τά ἕγχρωμα σλάϊντς	ta engkhroma slaeedz
(to) develop	ἐμφανίζω	emfaneezo
flash bulbs	οἱ λαμπτῆρες φλάς	ee lampteeres flas
lens	ὁ φακός	o fakos
lens cap	τό καπάκι φακοῦ	to kapakee fakoo
long-focus lens	ὁ τηλεφακός	o teelefakos
photograph	ἡ φωτογραφία	ee fotoghrafeea
photographer	ὁ φωτογράφος	o fotoghrafos
(to) print	ἐκτυπώνω	ekteepono
range finder	τό μέτρο ἀποστάσεως	to metro apostaseos
red filter	τό κόκκινο φίλτρο	to kokeeno feeltro
shutter	τό διάφραγμα	to dheeafraghma
ultraviolet	τό ὑπεριῶδες	to eepereeodhes
wide-angle lens	ὁ εὐρυγώνιος φακός	o evreeghoneeos fakos
yellow filter	τό κίτρινο φίλτρο	to keetreeno feeltro

Bookshop/Stationer's

On which shelf are the books on art/history/politics/sport?	Σέ ποιό ράφι εἶναι τά βιβλία se pyo rafee eene ta veevleea καλλιτεχνίας/ἱστορίας/γιά τήν πολιτική/γιά τά σπόρ; kaleetekhneeas/eestoreeas/ya teen poleeteekee/ya ta spor
Where are the guide books?	Ποῦ εἶναι οἱ ὁδηγοί περιηγήσεως; poo eene ee odheeyee peree-eeyeeseos
I want a pocket dictionary.	Θέλω ἕνα λεξικό τῆς τσέπης. thelo ena lekseeko tees tsepees
Have you any English newspapers?	Ἔχετε Ἀγγλικές ἐφημερίδες; ekhete anggleekes efeemereedhes
Have you any English paperbacks?	Ἔχετε Ἀγγλικά φθηνά βιβλία; ekhete anggleeka ftheena veevleea
Can you recommend an easy-to-read book in Greek?	Μπορεῖτε νά μοῦ συστήσετε ἕνα εὔκολο Ἑλληνικό βιβλίο; boreete na moo seesteesete ena efkolo eleeneeko veevleeo
Do you sell second-hand books?	Πουλᾶτε μεταχειρισμένα βιβλία; poolate metakheereezmena veevleea
I want a map of the area.	Θέλω ἕνα χάρτη τῆς περιοχῆς. thelo ena khartee tees pereeokhees
The scale of this one is too small.	Ἡ κλίμακα αὐτοῦ τοῦ χάρτη εἶναι πολύ μικρή. ee kleemaka aftoo too khartee eene polee meekree
Have you got refills for this ballpoint pen?	Ἔχετε ἀνταλλακτικά γι' αὐτό τό μπίκ; ekhete andalakteeka yafto to beek
Can you please deliver the English newspaper every morning?	Μπορεῖτε νά μοῦ στέλνετε κάθε πρωΐ τήν Ἀγγλική ἐφημερίδα; boreete na moo stelnete kathe proee teen anggleekee efeemereedha

VOCABULARY

address book	τό καρνέ διευθύνσεων	to karne dhee-eftheenseon
box of crayons	τό κουτί μέ χρωματιστά μολύβια	to kootee me khromateesta moleevya
carbon paper	τό καρμπόν	to karbon
cellophane	ἡ σελλοφάνη	ee selofanee
drawing paper	τό χαρτί σχεδιάσεως	to khartee skhedheeaseos
drawing pins	οἱ πινέζες	ee peenezes
envelopes	τά φάκελλα	ta fakela
exercise book	τό τετράδιο	to tetradhyo
fountain pen	ὁ στυλογράφος	o steeloghrafos
glue	ἡ κόλλα	ee kola
greaseproof paper	τό λαδόχαρτο	to ladhokharto
ink	τό μελάνι	to melanee
label	ἡ ἐτικέττα	ee eeteeketa
magazines	τά περιοδικά	ta pereeodheeka
notebook	τό μπλόκ	to blok
notepaper	τό χαρτί ἀλληλογραφίας	to khartee aleeloghrafeeas
paste	ἡ γόμα	ee ghoma
pen	ὁ στυλός	o steelos
pencil	τό μολύβι	to moleevee
pencil sharpener	ἡ ξύστρα	ee kseestra
playing cards	ἡ τράπουλα	ee trapoola
postcards	τά κάρτ-ποστάλ	ta kart postal
rubber	ἡ γομολάστιχα	ee ghomolasteekha
ruler	ὁ χάρακας	o kharakas
silver foil	τό ἀσημόχαρτο	to aseemokharto
sketchpad	τό μπλόκ ζωγραφικῆς	to blok zoghrafeekees
tissue paper	τό μεταξοειδές χαρτί	to metaksoeedhes khartee
typewriter ribbon	ἡ ταινία γραφομηχανῆς	ee teneea ghrafomeekhanees
typing paper	τό χαρτί γραφομηχανῆς	to khartee ghrafomeekhanees
writing pad	τό μπλόκ ἀλλληλογραφίας	to blok aleeloghrafeeas

Buying Souvenirs

Are all these things made in Greece?	Εἶναι ὅλα αὐτά τά πράγματα Ἑλληνικῆς κατασκευῆς; eene ola afta ta praghmata eleeneekees kataskevees
This is a nice straw hat.	Αὐτό εἶναι ἕνα ὡραῖο ψάθινο καπέλλο. afto eene ena oreo psatheeno kapelo
I like this bag.	Μ' ἀρέσει αὐτή ἡ τσάντα. maresee aftee ee tsanda
Have you any costume jewellery?	Ἔχετε τίποτα φθηνά κοσμήματα; ekhete teepota ftheena kozmeemata
I'm looking for bracelet charms.	Ψάχνω γιά ἕνα βραχιόλι μέ μπιχλιμπίδια. psakhno ya ena vrakhyolee me beekhleebeedhya
I'd like to try on that ring.	Θά ἤθελα νά δοκιμάσω αὐτό τό δακτυλίδι. tha eethela na dhokeemaso afto to dhakteeleedhee
What is the bracelet made of?	Ἀπό τί εἶναι φτιαγμένο τό βραχιόλι; apo tee eene ftyaghmeno to vrakhyolee
I collect copper ware. Have you any pots?	Κάνω συλλογή ἀπό χάλκινα εἴδη. Ἔχετε κανένα δοχειάκι; kano seeloyee apo khalkeena eedhee. ekhete kanena dhokheeakee
I'd like some local pottery.	Θά ἤθελα πήλινα εἴδη τοῦ τόπου. tha eethela peeleena eedhee too topoo
Can you pack this carefully?	Μπορεῖτε νά τό πακετάρετε αὐτό προσεχτικά; boreete na to paketarete afto prosekteeka
Do you despatch things abroad?	Ἀποστέλνετε πράγματα στό ἐξωτερικό; apostelnete praghmata sto eksotereeko
I'm just looking around.	Ἀπλῶς ρίχνω μιά ματιά. aplos reekhno mya matya
I will come back later.	Θά ἐπιστρέψω ἀργότερα. tha epeestrepso arghotera

| Can I leave a deposit on it and return tomorrow? | Μπορῶ ν' ἀφήσω μιά προκαταβολή καί νά γυρίσω αὔριο;
boro nafeeso mya prokatavolee ke na yeereeso avreeo |
| Do you take foreign cheques with a Eurocard? | Δέχεστε ξένες ἐπιταγές μέ Eurocard;
dhekheste ksenes epeetayes me Eurocard |

VOCABULARY

beads	οἱ χάντρες	ee khandres
brooch	ἡ καρφίτσα	ee karfeetsa
chain	ἡ ἀλυσίδα	ee aleeseedha
cigarette lighter	ὁ ἀναπτήρας	o anapteeras
clock	τό ρολόϊ	to roloee
costumes	τά κουστουμάκια	ta koostoomakya
cufflinks	τά κουμπιά γιά μανικέτες	ta koombya ya maneeketes
dolls	οἱ κούκλες	ee kookles
earrings	τά σκουλαρίκια	ta skoolareekya
jewel box	ἡ κασετίνα γιά μπιζού	ee kaseteena ya beezoo
leatherwork	τά δερμάτινα εἴδη	ta dhermateena eedhee
music box	ἡ κασετίνα μέ μουσική	ee kaseteena me mooseekee
necklace	τό κολλιέ	to kolye
pewterware	τά εἴδη ἀπό πιούτερ	ta eedhee apo pyooter
pottery	τά πήλινα εἴδη	ta peeleena eedhee
rosary	τό κομπολόϊ προσευχῆς	to komboloee prosefkhees
silverware	τά ἀσημικά	ta aseemeeka
souvenir	τό σουβενίρ	to sooveneer
watchstrap	τό λουριδάκι γιά ρολόϊ	to looreedhakee ya roloee
wristwatch	τό ρολόϊ χειρός	to roloee kheeros

Entertainment

Out for the Evening

Nightclubs

Can you recommend	**Μπορεῖτε νά συστήσετε**
	boreete na seesteesete
a nightclub with a good show?	**ἕνα νυχτερινό κέντρο μέ καλή ἐπιθεώρηση;**
	ena neektereeno **ken**dro me kalee epeetheoreesee
a place with dancing and cabaret?	**ἕνα κέντρο μέ χορό καί καμπαρέ;**
	ena **ken**dro me khoro ke kabare
a disco?	**ἕνα ντισκοτέκ;**
	ena deeskotek
an open-air dance?	**μιά ὑπαίθρια πίστα;**
	mya eepethreea **pees**ta
a nightclub with hostesses?	**ἕνα νυχτερινό κέντρο μέ κοπέλλες;**
	ena neektere**eno ken**dro me kopeles
Is there an entrance fee?	**Ὑπάρχει εἰδική τιμή γιά τήν εἴσοδο;**
	ee**par**khee eedhee**kee** tee**mee** ya teen **ee**sodho
Does it include drinks?	**Περιλαμβάνει ἡ τιμή καί τά ποτά;**
	pereelam**va**nee ee tee**mee** ke ta po**ta**
What is the cost of drinks?	**Πόσο κοστίζουν τά ποτά;**
	poso kostee**zoon** ta po**ta**
What times does the show start?	**Τί ὥρα ἀρχίζει τό καμπαρέ;**
	tee ora arkhee**zee** to kabare
Is there a different price for drinks at the bar?	**Ἔχουν τά ποτά ἄλλη τιμή στό μπάρ;**
	ekhoon ta po**ta** alee tee**mee** sto **bar**
I do not want a photograph.	**Δέν θέλω φωτογραφία.**
	dhen **the**lo fotoghra**fee**a

Would you like to dance?	Θά θέλατε νά χορέψετε; tha thelate na khorepsete

Theatre/Opera

Is there a ticket agency near?	Ἔχει ἐδῶ κοντά κανένα πρακτορεῖο γιά εἰσιτήρια; ekhee edho konda kanena praktoreeo ya eeseeteereea
Is there another way of getting a ticket?	Ἔχει κανένα ἄλλο τρόπο γιά ν' ἀγοράσω εἰσιτήριο; ekhee kanena alo tropo ya naghoraso eeseeteereo
Are there any last-minute returns?	Ὑπάρχουν ἐπεστεραμμένα εἰσιτήρια; eeparkhoon epestramena eeseeteereea
Do I have to wear evening dress?	Πρέπει νά ντυθῶ τυπικά γιά βράδυ; prepee na deetho teepeeka ya vradhee
I'd like a souvenir programme.	Θά ἤθελα ἔνα εἰδικό πρόγραμμα γιά ἐνθύμιο. tha eethela ena eedheeko proghrama ya entheemeeo
What is the name of the prima donna?	Πῶς λέγεται ἡ πριμαντόνα; pos leyete ee preemadona
Who is the leading actor?	Ποιός εἶναι ὁ πρωταγωνιστής; pyos eene o protaghoneestees
How long is the interval?	Πόση ὥρα διαρκεῖ τό διάλειμμα; posee ora dhyarkee to dhyaleema
Where is the bar?	Ποῦ εἶναι τό μπάρ; poo eene to bar

VOCABULARY

applause	τό χειροκρότημα	to kheerokroteema
audience	οἱ ἀκροατές	ee akroates

baritone	ὁ βαρύτονος	o vareetonos
bass	ὁ μπάσσος	o basos
chorus	ὁ χορός	o khoros
composer	ὁ συνθέτης	o seenthetees
conductor	ὁ μαέστρος	o maestros
contralto	ἡ κοντράλτο	ee kontralto
encore	τό μπιζάρισμα	to beezareezma
encore!	μπίς!	bis
leading actor	ὁ πρωταγωνιστής	o protaghoneestees
leading actress	ἡ πρωταγωνίστρια	ee protaghoneestreea
opera	ἡ ὄπερα	ee opera
orchestra	ἡ ὀρχήστρα	ee orkheestra
playwright	ὁ δραματουργός	o dhramatoorghos
scenery	τά σκηνικά	ta skeeneeka
soprano	ἡ σοπράνο	ee soprano
stage	ἡ σκηνή	ee skeenee
tenor	ὁ τενόρος	o tenoros
theatre	τό θέατρο	to theatro

Cinema

What's on at the cinema?	Τί παίζει στό σινεμά; tee pezee sto seenema
Have you got a guide to what's on?	Ἔχετε ἕναν ὁδηγό γιά τά ἔργα πού παίζουν; ekhete enan odheegho ya ta ergha poo pezoon
Two tickets, please,	Δύο εἰσιτήρια παρακαλῶ. dheeo eeseeteereea parakalo
for the stalls/for the circle.	γιά τή πλατεῖα/γιά τόν ἐξώστη παρακαλῶ. ya tee plateea/ya ton eksostee parakalo
Will we have to queue for long?	Θά πρέπει νά κάνουμε σειρά πολλή ὥρα; tha prepee na kanoome seera polee ora
I want a seat	Θέλω μία θέση thelo meea thesee
near the front/at the back/in the middle.	μπροστά/πίσω/στή μέση. brosta/peeso/stee mesee

Do I tip the usherette?	Πρέπει νά δώσω πουρμπουάρ στή ταξιθέτρια; prepee na dhoso poorbooar stee takseethetreea	
I'd rather sit over there.	Θά προτιμούσα νά καθήσω ἐκεῖ πέρα. tha proteemoosa na katheeso ekee pera	
I have dropped something.	Μοῦ ἔπεσε κάτι. moo epese katee	
Is there an ice-cream seller?	Ὑπάρχει κάποιος πού πουλάει παγωτά; eeparkhee kapyos poo poolaee paghota	
At what time does the film start?	Τί ὥρα ἀρχίζει τό ἔργο; tee ora arkheezee to ergho	
Will you please move	Θά μπορούσατε νά μετακινηθεῖτε παρακαλῶ tha boroosate na metakeeneetheete parakalo	
to the right/to the left?	λίγο δεξιά/λίγο ἀριστερά; leegho dheksya/leegho areestera	

VOCABULARY

actor	ὁ ἠθοποιός	o eethopeeos
actress	ἡ ἠθοποιός	ee eethopeeos
director	ὁ σκηνοθέτης	o skeenothetees
dubbing	τό ντουμπλάρισμα	to dooblareezma
film	ἡ ταινία	ee teneea
interval	τό διάλειμμα	to dhyaleema
producer	ὁ παραγωγός	o paraghoghos
projector	ὁ προβολεύς	o provolefs
screen	ἡ ὀθόνη	ee othonee
sound	ὁ ἦχος	o eekhos
star	τό ἀστέρι	to asteree

Concert Hall

I want a seat from which I can see the pianist's hands.	Θά ἤθελα μιά θέση ἀπ' ὅπου μπορῶ νά βλέπω τά χέρια τοῦ πιανίστα.	
	tha eethela mya thesee apopoo boro na vlepo ta kherya too pyaneesta	
Can I buy the score?	Μπορῶ ν' ἀγοράσω τήν παρτιτούρα;	
	boro naghoraso teen parteetoora	
Who is conducting tonight?	Ποιός διευθύνει τήν ὀρχήστρα ἀπόψε;	
	pyos dhee-eftheenee teen orkheestra apopse	
Who is the soloist?	Ποιός εἶναι ὁ σολίστ;	
	pyos eene o soleest	

Vocabulary

bassoon	τό φαγκότο	to fagoto
brass	τά χάλκινα (ὄργανα)	ta khalkeena (orghana)
cello	τό βιολοντσέλλο	to vyolontselo
choir	ἡ χορωδία	ee khorodheea
clarinet	τό κλαρινέττο	to klareeneto
conductor	ὁ μαέστρος	o maestros
cymbals	τά κύμβαλα	ta keemvala
double-bass	ἡ μπασσαβιόλα	ee basavyola
drum	τό τύμπανο	to teembano
flute	τό φλάουτο	to flaooto
French horn	ἡ γαλλική κόρνα	ee ghaleekee korna
harp	ἡ ἄρπα	ee arpa
oboe	τό ὄμποε, ὁ ὀξύαλος	to oboe, o okseeavlos
percussion	τά κρουστά (ὄργανα)	ta kroosta (orghana)
saxophone	τό σαξόφωνο	to saksofono
strings	τά ἔγχορδα (ὄργανα)	ta engkhordha (orghana)
timpani	τά ἡμισφαιρικά τύμπανα	ta eemeesfereeka teembana
trombone	τό τρομπόνι	to trombonee
trumpet	ἡ τρομπέτα	ee trompeta
violin	τό βιολί	to vyolee
wind	τά πνευστά (ὄργανα)	ta pnefsta (orghana)

Casino

What games are played here?	Τί παιχνίδια παίζονται ἐδῶ;	tee pekhneedhya pezonde edho
Is there a minimum stake at this table?	Ἔχει ἕνα μίνιμουμ ποντάρισμα σ' αὐτό τό τραπέζι;	ekhee ena meeneemoom pondareezma safto to trapezee
Can I buy some chips?	Μπορῶ ν' ἀγοράσω μάρκες;	boro naghoraso markes
I should like 2000 drachmas' worth.	Θά ἤθελα μάρκες γιά 2000 δραχμές.	tha eethela markes ya dheeo kheelyadhes dhrakhmes
Excuse me, those are my chips.	Συγγνώμη, αὐτές οἱ μάρκες εἶναι δικές μου.	seeghnomee aftes ee markes eene dheekes moo
I'll take another card.	Μιά κάρτα ἀκόμα παρακαλῶ.	mya karta akoma parakalo
No more.	Ἀρκεῖ.	arkee
Pass me the dice please.	Δῶστε μου τά ζάρια παρακαλῶ.	dhoste moo ta zarya parakalo

VOCABULARY

ace	ὁ ἄσσος	o asos
banker	ὁ μπανκέρης	o bangkerees
bet	τό ποντάρισμα	to pondareezma
cards	τά χαρτιά	ta khartya
chemin de fer	τό σεμέν-ντέ-φέρ	to semen de fer
clubs	τά σπαθιά	ta spathya
craps	τά ζάρια, τό μπαρμπούτι	ta zarya, to barbootee
croupier	ὁ κρουπιέρης	o kroopyerees

diamonds	τά καρρά	ta kara
evens	ή ισοφάριση	ee eesofareesee
hearts	οί κούπες	ee koopes
jack	ό βαλές	o vales
joker	ό μπαλαντέρ	o balader
king	ό ρήγας	o reeghas
poker	τό πόκερ	to poker
pontoon	τό εἰκοσιένα	to eekoseeena
queen	ή ντάμα	ee dama
shoe	ή θήκη	ee theekee
spades	τά μπαστούνια	ta bastoonya

Out for the Day

On the Beach

Does one have to pay to use this beach?	Χρειάζεται νά πληρώσεις γι' αὐτή τήν πλάζ;
	khreeazete na pleerosees yaftee teen plaz
Is there a free section of the beach?	Έχει ἕνα μέρος ἄνευ πληρωμῆς σ' αὐτή τήν ἀκρογιαλιά;
	ekhee ena meros anef pleeromees saftee teen akroyalya
Is it clean?	Εἶναι καθαρό;
	eene katharo
How much does it cost to hire	Πόσο νοικιάζεται
	poso neekyazete
a cabin?	μιά καμπίνα;
	mya kambeena
a deckchair?	μιά πολυθρόνα;
	mya poleethrona
an air mattress?	ἕνα ἀερόστρωμα;
	ena aerostroma
a sun umbrella?	μιά ὀμπρέλλα τοῦ ἡλίου;
	mya ombrela too eeleeoo

per day?

γιά τήν ἡμέρα;
ya teen eemera

per week?

γιά τήν ἔβδομάδα;
ya teen evdhomadha

May I leave valuables in the cabin?

Μπορῶ ν' ἀφήσω πράγματα ἀξίας στήν καμπίνα;
boro nafeeso praghmata akseeas steen kambeena

Is the ticket valid all day?

'Ισχύει τό εἰσιτήριο γιά ὅλη τήν ἡμέρα;
eeskheeee to eeseeteereeo ya olee teen eemera

Does the beach slope steeply?

Πάει ἀπότομα μέσα ἡ ἀκρογιαλιά;
paee apotoma mesa ee akroyalya

Is it safe for swimming?

Εἶναι ἀκίνδυνο γιά κολύμπι;
eene akeendheeno ya koleembee

Are there any currents?

Ἔχει ρεύματα;
ekhee revmata

Is it safe to dive off the rocks?

Εἶναι ἀκίνδυνο νά βουτήσεις ἀπ' τούς βράχους;
eene akeendheeno na vooteesees aptoos vrakhoos

Where is the freshwater shower?

Ποῦ εἶναι τό ντούς;
poo eene to doos

Have you any tar remover?

Ἔχετε κάτι πού βγάζει τήν πίσσα;
ekhete katee poo vghazee teen peesa

Can I hire a swimsuit?

Μπορῶ νά νοικιάσω μαγιό;
boro na neekyaso mayo

I've cut my foot. Have you any elastoplast?

Ἔκοψα τό πόδι μου. Ἔχετε λευκοπλάστη;
ekopsa to podhee moo. ekhete lefkoplastee

Is there a lost property office?

Ἔχει ἕνα γραφεῖο ἀπολεσθέντων εἰδῶν;
ekhee ena ghrafeeo apolesthendon eedhon

Is there a children's beach club?

'Υπάρχει στήν πλάζ ἕνα κλάμπ γιά παιδιά;
eeparkhee steen plaz ena klab ya pedhya

At what time are the keep fit classes?

Τί ὥρα γίνεται τό κόρς γυμναστικῆς;
tee ora yeenete to kors yeemnasteekees

Is there water ski tuition available?	Έχει μαθήματα γιά θαλάσσιο σκί;	ekhee matheemata ya thalaseeo skee
Does it matter if I can't swim?	Πειράζει πού δέν ξέρω κολύμπι;	peerazee poo dhen ksero koleembee
Where is the nearest beach shop?	Πού εἶναι τό πλησιέστερο μαγαζί πού πουλάει πράγματα γιά τήν πλάζ;	poo eene to pleeseeestero maghazee poo poolaee praghmata ya teen plaz
Have you got a life jacket?	Έχετε ἕνα σωσίβιο;	ekhete ena soseeveeo
Is this a good place for skin diving?	Εἶναι τό μέρος αὐτό καλό γιά ὑποβρύχιο κολύμπι;	eene to meros afto kalo ya eepovreekheeo koleembee
Help! I'm in trouble.	Βοήθεια! Πνίγομαι.	voeethya! pneeghome

VOCABULARY

aqualung	ἡ συσκευή μέ πεπιεσμένον ἀέρα	ee seeskevee me pepee-ezmenon aera
beach ball	ἡ μπάλλα γιά τήν πλάζ	ee bala ya teen plaz
cactus	ὁ κάκτος	o kaktos
dinghy	ἡ βαρκούλα	ee varkoola
flippers	τά πέδιλα	ta pedheela
goggles	ἡ μάσκα	ee maska
harpoon gun	τό ψαροτούφεκο	to psarotoofeko
high tide	ἡ πλημμαδούρα	ee pleemadhoora
lilo	τό ἀερόστρωμα	to aerostroma
low tide	ἡ ἄμπωτη	ee ambotee
net	τό δίχτυ	to dheekhtee
pedalo	τό θαλάσσιο ποδήλατο	to thalaseeo podheelato
pines	τά πεῦκα	ta pefka

promenade	ὁ παραθαλάσσιος δρόμος περιπάτου	o parathalaseeos **dhromos** pereepatoo
raft	ἡ σχεδία	ee skhedheea
rocks	οἱ βράχοι	ee vrakhee
rowing boat	ἡ βάρκα μέ κουπιά	ee varka me koopya
sand	ἡ ἄμμος	ee amos
sandals	τά σανδάλια	ta sandhalya
sea	ἡ θάλασσα	ee thalasa
seaweed	τά φύκια	ta feekya
shells	τά καβούκια	ta kavookya
shingle	τά χαλίκια	ta khaleekya
snorkel	ὁ ἀναπνευστήρας	o anapnefsteeras
sun oil	τό λάδι ἡλιοθεραπείας	to ladhee eelyotherapeeas
surf	τό σέρφ	to **serf**
surf board	ἡ σανίδα τοῦ σέρφ	ee saneedha too **serf**
underwater	ὑποβρύχιος	eepovreekheeos
waterski instructor	ὁ δάσκαλος τοῦ θαλασσίου σκί	o dhaskalos too thalaseeoo skee
wetsuit	ἡ στολή	ee stolee
yacht	τό γιώτ	to **yot**

Sightseeing

Where can I get a good guide book?	Ποῦ μπορῶ ν' ἀγοράσω ἕνα καλόν ὁδηγό περιηγήσεως; **poo** boro naghoraso ena **kalon** odheegho peree-eeyeeseos
Is there an excursion round the city?	Ἔχει μιά ἐκδρομή πού κάνει τό γῦρο τῆς πόλης; ekhee mya ekdhromee poo **kanee** to **yeero** tees polees
Is it a conducted party?	Εἶναι ἕνα γκρούπ μέ ξεναγό; eene ena groop me ksenagho

Am I allowed to go round alone?	Ἐπιτρέπεται νά περιπλανοῦμαι μόνος (μόνη) μου; epeetrepete na pereeplanoome monos (monee) moo
Where do I find an official guide?	Ποῦ μπορῶ νά βρῶ ἕναν ἐπίσημο ξεναγό; poo boro na vro enan epeeseemo ksenagho
Does the whole day excursion include lunch?	Περιλαμβάνεται στήν τιμή τῆς ὁλομέρου ἐκδρομῆς καί τό μεσημεριανό φαγητό; pereelamvanete steen teemee tees oloeemeroo ekdhromees ke to meseemereeno fayeeto
Are the entrance fees extra?	Πληρώνεις ἐπί πλέον γιά νά ἐπισκεφτεῖς τά ἀξιοθέατα; pleeronees epeepleon ya na epeeskeftees ta aksyotheata
Should I tip the guide/the driver?	Πρέπει νά δώσω πουρμπουάρ prepee na dhoso poorbooar στόν ξεναγό/στόν ὁδηγό; ston ksenagho/ston odheegho
I'd like to stay here longer.	Θά ἤθελα νά μείνω ἐδῶ λίγο ἀκόμα. tha eethela na meeno edho leegho akoma
I'll meet the party later.	Θά ξανασυναντήσω τό γκρούπ ἀργότερα. tha ksanaseenandeeso to groop arghotera
Where will you be?	Ποῦ θά εἶστε; poo tha eeste
Will you please write it down?	Μπορεῖτε νά τό γράψετε παρακαλῶ; boreete na to ghrapsete parakalo
Can I hire an audioguide?	Μπορῶ νά νοικιάσω ἕνα ἀκουστικό; boro na neekyaso ena akoosteeko
What time does the boat leave for Delos?	Τί ὥρα φεύγει τό πλοῖο γιά τή Δῆλο; tee ora fevyee to pleeo ya tee dheelo
I would like to go on a trip to the island	Θά ἤθελα νά πάω ἕνα ταξίδι στό νησί . . . tha eethela na pao ena takseedhee sto neesee

In Churches

Do ladies have to cover their heads?	Πρέπει οἱ γυναῖκες νά ἔχουν καλυμμένο τό κεφάλι τους;	
	prepee ee yeenekes na ekhoon kaleemeno to kefalee toos	
Is it all right to enter like this?	Εἶναι ἐντάξει νά μπῶ ἔτσι;	
	eene endaksee na bo etsee	
How old is this church?	Πόσο παλιά εἶναι αὐτή ἡ ἐκκλησία;	
	poso palya eene aftee ee ekleeseea	
Who founded it?	Ποιός τήν ἴδρυσε;	
	pyos teen eedhreese	
Are the stained glass windows original?	Εἶναι πρωτότυπα τά ὑαλογραφήματα;	
	eene prototeepa ta eealoghrafeemata	
Can one illuminate the fresco?	Εἶναι δυνατόν νά φωτιστεῖ ἡ τοιχογραφία;	
	eene dheenaton na foteestee ee teekhoghrafeea	
Is one allowed to go up the bell tower?	Ἐπιτρέπεται τό ἀνέβασμα στό καμπαναριό;	
	epeetrepete to anevazma sto kambanaryo	
Is there a book about the church?	Ὑπάρχει ἕνα βιβλίο πού λέει γιά τήν ἐκκλησία;	
	eeparkhee ena veevleeo poo leee ya teen ekleeseea	
May I leave a small contribution?	Μπορῶ ν' ἀφήσω μιά μικρή δωρεά;	
	boro nafeeso mya meekree dhorea	

Vocabulary

abbey	τό μοναστήρι	to monasteeree
aisles	τά κλίτη	ta kleetee
altar	ἡ Ἁγία Τράπεζα	ee ayeea trapeza
arch	ἡ καμάρα	ee kamara
basilica	ἡ βασιλική	ee vaseeleekee
candle	τό κερί	to keree
cathedral	ὁ καθεδρικός ναός	o kathedhreekos naos
chapel	τό παρεκκλήσι	to parekleesee

choir	τό χοροστάσιο	to khorostasyo
cloister	τό περιστύλιο	to pereesteeleeo
column	ἡ στήλη	ee steelee
convent	ἡ μονή	ee monee
crucifix	ὁ ἐσταυρωμένος	o estavromenos
crypt	ἡ κρύπτη	ee kreeptee
font	ἡ κολυμβήθρα	ee koleemveethra
fresco	ἡ τοιχογραφία	ee teekhoghrafeea
monastery	τό μοναστήρι	to monasteeree
nave	τό καθολικό	to katholeeko
rood	ὁ 'Εσταυρωμένος	o estavromenos
sculpture	ἡ γλυπτική	ee ghleepteekee
shrine	τό εἰκονοστασιάκι	to eekonostaseeakee
west front	ἡ δυτική πρόσοψη	ee dheeteekee prosopsee

SIGNS

'Απαγορεύεται ἡ λῆψις φωτογραφιῶν	apaghorevete ee leepsees fotoghrafeeon	No photographs
Κλειστόν λόγω ἐπισκευῶν	kleeston logho epeeskevon	Closed for repair
Κλειστόν λόγω ἀνακαινήσεως	kleeston logho anakeneeseos	Closed for restoration

Art Galleries and Museums

Have you	Ἔχετε ekhete	
a catalogue?	ἕναν κατάλογο; enan katalogho	
an illustrated catalogue?	ἕναν εἰκονογραφημένο κατάλογο; enan eekonoghrafeemeno katalogho	
Are there any plaster casts?	Ἔχει γύψινα ἐκμαγεῖα; ekhee yeepseena ekmayeea	
Do you sell transparencies?	Πουλᾶτε σλάϊντς; poolate slaeedz	

Am I allowed to photograph?	Ἐπιτρέπεται νά βγάλω φωτογραφίες;	
	epeetrepete na vghalo fotoghrafeees	
May I use my tripod?	Ἐπιτρέπεται νά χρησιμοποιήσω τό τρίποδό μου;	
	epeetrepete na khreeseemopeeeeso to **treepodho moo**	
Is the museum open every day?	Εἶναι ἀνοικτό τό μουσεῖο κάθε μέρα;	
	eene aneekto to mooseeo **kathe mera**	
Is the gallery open on Sunday?	Εἶναι ἀνοικτό τό μουσεῖο τήν Κυριακή;	
	eene aneekto to mooseeo teen keeryakee	
Is it free?	Εἶναι ἡ εἴσοδος ἄνευ πληρωμῆς;	
	eene ee eesodhos anef pleeromees	
Where can I find the modern paintings?	Ποῦ μπορῶ νά βρῶ τούς μοντέρνους πίνακες ζωγραφικῆς;	
	poo boro na vro toos **modernoos peenakes** zoghrafeekees	
Do you make photocopies	Κάνετε φωτοαντίγραφα;	
	kanete fotoandeeghrafa	
Where can we buy postcards?	Ποῦ μποροῦμε ν' ἀγοράσουμε κάρτ-ποστάλ;	
	poo boroome naghorasoome **kart** postal	
Where is the library?	Ποῦ εἶναι ἡ βιβλιοθήκη;	
	poo eene ee veevleeotheekee	

Vocabulary

antique books	τά παλιά βιβλία	ta palya veevleea
bas relief	τό ἀνάγλυφο	to anaghleefo
china	ἡ πορσελάνη	ee porselanee
costumes	οἱ ἐνδυμασίες	ee endheemaseees
drawing	τό σχέδιο	to skhedheeo
engraving	τό ἔργο χαρακτικῆς	to ergho kharakteekees
etching	ἡ μεταλλογραφία	ee metaloghrafeea
frame	ἡ κορνίζα	ee korneeza
furniture	τά ἔπιπλα	ta epeepla

gallery	ἡ πινακοθήκη	ee peenakotheekee
jewellery	τά κοσμήματα	ta kozmeemata
lithograph	ἡ λιθογραφία	ee leethoghrafeea
miniature	ἡ μικρογραφία	ee meekroghrafeea
porcelain	ἡ πορσελάνη	ee porselanee
pottery	ἡ ἀγγειοπλαστική	ee anggeeoplasteekee
silverware	τά ἀσημικά	ta aseemeeka

Historical Sights

Will there be far to walk?	**Θά πρέπει νά περπατήσουμε πολύ;** tha **prepee** na perpateesoome polee
Can I wait here till you return?	**Μπορῶ νά περιμένω ἐδῶ μέχρι νά γυρίσεις;** boro **na** pereemeno **edho mekhree** na yeereesees
Is there a souvenir stall?	**῾Υπάρχει ἕνα περίπτερο μέ σουβενίρ;** eeparkhee ena pereeptero me sooveneer
Where can we get a cold drink?	**Ποῦ μποροῦμε νά πάρουμε ἕνα ἀναψυκτικό;** poo boroome na paroome ena anapseekteeko
Is there a plan of the grounds?	**῾Υπάρχει ἕνα σχεδιάγραμμα τοῦ κήπου;** eeparkhee ena skhedhyaghrama too keepoo
I would like to walk round the gardens.	**Θά ἤθελα νά κάνω τό γῦρο τοῦ κήπου.** tha eethela na kano to yeero too keepoo

Vocabulary

acropolis	ἡ ἀκρόπολις	ee akropolees
amphitheatre	τό ἀμφιθέατρο	to amfeetheatro
aqueduct	τό ὑδραγωγεῖο	to eedhraghoyeeo
arena	ἡ παλαίστρα	ee palestra
armour	ἡ πανοπλία	ee panopleea
bas relief	τό ἀνάγλυφο	to anaghleefo
castle	τό κάστρο	to kastro
column	ἡ στήλη	ee steelee

Corinthian style	Κορινθιακός ϱυθμός	koreentheeakos reethmos
courtyard	ἡ αὐλή	ee avlee
crossbow	ἡ βαλλιστϱίς	ee valeestrees
Doric style	Δωϱικός ϱυθμός	dhoreekos reethmos
fort	τό φϱούϱιο	to frooreeo
fortifications	τά ὀχυϱώματα	ta okheeromata
forum	ἡ ἀϱχαία ἀγοϱά	ee arkhea aghora
fountain	τό συντϱιβάνι	to seendreevanee
gate	ἡ πύλη	ee peelee
Ionic style	Ἰωνικός	eeoneekos reethmos
marble	τό μάϱμαϱο	to marmaro
palace	τά ἀνάκτοϱα, τό παλάτι	ta anaktora, to palatee
pediment	τό ἀέτωμα	to aetoma
temple	ὁ ναός	o naos
tower	ὁ πύϱγος	o peerghos
viaduct	ἡ ἐπίσημος γέφυϱα	ee epeeseemos yefeera
wall	τό τεῖχος	to teekhos

Gardens

Are these gardens open to the public?	Εἶναι αὐτός ὁ κῆπος ἀνοικτός γιά τό κοινό;	eene aftos o keepos aneektos ya to keeno
Can we walk where we like?	Μποϱοῦμε νά πεϱπατήσουμε ὅπου θέλουμε;	boroome na perpateesoome opoo theloome
How long will it take to walk around?	Πόση ὥϱα θέλει ὁ γῦϱος μέ τά πόδια;	posee ora thelee o yeeros me ta podhya
At what time do you close?	Τί ὥϱα κλείνετε;	tee ora kleenete
Is there a plan of the gardens?	Ὑπάϱχει ἕνα σχεδιάγϱαμμα τοῦ κήπου;	eeparkhee ena skhedhyaghrama too keepoo
May we sit on the grass?	Μποϱοῦμε νά καθήσουμε στό γϱασίδι;	boroome na katheesoome sto ghraseedhee

What is the name of that	Πῶς λέγεται αὐτό τό	
	pos leyete afto to	
plant/flower/ tree?	φυτό/λουλούδι/δέντρο;	
	feeto/looloodhee/dhendro	

Is there a	Ἔχει μιά	
	ekhee mya	
lake/pond?	λίμνη/λιμνούλα;	
	leemnee/leemnoola	

Who designed these gardens?	Ποιός σχεδίασε αὐτόν τόν κῆπο;	
	pyos skhedheease afton ton keepo	

VOCABULARY

ash	ἡ φλαμουριά	ee flamoorya
beech	ἡ ὀξυά	ee oksya
birch	ἡ σημύδα	ee seemeedha
bougainvillea	ἡ μπουγκενβίλλια	ee boogenveelya
carnation	τό γαρύφαλλο	to ghareefalo
cherry tree	ἡ κερασιά	ee kerasya
chestnut	ἡ καστανιά	ee kastanya
chrysanthemum	τό χρυσάνθεμο	to khreesanthemo
clematis	ἡ κληματίδα	ee kleemteedha
conifer	τό κωνοφόρον	to konoforon
daffodil	ὁ ψευδονάρκισσος	o psevdhonarkeesos
dahlia	ἡ ντάλια	ee dalya
daisy	ἡ μαργαρίτα	ee marghareeta
deciduous tree	τό φυλλοβόλο δέντρο	to feelovolo dhendro
elm	ἡ φτελιά	ee ftelya
evergreen	τό ἀειθαλές	to aeethales
fir	τό ἔλατο	to elato
geranium	τό γεράνιο	to yeraneeo
herbaceous border	ἡ πρασιά (μέ ποώδη φυτά)	ee prasya (me poodhee feeta)
ivy	ὁ κισσός	o keesos
lily	ὁ κρίνος	o kreenos
moss	τά βρύα	ta vreea

nasturtium	τό ναστούρτιο	to nastoorteeo
oak	ἡ βελανιδιά	velaneedhya
palm tree	τό φοινικόδεντρο	to feeneekodhendro
pear tree	ἡ ἀχλαδιά	ee akhladhya
pine	τό πεῦκο	to pefko
plane	ὁ πλάτανος	o platanos
poplar	ἡ λεύκα	ee lefka
rose	τό τριαντάφυλλο	to treeandafeelo
tulip	ἡ τουλίπα	ee tooleepa
violet	ἡ βιολέττα	ee vyoleta
wisteria	ἡ οὐϊσταρία	ee ooeestareea

The Zoo

The children would like to visit the zoo.	**Τά παιδιά θά ἤθελαν νά πᾶνε στό ζωολογικό κῆπο.** ta pedhya tha eethelan na pane sto zo-oloyeeko keepo
Is it open every day?	**Εἶναι ἀνοικτός κάθε μέρα;** eene aneektos kathe mera
Where can we park the car?	**Ποῦ μποροῦμε νά παρκάρουμε τό αὐτοκίνητο;** poo boroome na parkaroome to aftokeeneeto
Can we feed the animals?	**Ἐπιτρέπεται νά ταΐσουμε τά ζῶα;** epeetrepete na taeesoome ta zoa
Where can one buy animal food?	**Ποῦ μπορεῖ κανείς νά ἀγοράσει τροφή γιά τά ζῶα;** poo boree kanees naghorasee trofee ya ta zoa
When is feeding time?	**Πότε ταΐζουν τά ζῶα;** pote taeezoon ta zoa
Is there an insect house?	**Ὑπάρχει ἕνα εἰδικό τμῆμα γιά τά ἔντομα;** eeparkhee ena eedheeko tmeema ya ta endoma

Vocabulary

antelope	ἡ ἀντιλόπη	ee andee**lope**e
ants	τά μυρμήγκια	ta meer**meeng**gya
aquarium	τό ἐνυδρεῖο	to enee**dhree**o
baboon	ὁ μπαμπουῖνος	o baboo**eenos**
bat	ἡ νυκτερίδα	ee neektee**reedha**
bird	τό πουλί	to poo**lee**
bison	τό μπούφφαλο	to **boo**falo
cat	ἡ γάτα	ee **ghata**
crocodile	ὁ κροκόδειλος	o kro**kodheelos**
dog	τό σκυλί	to skee**lee**
frog	ὁ βάτραχος	o **vatrakhos**
giraffe	ἡ καμηλοπάρδαλη	ee kameelo**pardhalee**
hippopotamus	ὁ ἱπποπόταμος	o eepo**potamos**
horse	τό ἄλογο	to **alogho**
hyena	ἡ ὕαινα	ee **eeena**
leopard	ἡ λεοπάρδαλη	ee leo**pardhalee**
lion	τό λιοντάρι	to lyon**daree**
monkey	ὁ πίθηκος	o **peetheekos**
parrot	ὁ παπαγάλος	o papa**ghalos**
rhinoceros	ὁ ρινόκερος	o ree**nokeros**
seal	ἡ φώκια	ee **fokya**
snake	τό φίδι	to **feedhee**
tiger	ἡ τίγρις	ee **teeghrees**
turtle	ἡ (θαλασσινή) χελώνα	ee (thalasee**nee**) khelona
zebra	ὁ ζέβρος	o **zevros**

Sport

Greece is not well provided with sports facilities although amateur foot-
ball is followed with great enthusiasm and there are plenty of aquatic
sports for the visitor, including water skiing and underwater fishing.
Yachting is also growing in popularity among the Greeks and there are
local sailing clubs at some resorts. There are few golf courses, the best
known being at Glyfada (Γλυφάδα) near Athens. There is also a small
one on Corfu, and one on Rhodes. As might be expected in the country
that gave birth to the Olympics, there is a large stadium in Athens for
athletics.

Football

Where is the stadium?	**Ποῦ εἶναι τό γήπεδο;** poo eene to yeepedho
How does one get there?	**Πῶς μπορῶ νά πάω ἐκεῖ;** pos boro na pao ekee
Should I book tickets?	**Πρέπει νά κρατήσω εἰσιτήρια ἀπό μπροστά;** prepee na krateeso eeseeteereea apo brosta
Will it be very crowded?	**Θά ἔχει πολυκοσμία;** tha ekhee poleekozmeea
Who is playing?	**Ποιά ὁμάδα παίζει;** pya omadha pezee
Is there a local team?	**Ἔχει μιά τοπική ὁμάδα;** ekhee mya topeekee omadha
I want a ticket	**Θέλω ἕνα εἰσιτήριο** thelo ena eeseeteereeo
for the main stand/under cover/in the open.	*γιά τήν κυρία ἐξέδρα/σέ ὑπόστεγο/στό ἀστέγαστο.* ya teen keereea eksedhra/see eeposteegho/sto asteghasto

| May I have a programme? | **Μπορῶ νά ἔχω ἕνα πρόγραμμα;** boro na ekho ena proghrama |
| What is the score? | **Τί εἶναι τό σκόρ;** tee eene to skor |

Vocabulary

area	ἡ περιοχή	ee pereeokhee
attack	ἡ ἐπίθεση	ee epeethesee
centre half	τό σέντρα χάφ	to sendra khaf
defence	ἡ ἄμυνα	ee ameena
fans	οἱ ὀπαδοί	ee opadhee
football (ball)	ἡ μπάλλα	ee bala
football (game)	τό ποδόσφαιρο	to podhosfero
forwards	οἱ κυνηγοί	ee keeneeyee
foul	τό φάουλ	to faool
goal	τό γκόλ	to gol
goalkeeper	ὁ τερματοφύλακας	o termatofeelakas
goal posts	τά δοκάρια	ta dhokarya
halfway line	ἡ σέντρα	ee sendra
linesmen	οἱ λάϊνσμαν	ee laeenzman
offside	ὀφσάϊντ	ofsaeed
penalty area	ἡ μικρή περιοχή	ee meekree pereeokhee
penalty kick	τό πέναλτυ	to penaltee
players	οἱ παῖχτες	ee pekhtes
referee	ὁ διαιτητής	o dhyeteetees
team	ἡ ὁμάδα	ee omadha
wing	ὁ ἔξω	o ekso

Race Meeting

| I would like | **Θά ἤθελα** tha eethela |
| a ticket for the paddock. | **ἕνα εἰσιτήριο γιά τό πάντοκ.** ena eeseeteereeo ya to padok |

| a grandstand seat. | μιά θέση στή μεγάλη ἐξέδρα. |
| | mya **thee**see stee me**gha**lee ek**sed**hra |

| Where can I place a bet? | **Ποῦ μπορῶ νά βάλω στοίχημα;** |
| | poo bo**ro** na **va**lo **stee**kheema |

| What are the odds on number 5? | **Πόσες φορές παίζεται τό νούμερο 5;** |
| | **po**ses fo**res pe**zete to **noo**mero **pen**de |

I'd like to back it	**Θά ἤθελα νά τό παίξω**
	tha **ee**thela na to **pek**so
to win/each way/for a place.	γκανιάν/γκανιάν καί πλασέ/πλασέ.
	gan**yan**/gan**yan** ke pla**se**/pla**se**

| Which is the favourite? | **Ποιό εἶναι τό φαβορί;** |
| | pyo **ee**ne to favo**ree** |

| I will back the outsider. | **Θά ποντάρω τό ἀουτσάιντερ.** |
| | tha pon**da**ro to aoo**tsa**eeder |

| Is the jockey well known? | **Εἶναι πασίγνωστος ὁ τζόκεϋ;** |
| | **ee**ne pa**seegh**nostos o **dzo**ke-ee |

VOCABULARY

course	ὁ ἱππόδρομος	o ee**po**dhromos
filly	ἡ πουλάρα	ee poo**la**ra
flat	ἡ κούρσα χωρίς ἐμπόδια	ee **koor**sa kho**rees** em**bo**dheea
horse	τό ἄλογο	to **a**logho
hurdles	τά ἐμπόδια	ta em**bo**dheea
jockey	ὁ τζόκεϋ	o **dzo**ke-ee
owner	ὁ ἰδιοκτήτης	o eedhyok**tee**tees
photo finish	τό φωτο-φίνις	to foto**fee**nees
rails	τά κάγκελα	ta **kang**gela
stable	ὁ σταῦλος	o **stav**los
starting gate	ἡ ἀφετηρία	ee afetee**ree**a
tote	ἡ ἀθροιστική μηχανή (στοιχημάτων)	ee athreestee**kee** mee**kha**nee (steekhee**ma**ton)
trainer	ὁ προπονητής	o propo**nee**tees

Tennis

Is there a tennis club near here?	Ὑπάρχει ἕνας σύλλογος γιά τέννις ἐδῶ κοντά; eeparkhee enas seeloghos ya tenees edho konda
Where is the championship being held?	Ποῦ παίζεται τό πρωτάθλημα; poo pezete to protathleema
How can I get tickets?	Πῶς μπορῶ νά πάρω εἰσιτήρια; pos boro na paro eeseeteereea
Should I arrive early?	Πρέπει νά εἶμαι ἐκεῖ ἐνωρίς; prepee na eeme ekee enorees
Who is playing?	Ποιός παίζει; pyos pezee
Is it on hard courts or grass?	Εἶναι σέ σκληρό γήπεδο ἤ σέ γρασίδι; eene se skleero yeepedho ee se ghraseedhee
I want to watch	Θέλω νά δῶ thelo na dho
the men's singles/the doubles/the mixed doubles.	τή μονομαχία ἀνδρῶν/τό διπλό/τό μιχτό διπλό. tee monomakheea andhron/to dheeplo/to meekto dheeplo
How do you score in Greek?	Πῶς λέγονται οἱ πόντοι στά Ἑλληνικά; pos leghonde ee pondee sta eleeneeka
15, 30, 40, deuce, advantage in/out, game, set, match.	15, 30, 40, ντιούς, ἀντβάντιτζ ἴν/ἄουτ, γκέϊμ, σέτ, μάτς. dhekapende, treeanda, saranda, dyoos, advanteedz in/aoot, geeem, set, mats
Shall we toss for service?	Θά στρίψουμε τό νόμισμα γιά τό σερβί; tha streepsoome to nomeezma ya to servee
Let's adjust the net.	Νά ρυθμίσουμε τό φιλέ. na reethmeesoome to feele
It's too high/too low.	Εἶναι πολύ ψηλά/πολύ χαμηλά. eene polee pseela/polee khameela

That was out/in/on the line.
῏Ηταν ἄουτ/μέσα/στή γραμμή.
eetan aoot/mesa/stee ghramee

Good shot.
Καλή μπαλλιά.
kalee balya

Will you keep the score?
Θέλετε νά κρατήσετε τούς πόντους;
thelete na krateesete toos pondoos

Change ends.
Νά κάνουμε ἀλλαγή.
na kanoome alayee

Vocabulary

backhand	τό ρεβέρ	to rever
forehand	τό ντράϊβ	to draeev
net	ὁ φιλές	o feeles
racket	ἡ ρακέτα	ee raketa
rally	ἡ παρατεταμένη ἀνταλλαγή ἀπό καλές πάσσες	ee paratetamenee andalayee apo kales pases
smash	τό σμάς	to smas
spin	ἡ γυριστή μπαλλιά	ee yeereestee balya
tennis ball	ἡ μπάλλα τοῦ τέννις	ee bala too tenees
umpire	ὁ διαιτητής	o dhyeteetees
volley	τό βόλεϋ	to vole-ee

Golf

Is there a golf course nearby?
Ὑπάρχει ἕνα γήπεδο γκόλφ ἐδῶ κοντά;
eeparkhee ena yeepedho golf edho konda

Does one have to be a member?
Πρέπει νά εἶσαι μέλος;
prepee na eese melos

Is there temporary membership?
Ἔχει προσωρινά μέλη;
ekhee prosoreena melee

How much does it cost to play?
Πόσο κοστίζει τό παιγνίδι;
poso kosteezee to pekhneedhee

I'd like a caddy.	**Θά ἤθελα ἕνα κάντη.** tha eethela ena kadee
Are there any trolleys for hire?	**Εἶναι δυνατόν νά νοικιάσεις καροτσάκια;** eene dheenaton na neekyasees karotsakya
I'd like to speak to the professional.	**Θά ἤθελα νά μιλήσω στόν προπονητή.** tha eethela na meeleeso ston proponeetee
Are you free for lessons?	**Εἶστε ἐλεύθερος γιά μαθήματα;** eeste eleftheros ya matheemata
Will you play a round with me?	**Θέλετε νά παίξετε ἕνα ράουντ μαζί μου;** thelete na peksete ena raoond mazee moo
My handicap is eighteen.	**Τό χάντικάπ μου εἶναι δεκαοκτώ.** to khandeekap moo eene dhekaokto
My problem is	**Τό πρόβλημά μου εἶναι** to provleema moo eene
the slice/the hook.	**τό σλάϊς/τό χούκ.** to slaees/to khook
I can't get any length on my drive.	**Δέν ἔχω μῆκος στά ντράϊβ μου.** dhen ekho meekos sta draeev moo
My approach shots are weak.	**Τά ἀπρόουτς σότς μου (τό κοντό παιχνίδι μου) δέν εἶναι πολύ σπουδαῖο.** ta aproots sots moo (to kondo pekhneedhee moo) dhen eene polee spoodheo
I'll do some putting while I wait for you.	**Θά κάνω πάττιγγ (μερικά συρτά κτυπήματα) καθώς περιμένω.** tha kano pateengg (mereeka seerta kteepeemata) kathos pereemeno
Can I hire some clubs?	**Μπορῶ νά νοικιάσω κλάμπς (μπαστούνια);** boro na neekyaso klabz (bastoonya)
May I have a scorecard?	**Μπορῶ νά ἔχω ἕνα σκόρ-κάρτ;** boro na ekho ena skor kart

VOCABULARY

birdie	τό μπέρντι	to berdee
bunker	τό ἐμπόδιο	to embodheeo
club house	τό ἐντευκτήριο	to endefkteereeo
eagle	τό ἦγκελ	to eegel
fairway	ὁ διάδρομος	o dhyadhromos
golf bag	ὁ σάκκος τοῦ γκόλφ	o sakos too golf
green	τό γκρίν	to green
irons	τά σίδερα	ta seedhera
mashie	τό μάσι	to masee
niblick	τό νίμπλικ	to neebleek
par	τό πάρ	to par
the rough	τό ράφ, τά ψηλά χόρτα	to raf, ta pseela khorta
tee	τό τῆ (τό σημεῖο ἀφετηρίας)	to tee (to seemeeo afeteereeas)

Water-Skiing

I have never skiied before.	Δέν ἔχω κάνει σκί ποτέ πρίν. dhen ekho kanee skee pote prin
I am not a good swimmer.	Δέν ξέρω καλά κολύμπι. dhen ksero kala koleembee
Do I wear a life jacket?	Πρέπει νά φορέσω σωσίβιο; prepee na foreso soseeveeo
Will you please help me to put on the skis?	Μπορεῖτε νά μέ βοηθήσετε νά φορέσω τά σκί; boreete na me voeetheesete na foreso ta skee
Please pass me the rope.	Δῶστε μου τό σχοινί, παρακαλῶ. dhoste moo to skheenee parakalo
May I ride on the speed boat?	Μπορῶ νά πάω στό ταχύπλοο; boro na pao sto takheeplo-o
Can I borrow a wetsuit?	Μπορῶ νά δανειστῶ μιά λαστιχένια φόρμα; boro na dhaneesto mya lasteekhenya forma

I'm ready now.	**Εἶμαι ἕτοιμος (ἕτοιμη) τώρα.**	
	eeme eteemos (eteemee) tora	
Just a moment.	**Μιά στιγμή.**	
	mya steeghmee	

VOCABULARY

aquaplane	**τό ἀκουαπλέϊν, ἡ**	to akooaple-een, ee
	ὑποβρύχιος σανίδα	eepovreekheeos saneedha
bathing hat	**τό σκουφί γιά τό**	to skoofee ya to koleembee
	κολύμπι	
course	**ἡ σειρά μαθημάτων**	ee seera matheematon
goggles	**ἡ μάσκα**	ee maska
jump	**τό ἅλμα**	to alma
monoski	**τό μονοσκί**	to monoskee
slalom	**τό σλάλομ**	to slalom

Riding

Is there a riding stable in the area?	**Ὑπάρχουν σταῦλοι γιά τήν ἱππασία στήν περιοχή;**
	eeparkhoon stavlee ya teen eepaseea steen pereeokhee
Can I hire a horse for riding?	**Μπορῶ νά νοικιάσω ἕνα ἅλογο γιά ἱππασία;**
	boro na veekyaso ena alogho ya eepaseea
Do you give lessons?	**Δίνετε μαθήματα;**
	dheenete matheemata
I'd like to go for a ride.	**Θά ἥθελα νά κάνω βόλτα μέ ἅλογο.**
	tha eethela na kano volta me alogho
I want a quiet horse.	**Θέλω ἕνα ἥρεμο ἅλογο.**
	thelo ena eeremo alogho
Have you any ponies?	**Ἔχετε πουλάρια;**
	ekhete poolarya

Will an instructor accompany the ride?	**Θά μᾶς συνοδέψει ἕνας δάσκαλος;** tha mas seenodhepsee enas dhaskalos	
I'd like to practise jumping.	**Θά ἤθελα νά κάνω ἀσκήσεις ἅλματος.** tha eethela na kano askeesees almatos	
I am	**Εἶμαι** eeme	
an experienced rider/a novice.	**ἔμπειρος καβαλλάρης/ἀρχάριος.** embeeros kavalarees/arkhareeos	
Do you have English saddles?	**Ἔχετε Ἀγγλικές σέλλες;** ekhete anggleekes seles	
This horse has gone lame.	**Αὐτό τό ἅλογο κουτσαίνει.** afto to alogho kootsenee	
The girth is too loose.	**Ἡ ἴγγλα εἶναι πολύ χαλαρή.** ee eenggla eene polee khalaree	
Will you please adjust my stirrups?	**Μπορεῖτε νά ρυθμίσετε τούς ἀναβολεῖς μου;** boreete na reethmeesete toos anavolees moo	
Will you hold my horse while I get on?	**Μπορεῖτε νά κρατήσετε τό ἅλογό μου μέχρι ν' ἀνέβω;** boreete na krateesete to alogho moo mekhree nanevo	
Will you give me a leg-up?	**Μοῦ δίνετε ἕνα χέρι ν' ἀνέβω;** moo dheenete ena kheree nanevo	

Vocabulary

bit	**ἡ στομίς**	ee stomees
bridle	**τό χαλινάρι**	to khaleenaree
gelding	**τό εὐνουχισμένο**	to evnookheezmeno
harness	**τά χάμουρα**	ta khamoora
hock	**ὁ ταρσός**	o tarsos
hoof	**ἡ ὁπλή**	ee oplee
mare	**ἡ φοράδα**	ee foradha
pony	**τό ἀλογάκι**	to aloghakee

reins	τά γκέμια	ta gemya
saddle	ή σέλλα	ee sela
stallion	τό βαρβάτο	to varvato
withers	τό άκρώμιο	to akromeeo

Fishing

Where can I get a permit?	Πού μπορῶ νά βγάλω ἄδεια γιά ψάρεμα; poo boro na vghalo adheea ya psarema
Is there fishing in this area?	Ὑπάρχουν μέρη γιά ψάρεμα σ' αὐτήν τήν περιοχή; eeparkhoon meree ya psarema safteen teen pereeokhee
How much does a day's fishing cost?	Πόσο κοστίζει γιά νά ψαρέψεις γιά μία ἡμέρα; poso kosteezee ya na psarepsees ya meea eemera
Is that per rod?	Εἶναι αὐτό γιά κάθε ἄτομο; eene afto ya kathe atomo
Where can I get some bait?	Πού μπορῶ ν' ἀγοράσω δόλωμα; poo boro naghoraso dholoma
Is there a minimum size that I am allowed to keep?	Ὑπάρχει ἕνα μίνιμουμ μέγεθος ψαριοῦ πού ἐπιτρέπεται νά τό κρατήσω; eeparkhee ena meeneemoom meyethos psaryoo poo epeetrepete na to krateeso
What is the best time of day to go out?	Ποιά εἶναι ἡ καλύτερη ὥρα τῆς ἡμέρας γιά νά πάμε γιά ψάρεμα; pya eene ee kaleeteree ora tees eemeras ya na pame ya psarema
Is it safe to skin dive here?	Εἶναι ἀκίνδυνο ἐδῶ τό ὑποβρύχιο κολύμπι μέ μάσκα καί ἀναπνευστήρα; eene akeendheeno edho to eepovreekheeo koleembee me maska ke anapnefsteera
Where can I hire diving equipment?	Πού μπορῶ νά νοικιάσω τά ἀναγκαῖα γιά καταδύσεις; poo boro na neekyaso ta ananggea ya katadheesees

Is there an underwater swimming school?	Ὑπάρχει καμμιά σχολή γιά ὑποβρύχιο κολύμπι; eeparkhee kamya skholee ya eepovreekheeo koleembee
Are there any boats that will take me deep sea fishing?	Ὑπάρχουν βάρκες γιά ψάρεμα στ' ἀνοιχτά; eeparkhoon varkes ya psarema staneekhta
Do they provide tackle?	Προμηθεύουν καί τά σύνεργα; promeethevoon ke ta seenergha

VOCABULARY

(to) cast	πετάω	petao
fishing season	ἡ ἐποχή ψαρεύματος	ee epokhee psarevmatos
flippers	τά πέδιλα	ta pedheela
fly	ἡ μύγα	ee meegha
gaff	ὁ γάντζος	o ghandzos
goggles	ἡ μάσκα	ee maska
hook	τό ἀγκίστρι	to anggeestree
line	ἡ πετονιά	ee petonya
lure	τό δόλωμα	to dholoma
net	τό δίχτυ	to dheekhtee
oxygen cylinders	οἱ φιάλες ὀξυγόνου	ee fyales okseeghonoo
reel	τό καρούλι	to karoolee
snorkel	ὁ ἀναπνευστήρας	o anapnefsteeras
spinner	τό κουταλάκι	to kootalakee
weights	τά βαρίδια	ta vareedhya
wetsuit	ἡ φόρμα	ee forma

Shooting

Where can I shoot?	Ποῦ μπορῶ νά κυνηγήσω; poo boro na keeneeyeeso
Do I need a licence?	Χρειάζομαι ἄδεια; khreeazome adheea

I'd like to borrow a 12-bore shotgun.	Θά ἤθελα νά δανειστῶ ἕνα ὅπλο δωδεκάρι;	tha eethela na dhaneesto ena oplo dhodhekaree
I have my own rifle.	Ἔχω τό δικό μου ὅπλο.	ekho do dheeko moo oplo
Is there a shooting party I could join?	Ὑπάρχει κανένα γκρούπ γιά κυνήγι πού μπορῶ νά λάβω μέρος;	eeparkhee kanena groop ya keeneeyee poo boro na lavo meros
Is there a clay pigeon shoot?	Ὑπάρχει ἕνα τέστ μέ πήλινους δίσκους γιά σκοποβολή;	eeparkhee ena test me peeleenoos dheeskoos ya skopovolee
Is there a rifle range near?	Ὑπάρχουν στόχοι ἐδῶ κοντά;	eeparkhoon stokhee edho konda

VOCABULARY

backsight	τό κλισιοσκόπιο	to kleeseeoskopeeo
barrel	ἡ κάννη	ee kanee
bullets	τά βόλια	to volya
butt	τό κοντάκι	to kondakee
cartridges	τά φυσίγγια	ta feeseenggya
catch	ὁ σύρτης	o seertees
ejector	ὁ ἐξολκεύς	o eksolkefs
foresight	τό στόχαστρο	to stokhastro
hammer	ὁ ἐπικρουστήρας	o epeekroosteeras
revolver	τό περίστροφο	to pereestrofo
safety catch	ἡ ἀσφάλεια	ee asfalya
telescopic sight	ἡ διόπτρα σκοπεύσεως	ee dhyoptra skopefseos
trigger	ἡ σκανδάλη	ee skandhalee

Sailing and Cruising

Is there a boat hire agent here?	Ὑπάρχει ἐδῶ κοντά κανένα πρακτορείο πού νοικιάζει βάρκες; eeparkhee 'edho konda kanena praktoreeo poo neekyazee varkes
I'd like to hire	Θά ἤθελα νά νοικιάσω tha eethela na neekyaso
a dinghy/a boat.	μιά βαρκούλα/μιά βάρκα. mya varkoola/mya varka
Is an outboard motor extra?	Πληρώνεις παραπάνω γιά ἐξωλέμβιο; pleeronees parapano ya eksolemveeo
Does this have an auxiliary engine?	Ἔχει αὐτό βοηθητική μηχανή; ekhee afto voeetheeteekee meekhanee
How many berths are there?	Πόσα κρεββάτια ἔχει; posa krevatya ekhee
How much water does it draw?	Τί εἶναι τό βύθισμά του; tee eene to veetheezma too
Is there	Ἔχει ekhee
a stove/a sink/a chemical toilet?	μιά κουζίνα/ἕνα νεροχύτη/μιά χημική τουαλέττα; mya koozeena/ena nerokheetee/mya kheemeekee tooaleta
Are all cutlery, china and cooking utensils included?	Περιλαμβάνονται ὅλα τά μαχαιροπήρουνα, τά πιατικά καί τά σκεύη κουζίνας; perrelamvanonde ola ta makheropeeroona, ta pyateeka ke ta skevee koozeenas
Are sheets and blankets provided?	Παρέχονται σεντόνια καί κουβέρτες; parekhonde sedonya ke koovertes
Where can I join a sailing yacht party?	Ποῦ μπορῶ νά λάβω μέρος σ' ἕνα γκρούπ γιά ἱστιοπλοΐα μέ γιώτ; poo boro na lavo meros sena groop ya eesteeoploeea me yot

Do you hire this yacht with a crew?	**Νοικιάζετε αὐτό τό γιώτ μαζί μέ πλήρωμα;** neekyazete afto to yot mazee me pleeroma
I will sail it myself.	**Θά τό κυβερνήσω ἐγώ.** tha to keeverneeso egho
How far is it to the next place where I can get fuel?	**Πόσο μακριά εἶναι τό πλησιέστερο μέρος ὅπου μπορῶ νά πάρω καύσιμα;** poso makreea eene to pleeseeestero meros opoo boro na paro kafseema
Will you please give me a tow?	**Μπορεῖτε νά μέ ρυμουλκήσετε παρακαλῶ;** boreete na me reemoolkeesete parakalo
May I	**Μπορῶ νά** boro na
anchor here/moor here?	**ἀγκυροβολήσω ἐδῶ/προσδέσω ἐδῶ;** anggeerovoleeso edho/prozdheso edho
How deep is it?	**Τί βάθος ἔχει;** tee vathos ekhee
I draw ... feet/metres.	**Τό βύθισμά μου εἶναι . . . πόδια/μέτρα.** to veetheezma moo eene . . . podhya/metra
Do I need an anchor light?	**Χρειάζομαι ἕνα φῶς ἀγκυροβολίας;** khreeazome ena fos anggeerovoleeas
Where can I find	**Ποῦ μπορῶ νά βρῶ** poo boro na vro
fresh water/ diesel/petrol/ gas/paraffin?	**γλυκό νερό/πετρέλαιο/βενζίνη/γκάζι/ παραφίνη;** ghleeko nero/petreleo/venzeenee/gazee/ parafeenee
Where can I find the chandler?	**Ποῦ μπορῶ να βρῶ τόν τροφοδότη;** poo boro na vro ton trofodhotee
How much is the harbour due?	**Πόσο εἶναι τό δικαίωμα ἐλλιμενισμοῦ;** poso eene to dheekeoma eleemeneezmoo
Where is the Customs Office?	**Ποῦ εἶναι τό Τελωνεῖο;** poo eene to teloneeo

I am awaiting customs clearance.	Ἀναμένω τελωνειακή ἄδεια ἀπόπλου.	anameno teloneeakee adheea apoploo
I am bound for/I have left . . .	Ὁ προορισμός μου εἶναι/Ἀπόπλευσα ἀπό . . .	o pro-oreezmos moo eene/apoplefsa apo
Can you take my line (mooring rope), please.	Μπορεῖτε νά πάρετε τό παλαμάρι μου παρακαλῶ;	borette na parete to palamaree moo parakalo
I have damaged	Ἔγιναν ζημιές	eyeenan zeemyes
my hull/my rudder/my mast/my rigging.	στό σκάφος μου/στό τιμόνι μου/στό κατάρτι μου/στά ἀρμενά μου.	sto skafos moo/sto teemonee moo/sto katartee moo/sta armena moo
My engine has broken down. Is there an engineer or shipyard here?	Ἡ μηχανή μου ἔχει χαλάσει. Ἔχει ἐδῶ κανένα μηχανικό ἤ ναυπηγεῖο;	ee meekhanee moo ekhee khalasee. ekhee edho kanena meekhaneeko ee nafpeeyeeo
I am aground.	Εἶμαι προσαραγμένος.	eeme prosaraghmenos
What is the weather going to be?	Τί καιρό θά ἔχουμε;	tee kero tha ekhoome

VOCABULARY

anchor	ἡ ἄγκυρα	ee anggeera
antifoul (paint)	τό παλάμι (χρῶμα), τό ἀντιρρυπαντικό ὑφαλόχρωμα	to palamee (khroma), to andeereepandeeko eefalokhroma
beacon	ὁ ραδιοφάρος	o radheeofaros
boat	ἡ βάρκα, ἡ λέμβος	ee varka, ee lemvos
boathook	τό κοντάρι μέ γάντζο	to kondaree me ghandzo
boom	ἡ μπούμα	ee booma
bows	ἡ πρώρα, ἡ πλώρη	ee prora, ee ploree
buoy	ἡ σημαδούρα	ee seemadhoora

canoe	τό κανώ	to kano
chart	ὁ χάρτης	o khartees
coast	ἡ ἀκτή	ee aktee
compass	ἡ πυξίδα	ee peekseedha
current	τό ῥεῦμα	to revma
deck	ἡ κουβέρτα,	ee kooverta.
	τό κατάστρωμα	to katastroma
diesel engine	ἡ μηχανή ντῆζελ	ee meekhanee deezel
dinghy	ἡ βαρκούλα	ee varkoola
dock	ὁ ντόκος	o dokos
east	ἀνατολικά	anatoleeka
fender	τό μπαλλόνι	to balonee
fibreglass	τό φαϊμπεργκλάς	to faeeberglas
fog	ἡ ὀμίχλη	ee omeekhlee
gale warning	ἡ προειδοποίησις	ee proeedhopeeeesees
	καταιγίδας	kateyeedhas
grease	τό λίπος	to leepos
halyards	τά μαντάρια	to mandarya
hull	τό σκάφος	to skafos
jib	ὁ φλόκος	o flokos
keel	ἡ καρίνα	ee kareena
leak	ἡ διαρροή	ee dhyaroee
lifebelt	ἡ κουλούρα	ee kooloora
lifejacket	τό σωσίβιο	to soseeveeo
lighthouse	ὁ φάρος	o faros
mainsail	τό κύριο πανί	to keereeo panee
marine ply	τό κόντρα πλακέ	to kondra plake thalasees
	θαλάσσης	
mast	τό κατάρτι	to katartee
mooring	ἡ πρόσδεση	ee prozdhese
motor boat	ἡ μηχανοκίνητη	ee meekhanokeeneetee
	λέμβος	lemvos
north	βόρεια	voreea
oars	τά κουπιά	ta koopya
oil	τό λάδι	to ladhee
outboard motor	ὁ ἐξωλέμβιος	o eksolemveeos
paddle	τό κουπί	to koopee
paint	ἡ μπογιά	ee boya

pennant	ἡ μπαντιέρα	ee bandyera
port (left)	ἀριστερά	areestera
propeller	ἡ ἕλικα, ἡ προπέλλα	ee eleeka. ee propela
rocks	οἱ βράχοι	ee vrakhee
rowing boat	ἡ βάρκα μέ κουπιά	ee varka me koopya
safe harbour	τό ὑπήνεμο λιμάνι	to eepeenemo leemanee
sail	τό πανί	to panee
shackle	τό κλειδί	to kleedhee
shallow	ἀβαθής	avathees
sheets	οἱ σκότες	ee skotes
south	νότια	notya
starboard (right)	δεξιά	dheksya
(to) steer	κυβερνῶ	keeverno
stern	ἡ πρύμνη	ee preemnee
storm	ἡ θύελλα	ee theeela
tiller	τό τιμόνι	to teemonee
varnish	τό βερνίκι	to verneekee
west	δυτικά	dheeteeka
winch	τό βίντζι	to veendzee
wind	ὁ ἄνεμος	o anemos
wire	τό σύρμα	to seerma
yacht	τό γιώτ	to yot

General Services

If you are travelling independently or having a self-catering holiday at a villa or apartment, phrases for dealing with electrical and plumbing problems will be indispensable. But even when that is taken care of by someone else it is useful to be able to communicate with Post Office staff, telephone operators and other officials in their own language.

Post Office

Post offices in Greece have the word **ΤΑΧΥΔΡΟΜΕΙΟΝ** outside them. Many of their letter boxes are painted yellow.

Where is the nearest post office?
Ποῦ εἶναι τό πλησιέστερο ταχυδρομεῖο;
poo eene to pleeseeestero takheedhromeeo

What are the opening hours?
Ποιές ὧρες εἶναι ἀνοικτό;
pyes ores eene aneekto

Can I cash an international money order here?
Μπορῶ νά ἐξαργυρώσω μιά διεθνή ἐπιταγή ἐδῶ;
boro na eksaryeeroso mya dhee-ethnee epeetayee edho

I want some stamps for a letter to Britain.
Θέλω γραμματόσημα γιά ἕνα γράμμα γιά τή Βρεττανία.
thelo ghramatoseema ya ena ghrama ya teen vretaneea

What is the postcard postage rate for the U.S.A.?
Τί εἶναι ἡ τιμή γιά κάρτ-ποστάλ γιά τίς Ἡνωμένες Πολιτεῖες;
tee eene ee teemee ya kart postal ya tees eenomenes poleeteees

I'd like to register this letter.
Θέλω νά στείλω αὐτό τό γράμμα συστημένο.
thelo na steelo afto to ghrama seesteemeno

I want to send it
Θέλω νά τό στείλω
thelo na to steelo

airmail.	**ἀεροπορικῶς.** aeroporeekos
express.	**ἐπεῖγον.** epeeghon
surface.	**σιδηροδρομικῶς, μέ τό πλοῖο.** seedheerodhromeekos (train), me to pleeo (ship)
printed matter rate.	**μέ τήν τιμή γιά τυπωμένα.** me teen teemee ya teepomena
Where do I post parcels?	**Ποῦ μπορῶ νά ταχυδρομήσω δέματα;** poo boro na takheedhromeeso dhemata
Do I need a customs form?	**Χρειάζομαι ἕνα ἔντυπο δηλώσεως γιά τό Τελωνεῖο;** khreeazome ena endeepo dheeloseos ya to teloneeo
Is there a poste restante here?	**Ὑπάρχει πόστ-ρεστάντ ἐδῶ;** eeparkhee post restant edho
Have you a letter for me?	**Ἔχετε ἕνα γράμμα γιά μένα;** ekhete ena ghrama ya mena
May I have a telegram form?	**Μπορῶ νά ἔχω ἕνα ἔντυπο τηλεγραφήματος;** boro na ekho ena endeepo teeleghrafeematos
I'll send it by the	**Θά τό στείλω μέ τή** tha to steelo me tee
cheap/normal rate.	**φθηνή/κανονική τιμή.** ftheenee/kanoneekee teemee
When will it arrive?	**Πότε θά φθάσει;** pote tha fthasee
I want to make	**Θέλω νά τηλεφωνήσω** thelo na teelefoneeso
a local/an international telephone call.	**στήν περιφέρεια/στό ἐξωτερικό.** steen pereefereea/sto eksotereeko
Can you reverse the charges?	**Εἶναι δυνατόν νά χρεωθεῖ ὁ παραλήπτης;** eene dheenaton na khreothee o paraleeptees

Switchboard, the line is engaged. Please try again later.	**Δεσποινίς, ἡ γραμμή εἶναι ἀπασχολημένη. Παρακαλῶ νά πάρετε πάλι ἀργότερα.** dhespeenees, ee ghramee eene apaskholeemenee. parakalo na parete palee arghotera

The Police Station

I am a visitor to your country.	**Εἶμαι ἐπισκέπτης στήν χώρα σας.** eeme epeeskeptees steen khora sas
I would like to report	**Θέλω νά ἀναφέρω** thelo na anafero
a theft/a loss/an accident/a crime.	**μιά κλοπή/μία ἀπώλεια/ἔνα ἀτύχημα/ἔνα ἔγκλημα.** mya klopee/mya apoleea/ena ateekheema/ena enggleema
Someone has stolen my wallet.	**Κάποιος ἔχει κλέψει τό πορτοφόλι μου.** kapyos ekhee klepsee to portofolee moo
Something was stolen from my car/my hotel room.	**Κάτι κλέφτηκε ἀπό** katee klefteeke apo **τό αὐτοκίνητό μου/τό δωμάτιό μου.** to aftokeeneeto moo/to dhomateeo moo
The theft occurred in Athinas Street at about four o'clock.	**Ἡ κλοπή ἔγινε στήν ὁδό Ἀθηνᾶς κατά τίς τέσσερες.** ee klopee eyeene steen odho atheenas kata tees teseres
I have lost my watch on the beach.	**Ἔχασα τό ρολόϊ μου στήν ἀκρογιαλιά.** ekhasa to roloee moo steen akroyalya
It is valuable. It has sentimental value.	**Εἶναι μεγάλης ἀξίας. Ἔχει ἀξία γιά συναισθηματικούς λόγους.** eene meghalees akseeas. ekhee akseea ya seenestheemateekoos loghoos
I will offer a reward.	**Θά προσφέρω ἀμοιβή.** tha prosfero ameevee

Someone has been knocked down.	**Κάποιος ἔχει κτυπηθεῖ ἀπό αὐτοκίνητο.** kapyos ekhee kteepeethee apo aftokeeneeto
A lady has broken her leg.	**Μία κυρία ἔχει σπάσει τό πόδι της.** meea keereea ekhee spasee to podhee tees
There is man molesting women on the promenade.	**Ἕνας ἄντρας πειράζει τίς γυναίκες στό δρόμο μπροστά στή θάλασσα.** enas andras peerazee tees yeenekes sto dhromo brosta stee thalasa
I have been swindled.	**Ἔχω ἀπατηθεῖ.** ekho apateethee
Can a police officer come with me?	**Μπορεῖ ἕνας ἀστυνομικός νά ᾽ρθεῖ μαζί μου;** boree enas asteenomeekos narthee mazee moo
I will be a witness.	**Θά εἶμαι μάρτυρας.** tha eeme marteeras
I cannot be a witness. I did not see what was happening.	**Δέν μπορῶ νά γίνω μάρτυρας. Δέν εἶδα τί συνέβηκε.** dhen boro na yeeno marteeras. dhen eedha tee seeneveke
Is there anyone here who speaks English?	**Ἔχει κάποιον ἐδῶ πού μιλάει Ἀγγλικά;** ekhee kapyon edho poo meelaee anggleeka

Electricity

The lights have gone out.	**Τά φῶτα ἔχουν σβήσει.** ta fota ekhoon zveesee
The power plug is not working.	**Ἡ πρίζα ρεύματος δέν λειτουργεῖ.** ee preeza revmatos dhen leetooryee
The fuse has gone.	**Ἡ ἀσφάλεια ἔχει καεῖ.** ee asfalya ekhee kaee
I think it is the switch.	**Νομίζω ὅτι εἶναι ὁ διακόπτης.** nomeezo otee eene o dhyakoptees

There is a smell of burning.	**Μυρίζει ἀπό φωτιά.** meereezee apo fotya
The cooker doesn't work.	**Ἡ κουζίνα δέν λειτουργεῖ.** ee koozeena **dhen** leetooryee
The heating has broken down.	**Τό καλοριφέρ ἔχει χαλάσει.** to kaloree**fer** ekhee khalasee
Can you mend it straight away?	**Μπορεῖτε νά τό ἐπισκευάσετε ἀμέσως;** boreete na to epeeskevasete amesos
Where is the fuse box?	**Ποῦ εἶναι τό κιβώτιο ἀσφαλειῶν;** poo eene to keevoteeo asfalee**on**
Which is the main switch?	**Ποιός εἶναι ὁ κύριος διακόπτης;** pyos eene o **kee**reeos dhyakoptees

VOCABULARY

adaptor	**ὁ σταυρός**	o stavros
bulb	**ἡ λάμπα**	ee lamba
cooker	**ἡ κουζίνα**	ee koozeena
electric fire	**ἡ ἠλεκτρική σόμπα**	ee eelektree**kee** somba
extension lead	**τό καλώδιο ἐπεκτάσεως**	to kalodheeo epektaseos
fuse wire	**τό σύρμα ἀσφάλειας**	to seerma asfalyas
hairdryer	**τό σεσουάρ**	to sesooar
insulating tape	**ἡ ἀπομονωτική ταινία**	ee apomonoteekee teneea
iron	**τό σίδερο**	to seedhero
oven	**ὁ φοῦρνος**	o foornos
plug	**ἡ πρίζα**	ee preeza
radio	**τό ραδιόφωνο**	to radheeofono
razor point	**ἡ πρίζα γιά ξυριστική μηχανή**	ee preeza ya kseereesteekee meekhanee
refrigerator	**τό ψυγεῖο**	to pseeyeeo
spotlight	**ὁ προβολεύς**	o provelefs
television	**ἡ τηλεόραση**	ee teeleorasee

| torch | ὁ φακός | o fakos |
| water heater | τό θερμοσίφωνο | to thermoseefono |

Plumbing

Are you the plumber?	Εἴστε ὁ ὑδραυλικός;	eeste o eedhravleekos
The sink is stopped up.	Ὁ νεροχύτης εἶναι βουλωμένος.	o nerokheetees eene voolomenos
There is a blockage in the pipe.	Ἔχει ἐμπόδιο στό σωλήνα.	ekhee embodheeo sto soleena
The tap is dripping.	Ἡ βρύση στάζει συνεχῶς.	ee vreesee stazee seenekhos
The tap needs a new washer.	Ἡ βρύση θέλει μιά καινούργια ροδέλα.	ee vreesee thelee mya kenoorya rodhela
This water pipe is leaking.	Αὐτός ὁ σωλήνας νεροῦ στάζει.	aftos o soleenas neroo stazee
The lavatory cistern won't fill.	Τό καζανάκι τῆς τουαλέττας δέν γεμίζει.	to kazanakee tees tooaletas dhen yemeezee
The valve is stuck.	Ἡ βαλβίδα ἔχει κολλήσει.	ee valveedha ekhee koleesee
The float is punctured.	Ὁ πλωτήρας εἶναι τρυπημένος.	o ploteeras eene treepeemenos
The water tank has run dry.	Ἡ δεξαμενή νεροῦ εἶναι ἐντελῶς ἄδεια.	ee dheksamenee neroo eene endelos adhya
The tank is overflowing.	Ἡ δεξαμενή ξεχειλίζει.	ee dheksamenee ksekheeleezee

VOCABULARY

basin	ὁ νιπτήρας	o neepteeras
bath	ἡ μπανιέρα	ee banyera
cesspool	ὁ βόθρος	o vothros
drain	ὁ ὑπόνομος	o eeponomos
immersion heater	τό ἠλεκτρικό θερμοσίφωνο	to eelektreeko thermoseefono
main drainage	ἡ κεντρική ἀποχέτευση	ee kendreekee apokhetefsee
mains water	τό νερό κεντρικῆς παροχῆς	to nero kendreekees parokhees
overflow pipe	ὁ σωλήνας ἀσφαλείας	o soleenas asfaleeas
plug	τό βούλωμα	to vooloma
plumber	ὁ ὑδραυλικός	o eedhravleekos

Personal Services

This section suggests useful phrases for such occasions as a visit to a doctor, dentist, hairdresser, hospital or beautician.

At the Doctor's

Can you recommend a good doctor?	Μπορεῖτε νά συστήσετε ἕνα καλό γιατρό; boreete na seesteesete ena kalo yatro
Is there an English-speaking doctor in the area?	Ἔχει ἕνα γιατρό στήν περιφέρεια πού μιλάει Ἀγγλικά; ekhee ena yatro steen pereefereea poo meelaee anggleeka
Where is the surgery?	Ποῦ εἶναι τό ἰατρεῖο; poo eene to eeatreeo
I have an appointment. My name is . . .	Ἔχω κλείσει ραντεβού. Ὀνομάζομαι . . . ekho kleesee randevoo. onomazome
Can the doctor come	Μπορεῖ ὁ γιατρός νά 'ρθεῖ boree o yatros narthee
to the hotel/to the house?	στό ξενοδοχεῖο/στό σπίτι; sto ksenodhokheeo/sto speetee
I'm not feeling well.	Δέν αἰσθάνομαι καλά. dhen esthanome kala
I feel	Αἰσθάνομαι esthanome
sick/faint.	ἀναγούλα/λιποθύμηση. anaghoola/leepotheemeesee
dizzy.	ζαλάδα. zaladha
I feel shivery.	Ἔχω ρίγη. ekho reeyee

The pain is here.	'Ο πόνος εἶναι ἐδῶ. o ponos eene edho
I have	Ἔχω ekho
a temperature/a headache/sunburn.	πυρετό/πονοκέφαλο/ἡλιοκαύματα. peereto/ponokefalo/eelyokavmata
I have	Πονάει ponaee
back ache/a sore throat.	ἡ μέση μου/ὁ λαιμός μου. ee mesee moo/o lemos moo
I have diarrhoea.	Ἔχω διάρροια. ekho dhyareea
I have been like this since yesterday.	Εἶμαι ἔτσι ἀπό χθές. eeme etsee apo khthes
I have been vomiting.	Ἔκανα ἐμετό. ekana emeto
I am constipated.	Εἶμαι δυσκοίλιος (δυσκοίλια). eeme dheeskeeleeos (dheeskeeleea)
My . . . hurts.	Μέ πονάει ὁ (ἡ, τό) . . . μου. me ponaee o (ee, to) . . . moo
Must I undress?	Πρέπει νά ξεντυθῶ; prepee na ksedeetho
Is it serious?	Εἶναι τίποτα τό σοβαρό; eene teepota to sovaro
Should I stay in bed?	Πρέπει νά παραμείνω στό κρεββάτι; prepee na parameeno sto krevatee
Should I arrange to go home?	Πρέπει νά κανονίσω νά ἐπιστρέψω στή χώρα μου; prepee na kanoneeso na epeestrepso stee khora moo
I am allergic to . . .	Εἶμαι ἀλλεργικός (ἀλλεργική) εἰς . . . eeme aleryeekos (aleryeekee) ees . . .

I have a heart condition.	**Εἶμαι καρδιακός (καρδιακή).** eeme kardheeakos (kardheeakee)	
I am asthmatic.	**Ὑποφέρω ἀπό ἄσθμα.** eepofero apo asthma	
I am diabetic.	**Εἶμαι διαβητικός (διαβητική).** eeme dhyaveeteekos (dhyaveeteekee)	
I am pregnant.	**Εἶμαι ἔγκυος.** eeme enggeeos	
What attention do I get free under the national health arrangements?	**Τί θεραπεία δικαιοῦμαι βάσει τῶν συμφωνιῶν κοινωνικῆς ἀσφαλείας;** tee therapeea dheekeeoome vasee ton seemfoneeon keenoneekees asfaleeas	
Do I have to pay for hospitalization and medicines?	**Πρέπει νά πληρώσω γιά τό νοσοκομεῖο καί τά φάρμακα;** prepee na pleeroso ya to nosokomeeo ke ta farmaka	

Vocabulary

Parts of the body

ankle	**ὁ ἀστράγαλος**	o astraghalos
appendix	**ἡ σκωληκοειδής ἀπόφυσις**	ee skoleekoeedhees apofeesees
arm	**τό χέρι**	to kheree
artery	**ἡ ἀρτηρία**	eé arteereea
back	**ἡ ῥάχη**	ee rakhee
bladder	**ἡ κύστις**	ee keestees
blood	**τό αἷμα**	to ema
bone	**τό κόκκαλο**	to kokalo
bowels	**τά ἔντερα**	ta endera
breast	**τό στῆθος**	to steethos
cheek	**τό μάγουλο**	to maghoolo
chest	**τό στῆθος, ὁ θώρακας**	to steethos, o thorakas

chin	τό πηγούνι	to pee**ghoo**nee
collar bone	ὁ κλείς	o **klees**
ear	τό αὐτί	to af**tee**
elbow	ὁ ἀγκώνας	o ang**go**nas
eye	τό μάτι	to **ma**tee
face	τό πρόσωπο	to **pro**sopo
finger	τό δάκτυλο	to **dha**kteelo
foot	τό πόδι, ἡ πατούσα	to **po**dhee, ee pa**too**sa
forehead	τό μέτωπο	to **me**topo
gland	ὁ ἀδένας	o a**dhe**nas
hand	τό χέρι, ἡ παλάμη	to **khe**ree, ee pa**la**mee
head	τό κεφάλι	to ke**fa**lee
heart	ἡ καρδιά	ee kar**dhya**
heel	ἡ πτέρνα	ee **pter**na
hip	ὁ γοφός	to gho**fos**
intestine	τό ἔντερο	to **en**dero
jaw	τό σαγόνι	to sa**gho**nee
joint	ἡ κλείδωση	ee **klee**dhosee
kidney	τό νεφρό	to ne**fro**
knee	τό γόνατο	to **gho**nato
leg	τό πόδι	to **po**dhee
lip	τό χείλι	to **khee**lee
liver	τό συκώτι	to see**ko**tee
lung	τό πνευμόνι	to pnev**mo**nee
mouth	τό στόμα	to **sto**ma
muscle	ὁ μῦς	o **mees**
neck	ὁ τράχηλος	o **tra**kheelos
nerve	τό νεῦρο	to **nev**ro
nose	ἡ μύτη	ee **mee**tee
penis	τό πέος	to **pe**os
rib	τό πλευρό	to ple**vro**
shoulder	ὁ ὦμος	o **o**mos
skin	τό δέρμα	to **dher**ma
spine	ἡ σπονδυλική στήλη	ee spondhee**lee**kee **stee**lee
stomach	τό στομάχι	to sto**ma**khee
teeth	τά δόντια	to **dhon**dya
tendon	ὁ τένων	o **te**non
testicle	ὁ ὄρχις	o **or**khees

thigh	τό μπούτι	to bootee
throat	ὁ λάρυγγας, ὁ λαιμός	o lareenggas, o lemos
thumb	τό μεγάλο δάκτυλο	to meghalo dhakteelo
toe	τό δάκτυλο τοῦ ποδιοῦ	to dhakteelo too podhyoo
tongue	ἡ γλῶσσα	ee ghlosa
tonsils	οἱ ἀμυγδαλές	ee ameeghdhales
urine	τά οὖρα	ta oora
vein	ἡ φλέβα	ee fleva
vagina	ὁ κολεός	o koleos
wrist	ὁ καρπός	o karpos
womb	ἡ μήτρα	ee meetra

INDISPOSITIONS

abscess	τό ἀπόστημα	to aposteema
appendicitis	ἡ σκωλικοειδίτιδα	ee skoleekoeedheeteedha
arthritis	ἡ ἀρθρίτιδα	ee arthreeteedha
asthma	τό ἄσθμα	to asthma
bite (animal)	τό δάγκωμα	to dhanggoma
bite (insect)	τό τσίμπημα	to tseembeema
blisters	οἱ φουσκάλες	ee fooskales
boil	ὁ καλόγερος	o kaloyeros
bruise	ἡ μαυρίλα	ee mavreela
burn	τό ἔγκαυμα	to enggavma
chill, cold	τό κρυολόγημα	to kreeoloyeema
convulsions	οἱ σπασμοί	ee spazmee
cough	ὁ βήχας	o veekhas
cramp	τό πιάσιμο	to pyaseemo
cut	τό κόψιμο	to kopseemo
cyst	ἡ κύστις	ee keestees
diabetes	ὁ διαβήτης	o dhyaveetees
diarrhoea	ἡ διάρροια	ee dhyareea
dizziness	ἡ ζαλάδα	ee zaladha
haemorrhoids	οἱ αἱμορροείδες	ee emoroeedhes
hay fever	ὁ πυρετός τοῦ χόρτου	o peeretos too khortoo

high/low	ἡ ὑψηλή/χαμηλή	ee epseelee/khameelee
blood pressure	πίεση	peecsee
indigestion	ἡ δυσπεψία	ee dheespepseea
infection	ἡ μόλυνση	ee moleensee
inflammation	ἡ φλεγμονή	ee fleghmonee
influenza	ἡ γρίππη	ee ghreepee
irritation	ὁ ἐρεθισμός	o eretheezmos
nausea	ἡ ναυτία,	ee nafteea,
	ἡ ἀναγούλα	ee anaghoola
pneumonia	ἡ πνευμονία	ee pnevmoneea
rash	τό ἐξάνθημα	to eksantheema
rheumatism	ὁ ρευματισμός	o revmateezmos
scald	τό ἔγκαυμα	to engavma
shivers	τά ρίγη	ta reeyee
slipped disc	ἡ ὀλίσθηση δίσκου	ee oleestheesee dheeskoo
stiff neck	τό πιάσιμο τοῦ	to pyaseemo too trakheeloo
	τραχήλου	
sting	τό κέντρωμα	to kendroma
sunstroke	ἡ ἡλίαση	ee eeleeasee
swelling	τό πρήξιμο	to preekseemo
(high) temperature	ὁ πυρετός	o peeretos
tonsillitis	ἡ ἀμυγδαλίτις	ee ameeghdaleetees
ulcer	τό ἔλκος	to elkos
whooping cough	ὁ κοκκύτης	o kokeetees
wound	ἡ πληγή	ee pleeyee

At the Dentist's

Can you recommend a dentist?	**Μπορεῖτε νά συστήσετε ἕναν ὀδοντίατρο;** boreete na seesteesete enan odhondeeatro
I need an appointment as soon as possible.	**Χρειάζομαι ἕνα ραντεβού τό ἐνωρίτερο δυνατόν.** kreeazome ena randevoo to enoreetero dheenaton
I have	**Ἔχω** ekho
a toothache/an abscess.	**πονόδοντο/ἕνα ἀπόστημα.** ponodhondo/ena aposteema

| My gums are bleeding. | Τά οὖλα μου ματώνουν. |
| | ta oola moo matonoon |

| I have broken my dentures. | Ἔσπασα τή μασέλλα μου. |
| | espasa tee masela moo |

| Can you suggest a pain-killer until I can see you? | Μπορεῖτε νά συστήσετε ἕνα παυσίπονο μέχρι νά σᾶς δῶ; |
| | boreete na seesteesete ena pafseepono mekhree na sas dho |

The bad tooth is at the front/back/side.	Τό παλιό δόντι εἶναι
	to palyo dhondee eene
	μπροστά/πίσω/στήν πλευρά.
	brosta/peeso/steen plevra

| I have lost a filling. | Ἔχω χάσει ἕνα σφράγισμα. |
| | ekho khasee ena sfrayeezma |

| My gums are bleeding/sore. | Τά οὖλα μου ματώνουν/εἶναι ἐρεθισμένα. |
| | ta oola moo matonoon/eene eretheezmena |

| Can you extract it? | Μπορεῖτε νά τό βγάλετε; |
| | boreete na to vghalete |

| Does it need a filling? | Θέλει σφράγισμα; |
| | thelee sfrayeezma |

| Can you put in a temporary filling? | Μπορεῖτε νά κάνετε προσωρινό σφράγισμα; |
| | boreete na kanete prosoreeno sfrayeezma |

| Can I bite normally? | Μπορῶ νά μασῶ κανονικά; |
| | boro na maso kanoneeka |

| I'd prefer gas to an injection. | Προτιμῶ ἀέριο παρά ἔνεση. |
| | proteemo aereeon para enesee |

| What is your fee? | Πόσο παίρνετε γι' αὐτό; |
| | poso pernete yafto |

At the Optician's

Can you recommend an optician?	**Μπορεῖτε νά συστήσετε ἕναν ὀπτικό;** boreete na seesteesete enan opteeko
I have broken my glasses.	**῎Εσπασα τά γυαλιά μου.** espasa to yalya moo
Can you repair them temporarily?	**Μπορεῖτε νά τά ἐπιδιορθώσετε προσωρινά;** boreete na ta epeedhyorthosete prosoreena
The lens is broken. Can you get a new one quickly?	**῾Ο φακός ἔσπασε. Μπορεῖτε νά πάρετε γρήγορα ἕναν καινούργιο;** o fakos espase. boreete na parete ghreeghora enan kenooryo
Have you got contact lenses?	**῎Εχετε φακούς ἐπαφῆς;** ekhete fakoos epafees
I'd like a pair of tinted spectacles.	**Θά ἤθελα ἕνα ζευγάρι γυαλιά χρωματιστά.** tha eethela ena zevgharee yalya khromateesta
Do you sell	**Πουλᾶτε** poolate
binoculars/a magnifying glass/sunglasses?	**διόπτρες/μεγενθυντικό φακό/γυαλιά ἡλίου;** dheeoptres/meyentheendeeko fako/yalya eeleeoo
I had better have an eye test.	**Καλύτερα νά ἐξετασθοῦν τά μάτια μου.** keleetera na eksetasthoon ta matya moo
I am	**῎Εχω** ekho
shortsighted/ long sighted.	**μυωπία/ὑπερμετρωπία.** meeopeea/eepermetropeea
How long will it take to make me some new glasses?	**Πόσον καιρό θά χρειαστεῖ νά μοῦ φτιάξετε καινούργια γυαλιά;** poson kero tha khreeastee na moo ftyaksete kenoorya yalya
How much will they cost?	**Πόσο θά στοιχίσουν;** poso tha steekheesoon

At the Chiropodist's

Can you recommend a chiropodist?	**Μπορεῖτε νά συστήσετε ἕναν πεντικιουρίστα;** boreete na seesteesete enan pedeekyooreesta
I have a painful corn.	**Ἔχω ἕνα κάλο πού μέ πονάει.** ekho ena kalo poo me ponaee
Can you remove it?	**Μπορεῖτε νά τόν κόψετε;** boreete na ton kopsete
My bunion is rubbing against my shoe.	**Ὁ κάλος στήν πατούσα μου τρίβει στό παπούτσι μου.** o kalos steen patoosa moo treevee sto papootsee moo
I have a hard spot on the ball of my foot.	**Ἔχω ἕνα σκληρό σημεῖο στήν πατούσα μου.** ekho ena skleero seemeeo steen patoosa moo
My nails need attention. One of them is ingrowing.	**Τά νύχια μου χρειάζονται περιποίηση. Τό ἕνα μπαίνει μέσα στό δέρμα.** ta neekhya moo khreeazonde pereepeeeesee. to ena benee mesa sto dherma
Have you anything to soften them?	**Ἔχετε κάτι γιά νά τά μαλακώσει;** ekhete katee ya na ta malakosee
I have stubbed my toe.	**Ἔχω σκοντάψει τό δάκτυλο τοῦ ποδιοῦ μου.** ekho skondapsee to dhakteelo too podhyoo moo
The soles of my feet are very sore.	**Οἱ πατούσες μου μέ πονοῦν πολύ.** ee patooses moo me ponoon polee

At the Hairdresser's (Women's)

Where is the nearest hairdresser? Is there one in the hotel?	**Ποῦ εἶναι τό πλησιέστερο κομμωτήριο; Ἔχει κανένα στό ξενοδοχεῖο;** poo eene to pleeseeestero komoteereeo? ekhee kanena sto ksenodhokheeo
I'd like to make an appointment.	**Θά ἤθελα νά κλείσω ραντεβού.** tha eethela na kleeso randevoo

I'd like a shampoo and set.	**Θά ἤθελα λούσιμο καί μιζαμπλί.** tha eethela looseemo ke meezamblee
I want it cut and set.	**Θέλω κόψιμο καί μιζαμπλί.** thelo kopseemo ke meezamblee
I wear it brushed forward with a fringe.	**Τά ἔχω βουρτσισμένα ἐμπρός μέ φράντζα.** ta ekho voortseezmena embros me frandza
I like it brushed back.	**Μοῦ ἀρέσει νά εἶναι βουρτσισμένα πρός τά πίσω** moo aresee na eene voortseezmena pros ta peeso
Can you put in	**Μπορεῖτε νά βάλετε** boreete na valete
some waves/some curls?	**λίγες σγοῦρες/μπούκλες;** leeghes zghoores/bookles
Can you draw it back into a bun?	**Μπορεῖτε νά τά τραβήξετε πίσω σέ κότσο;** boreete na ta traveeksete peeso se kotso
Can you give me a colour rinse?	**Μπορεῖτε νά μοῦ τά βάψετε;** boreete na moo ta vapsete
I think I will have it dyed.	**Νομίζω ὅτι θά τά βάψω.** nomeezo otee tha ta vapso
Have you got a colour chart?	**Ἔχετε ἕνα πίνακα ἀποχρώσεων;** ekhete ena peenaka apokhroseon
No hairspray, thank you.	**Ὄχι λάκα, εὐχαριστῶ.** okhee laka, efkhareesto
I'd like a manicure.	**Θά ἤθελα ἕνα μανικιούρ.** tha eethela ena maneekyoor
What is the name of this varnish?	**Πῶς λέγεται αὐτό τό βερνίκι;** pos leyete afto to verneekee

VOCABULARY

auburn (hair)	**καστανοκόκκινα (μαλλιά)**	kastanokokeena (malya)

blonde	ξανθά	ksantha
brunette	σκούρα	skoora
brush	ἡ βούρτσα	ee voortsa
comb	ἡ χτένα	ee khtena
dryer	τό σεσουάρ	to sesooar
hairnet	ὁ φιλές	o feeles
hairpiece	τό περουκίνι	to perookeenee
hair pin	ἡ φουρκέτα	ee foorketa
razor	τό ξυράφι	to kseerafee
rollers	οἱ ρόλοι	ee rolee
scissors	τό ψαλίδι	to psaleedhee
shampoo	τό σαμπουάν	to sambooan
styling	τό μιζαμπλί, τό κτένισμα	to meezamblee, to kteneezma
wig	ἡ περούκα	ee perooka

At the Beauty Salon

I'd like	Θά ἤθελα tha eethela	
a complete beauty treatment/just a facial.	μιά ὁλοκληρωτική θεραπεία καλλωπισμοῦ/θεραπεία προσώπου μόνο. mya olokleeroteekee therapeea kalopeezmoo/therapeea prosopoo mono	
I'd like to change my make-up.	Θά ἤθελα ν' ἀλλάξω τό μακιγιάζ μου. tha eethela nalakso to makeeyaz moo	
I'd like	Θά ἤθελα tha eethela	
something more suitable for the seaside.	κάτι πιό κατάλληλο γιά τό ἀκρογιάλι. katee pyo kataleelo ya to akroyalee	
something lighter in tone.	κάτι σ' ἕνα πιό ἁπαλό τόνο. katee sena pyo apalo tono	
a more open-air look.	Μιά ἐμφάνιση πιό σπόρ. mya emfaneesee pyo spor	
something for the evening.	κάτι γιά τό βράδυ. katee ya to vradhee	

I have a delicate skin.	**Ἔχω πολύ εὐαίσθητο δέρμα.** ekho polee evestheeto **dh**erma
Can you please suggest a new eye make-up?	**Μπορεῖτε νά προτείνετε ἕνα ἄλλο μακιγιάζ γιά τά μάτια;** boreete na proteenete ena alo makeeyaz ya ta matya
I think that is too heavy.	**Νομίζω ὅτι αὐτό εἶναι πολύ βαρύ.** nomeezo otee afto eene polee varee
Have you any false eyelashes?	**Ἔχετε ψεύτικες βλεφαρίδες;** ekhete psefteekes vlefareedhes
I think my eyebrows need plucking.	**Νομίζω ὅτι τά φρύδια μου θέλουν βγάλσιμο.** nomeezo otee ta **freedh**ya moo **thel**oon vghalseemo
I'd like to see some new lipstick colours.	**Θά ἤθελα νά δῶ κάτι καινούργια χρώματα γιά κραγιόν.** tha eethela na **dh**o katee kenoorya khromata ya krayon

At the Laundry/Cleaner's

I'd like them washed and pressed, please.	**Αὐτά γιά πλύσιμο καί σιδέρωμα, παρακαλῶ.** afta ya **pl**eeseemo ke seedheroma parakalo
Will you iron the shirts?	**Μπορεῖτε νά σιδερώσετε τά πουκάμισα;** boreete na seed**h**erosete ta pookameesa
I will collect them tomorrow.	**Θά 'ρθῶ νά τά πάρω αὔριο.** thartho na ta paro avreeo
Do you deliver?	**Κάνετε διανομές;** kanete dhyanomes
Do you do mending?	**Κάνετε μανταρίσματα;** kanete mandareezmata
This tear needs patching.	**Αὐτό τό σχίσιμο θέλει μπάλωμα.** afto to skheeseemo thelee baloma

Can you sew this button on?	**Μπορείτε νά ράψετε αὐτό τό κουμπί;**	
	boreete na rapsete afto to koombee	
Will this stain come out?	**Θά βγεῖ αὐτός ὁ λεκές;**	
	tha vyee aftos o lekes	
It is	**Εἶναι ἀπό**	
	eene apo	
coffee/blood/ grease/biro.	**καφέ/αἷμα/λίπος/μπίχ.**	
	kafe/ema/leepos/beek	
Can you mend this invisibly?	**Μπορείτε νά κάνετε σ' αὐτό μαντάρισμα πού δέν φαίνεται;**	
	boreete na kanete sat:o mandareezma poo **dhen** fenete	
This suit is not mine.	**Αὐτό τό κοστούμι δέν εἶναι δικό μου.**	
	afto to kostoomee **dhen** eene dheeko moo	
My trousers are missing.	**Λείπει τό παντελόνι μου.**	
	leepee to pandelonee moo	
This was not torn when I brought it to you.	**Αὐτό δέν ἦταν σχισμένο ὅταν τό ἔφερα ἐδῶ.**	
	afto **dhen** eetan skheezmeno otan to efera edho	
How long does the launderette stay open?	**Μέχρι πότε εἶναι ἀνοιχτό αὐτό τό αὐτόματο πλυντήριο;**	
	mekhree pote eene aneekto afto to aftomato pleendeereeo	

VOCABULARY

bleach	**ἡ χλωρίνη**	ee khloreenee
(to) clean	**καθαρίζω**	kathareezo
cleaning fluid	**τό ὑγρό γιά καθάρισμα**	to eeghro ya kathareezma
clothes hanger	**ἡ κρεμάστρα**	ee kremastra
cold/hot/warm water	**κρύο/ζεστό/χλιαρό νερό**	kreeo/zesto/khlyaro nero

the dryer	ὁ στεγνωτήρας	o steghnoteeras
launderette	τό αὐτόματο πλυντήριο	to aftomato pleendeereeo
rinse	ξεπλένω	ksepleno
soap powder	ἡ σκόνη πλυσίματος	ee skonee pleeseematos
spin	στίβω στή μηχανή	steevo stee meekhanee
tumble dry	στεγνώνω μέ θέρμανση	steghnono me **ther**mansee
(the) washing	ἡ μπουγάδα	ee boo**gha**dha
washing machine	τό ἡλεκτρικό πλυντήριο	to eelektree**ko** pleendeereeo

At the Men's Hairdresser's

I want a haircut, please.	Θέλω κούρεμα, παρακαλῶ.	thelo koorema parakalo
Just a trim. I haven't much time.	Λίγο ψαλίδισμα μόνο. Δέν ἔχω πολλή ὥρα.	leegho psaleedheezma mono. **dhen** ekho polee ora
Please give me a shampoo.	Λούσιμο, παρακαλῶ.	looseemo parakalo
I would like it cut shorter.	Θά τά ἤθελα πιό κοντά.	tha ta eethela **pyo** konda
Leave it long.	Νά τ' ἀφήσετε μακριά.	na tafeesete makreea
You are taking too much off.	Τά κόβετε πάρα πολύ.	ta **ko**vete para polee
Take a little more off	Πάρτε τα λίγο περισσότερο	parte ta leegho pereesotero
the back/the sides/the top.	ἀπό πίσω/στίς πλευρές/στό πάνω μέρος.	apo **pee**so/stees plev**res**/sto **pa**no **me**ros
I part my hair on the	Τά χωρίζω	ta kho**ree**zo
left/right.	ἀριστερά/δεξιά.	areeste**ra**/dhe**ksya**

I'd like	**Θά ἤθελα** tha eethela
a singe/an alcohol rub.	**καψάλισμα/τρίψιμο μέ οἰνόπνευμα.** ka**psa**leezma/**tree**pseemo me eenopnevma
Please give me a shave.	**Ξυρίστε με, παρακαλῶ.** ksee**ree**ste me paraka**lo**
Please trim	**Μπορεῖτε νά μοῦ ψαλιδίσετε** bo**ree**te na moo psalee**dee**sete
my beard/my moustache/my sideboards.	**τά γένεια μου/τό μουστάκι μου/τίς φαβορίτες μου;** ta **ye**nya moo/to moo**sta**kee moo/tees favo**ree**tes moo
No, thank you. I do not want a facial massage.	**Ὄχι, εὐχαριστῶ. Δέν θέλω μασάζ τοῦ προσώπου.** **o**khee efkharee**esto. dhen the**lo masaz too pro**so**poo
I will have a manicure.	**Θά ἔχω ἕνα μανικιούρ.** tha **e**kho ena manee**kyoor**
May I have a hand towel?	**Μπορῶ νά ἔχω μιά πετσετούλα;** bo**ro** na **e**kho mya petse**too**la
Put some eau de cologne on but no cream.	**Νά βάλετε κολόνια, ἀλλ' ὄχι κρέμα ὅμως.** na **va**lete ko**lo**nya, a**lo**khee **kre**ma **o**mos
Move the mirror a bit more to the right.	**Νά κινήσετε τόν καθρέπτη λίγο περισσότερο δεξιά.** na kee**nee**sete ton ka**threp**tee **lee**gho peree**so**tero dhe**ksya**
Yes, that's fine.	**Ναί, αὐτό εἶναι ὡραῖο.** **ne**, af**to** eene o**reo**

Making Friends

Good morning/good afternoon/good evening.	**Καλημέρα (χαίρετε)/χαίρετε/καλησπέρα (χαίρετε).** kaleemera (**kh**erete)/**kh**erete/kaleespera (**kh**erete)
May I introduce	**Ἐπιτρέπεται νά συστήσω** epee**trepete** na sees**teeso**
myself/my friend John/my wife?	**τόν ἑαυτό μου/τό φίλο μου τό Γιάννη/τή γυναίκα μου;** ton eafto moo/to **fee**lo moo to **yanee**/tee yee**neka** moo
My name is . . .	**Μέ λένε . . .** me lene
How do you do?	**Χαίρω πολύ.** **kh**ero po**lee**
Are you staying	**Μένετε** **menete**
at this hotel/at this resort?	**σ' αὐτό τό ξενοδοχεῖο/σ' αὐτό τό μέρος;** safto to ksenodho**kheeo**/safto to **meros**
Are you enjoying your holiday?	**Χαιρόσαστε τίς διακοπές σας;** **kh**e**rosaste** tees dhya**kopes** sas
How long have you been on holiday?	**Πόσες ἡμέρες κάνετε διακοπές μέχρι τώρα;** **poses** ee**meres kanete** dhya**kopes mekh**ree **tora**
Do you always come here?	**Ἔρχεστε πάντα ἐδῶ;** er**kheste panda edho**
I'd like you to meet my friend . . .	**Θά ἤθελα νά συναντήσετε τό φίλο μου (τή φίλη μου);** tha **eethela** na seenan**deesete** to **fee**lo moo (tee **feelee** moo)
Would you care to have a drink with us?	**Θά θέλατε νά πιεῖτε κάτι μέ μᾶς;** tha **thelate** na **pyeete katee** me **mas**

| What would you like? | **Τί θά θέλατε;** |
| | tee tha thelate |

| Please, I insist that you let me pay. | **Παρακαλῶ, ἐπιμένω νά πληρώσω ἐγώ.** |
| | parakalo, epeemeno na pleeroso egho |

| I'm afraid that I don't speak Greek very well. | **Λυποῦμαι ἀλλά δέν μιλῶ πολύ καλά τά Ἑλληνικά.** |
| | leepoome ala dhen meelo polee kala ta eleeneeka |

| It is very nice to talk to a Greek person. | **Εἶναι πολύ εὐχάριστο νά μιλῶ μ' ἕναν Ἕλληνα (μέ μιά Ἑλληνίδα).** |
| | eene polee efkhareesto na meelo menan eleena (me mya eleeneedha) |

| Which part of Greece do you come from? | **Ἀπό ποιό μέρος τῆς Ἑλλάδας εἶστε;** |
| | apo pyo meros tees eladhas eeste |

| I am here with | **Εἶμαι ἐδῶ μέ** |
| | eeme edho me |

| my wife/my husband/my family/my friends. | **τή γυναίκα μου/τόν ἄντρα μου/τήν οἰκογένεια μου/τούς φίλους μου.** |
| | tee yeeneka moo/ton andra moo/teen eekoyenya moo/toos feeloos moo |

| Are you alone? | **Εἶστε μόνος σας (μόνη σας);** |
| | eeste monos sas (monee sas) |

| We come from | **Εἴμαστε ἀπό** |
| | eemaste apo |

| Ireland/ England/the United States. | **τήν Ἰρλανδία/τήν Ἀγγλία/τίς Ἡνωμένες Πολιτεῖες.** |
| | teen eerlandheea/teen anggleea/tees eenomenes poleeteees |

| Have you been to England? | **Ἔχετε πάει στήν Ἀγγλία;** |
| | ekhete paee steen anggleea |

| If you come, please let me know. | **Ἄμα θά 'ρθῆτε, παρακαλῶ νά μέ εἰδοποιήσετε.** |
| | ama thartheete parakalo na me eedhopeeeesete |

| This is my address. | **Αὐτή εἶναι ἡ διεύθυνσή μου.** |
| | aftee eene ee dhyeftheensee moo |

I hope to see you again soon.	Ἐλπίζω νά σᾶς ξαναδῶ σέ λίγο. elpeezo na sas ksanadho se leegho
Perhaps you would like to meet for a drink after dinner?	Μήπως θά θέλατε νά συναντηθοῦμε γιά νά πιοῦμε κάτι μετά τό δεῖπνο; meepos tha **the**late na seenandee**thoo**me ya na **pyoo**me **ka**tee meta to **dhee**pno
I would like to very much.	Πολύ εὐχαρίστως. polee efkha**ree**stos
At what time shall I come?	Τί ὥρα νά ’ρθῶ; tee ora nar**tho**
Have you got a family?	Ἔχετε οἰκογένεια; **e**khete eeko**ye**nya
Would you like to see some photos of our house and our children?	Θά θέλατε νά δεῖτε μερικές φωτογραφίες ἀπ’ τό σπίτι μας καί τά παιδιά μας; tha **the**late na **dhee**te me**ree**kes fotoghra**fee**es apto **spee**te mas ke ta pe**dhya** mas
Are you going to the gala?	Θά πᾶτε στή γιορτή; tha **pa**te stee yor**tee**
Would you like to make up a party?	Θά θέλατε νά κάνουμε παρέα; tha **the**late na **ka**noome pa**rea**
It has been so very nice to meet you.	Ἦταν τόσο ὡραῖο νά σᾶς συναντήσω. **ee**tan **to**so o**reo** na sas seenan**dee**so
You have been very kind.	Φερθήκατε πολύ εὐγενικά. fer**thee**kate po**lee** evye**nee**ka

Dating Someone

Are you on holiday?	Κάνετε διακοπές; **ka**nete dhya**ko**pes
Do you live here?	Μένετε ἐδῶ; **me**nete e**dho**

Do you like this place?	**Σᾶς ἀρέσει αὐτό τό μέρος;** sas aresee afto to meros
I've just arrived.	**Μόλις ἦρθα.** molees eertha
What is there to do?	**Τί μπορεῖ νά κάνει κανείς;** tee boree na kanee kanees
I don't know anyone here.	**Δέν ξέρω κανέναν ἐδῶ.** dhen ksero kanenan edho
I'm with a group of students.	**Εἶμαι μ' ἕνα γκρούπ ἀπό φοιτητές.** eeme mena groop apo feeteetes
I'm travelling alone.	**Ταξιδεύω μόνος μου (μόνη μου).** takseedhevo monos moo (monee moo)
I'm on my way round Europe.	**Κάνω τό γύρο τῆς Εὐρώπης.** kano to yeero tees evropees
I come	**Εἶμαι** eeme
from Scotland/ from Australia/ from New Zealand.	**ἀπό τή Σκωτία/ἀπό τήν Αὐστραλία/ἀπό τή Νέα Ζηλανδία.** apo tee skoteea/apo teen afstraleea/apo tee nea zeelandheea
Do you mind if I try my Greek on you?	**Θά σᾶς πειράξει ἄν δοκιμάσω τά Ἑλληνικά μου μέ σᾶς;** tha sas peeraksee an dhokeemaso ta eleeneeka moo me sas
My Greek is not very good.	**Τά Ἑλληνικά μου δέν εἶναι πολύ καλά.** ta eleeneeka moo dhen eene polee kala
Would you like a drink?	**Θά θέλατε νά πιεῖτε κάτι;** tha thelate na pyeete katee
What are you doing this evening?	**Τί θά κάνετε ἀπόψε;** tee tha kanete apopse

Would you like	**Θά θέλατε** tha thelate
to go to a discotheque/join our party?	**νά πᾶτε σ' ἕνα ντισκοτέκ/νά συμμετάσχετε** **στήν παρέα μας;** na pate sena deeskotek/na seemetaskhete steen parea mas
Do you like	**Σᾶς ἀρέσει** sas aresee
dancing/ swimming/ music?	**ὁ χορός/τό κολύμπι/ἡ μουσική;** o khoros/to koleembee/ee mooseekee
Can I walk along with you?	**Μπορῶ νά σᾶς συνοδέψω;** boro na sas seenodhepso
Which way are you going?	**Πρός τά ποῦ πᾶτε;** pros ta poo pate
Do you mind if I sit here?	**Σᾶς πειράζει ἄν καθήσω ἐδῶ;** sas peerazee an katheeso edho
This is my friend, Tom.	**Ὁρίστε ὁ φίλος μου ὁ Θωμᾶς.** oreeste o feelos moo o thomas
Do you have a girl friend?	**Ἔχετε φιλενάδα;** ekhete feelenadha
We could make a foursome.	**Θά μπορούσαμε νά κάνουμε μιά παρέα ἀπό** **τέσσερους.** tha boroosame na kanoome mya parea apo teseroos
Do you play tennis/golf?	**Παίζετε τέννις/γκόλφ;** pezete tenees/golf
Do you go swimming?	**Πηγαίνετε γιά κολύμπι;** peeyenete ya koleembee
Which beach do you go to?	**Σέ ποιά πλάζ πηγαίνετε;** se pya plaz peeyenete
Would you like to come for	**Θά θέλατε νά κάνουμε βόλτα** tha thelate na kanoome volta

a drive/a boat trip?	στό αὐτοκίνητο/σέ βάρκα; sto aftokeeneeto/se varka
It would be nice if you would.	Θά ἦταν ὡραῖο ἅμα θά θέλατε. tha eetan oreo ama tha thelate
Thanks for coming out with me.	Εὐχαριστῶ πού βγήκατε μαζί μου. efkhareesto poo vyeekate mazee moo
I enjoyed it.	Χάρηκα πολύ. khareeka polee
Can we meet again?	Μποροῦμε νά ξανασυναντηθοῦμε; boroome na ksnaseenandeethoome
How about tomorrow?	Τί λέτε γιά αὔριο; tee lete ya avreeo
Cheerio! See you tomorrow.	Γειά σας! Θά σᾶς δῶ αὔριο. ya sas! tha sas dho avreeo
No thanks, I'm busy.	Ὄχι εὐχαριστῶ, ἔχω δουλειές. okhee efkhareesto, ekho dhoolyes
Please stop bothering me.	Σταματεῖστε νά μέ ἐνοχλεῖτε, παρακαλῶ. stamateeste na me enokhleete parakalo

Mutual Interest

Do you play cards?	Παίζετε χαρτιά; pezete khartya
Would you like to make a four at bridge?	Θά θέλατε νά κάνουμε ἕνα καρρέ γιά μπρίτζ; tha thelate na kanoome ena kare ya breedz
We play	Ἐμεῖς παίζουμε emees pezoome
canasta/poker/ rummy.	κανάστα/πόκερ/ραμί. kanasta/poker/ramee
It is an English game.	Εἶναι ἕνα Ἀγγλικό παιχνίδι. eene ena anggleeko pekhneedhee

Are you a chess player?	Παίζετε σκάκι; pezete skakee
I'll ask the concierge if the hotel has a chess board.	Θά ρωτήσω τό (τή) θυρωρό ἄν ἔχει τό ξενοδοχεῖο ἕνα σκάκι. tha roteeso to (tee) theeroro an ekhee to ksenodhokheeo ena skakee
This is	Αὐτό εἶναι afto eene
the king/queen/ knight/bishop/ castle/pawn.	ὁ βασιλιάς/ἡ βασίλισσα/ὁ ἱππότης/ὁ τρελλός/τό κάστρο/ὁ στρατιώτης. o vaseelyas/ee vaseeleesa/o eepotees/o trelos/to kastro/o stratyotees
Do you play draughts or dominoes?	Παίζετε ντάμα ἤ ντόμινο; pezete dama ee domeeno
There is table tennis in the hotel. Would you care for a game?	Ἔχει ἕνα τραπέζι γιά πίνγκ-πόνγκ στό ξενοδοχεῖο. Ἔχετε κέφι γιά ἕνα παιχνίδι; ekhee ena trapezee ya peeng pongg sto ksenodhokheeo. ekhete kefee ya ena pekhneedhee
Do you read English?	Διαβάζετε Ἀγγλικά; dhyavazete angleeka
Would you like to borrow	Θά θέλατε νά δανειστεῖτε tha thelate na dhaneesteete
this book/this newspaper?	αὐτό τό βιβλίο/αὐτή τήν ἐφημερίδα; afto to veevleeo/aftee teen efeemereedha

Conversations

There are certain universal subjects of conversation which provide a bridge for communication with strangers all over the world. Among these are the weather, families, home, the cost of living and pets.

The following conversational phrases are designed to start you on an acquaintanceship with people who do not speak English.

About the Weather

It is a fine day.	**Εἶναι μιά ὡραία ἡμέρα.** eene mya orea eemera
It's not a very nice day.	**Ὁ καιρός δέν εἶναι πολύ καλός σήμερα.** o keros dhen eene polee kalos seemera
Do you think it will rain all day/ later/ tomorrow?	**Νομίζετε ὅτι θά βρέξει** nomeezete otee tha vreksee **ὅλη τήν ἡμέρα/ἀργότερα/αὔριο;** olee teen eemera/arghotera/avreeo
Today it's going to be hot/cold.	**Σήμερα θά κάνει** seemera tha kanee **ζέστη/κρύο.** zestee/kreeo
It's rather windy.	**Φυσάει ὁ ἄνεμος λίγο.** feesaee o anemos leegho
I think there is a thunderstorm coming.	**Νομίζω ὅτι θά ἔχουμε καταιγίδα καί ἀστραπές** nomeezo otee tha ekhoome kateyeedha ke astrapes
Look at the lightning.	**Δέστε τήν ἀστραπή.** dheste teen astrapee
It will soon clear up.	**Θά ξανοίξει σέ λίγο.** tha ksaneeksee se leegho
We don't get this kind of weather at home.	**Δέν ἔχουμε τέτοιον καιρό στήν χώρα μας.** dhen ekhoome tetyon kero steen khora mas
It's a pity it is so dull.	**Κρῖμα πού εἶναι τόσο γκρίζο.** kreema poo eene toso greezo
Did you see the beautiful sunset?	**Εἴδατε τήν ὡραία δύση τοῦ ἡλίου;** eedhate teen orea dheesee too eeleeoo

Last year we had a	**Εἴχαμε πέρσι ἕνα**	
	eekhame persee ena	
very good/very	**πολύ καλό καλοκαίρι/πολύ ἄσχημο καλοκαίρι.**	
poor summer.	polee kalo kalokeree/polee askheemo kalokeree	
There's a lot of haze	**῎Εχει πολλή καταχνιά σήμερα.**	
about today.	ekhee polee katakhnya seemera	
The atmosphere is	**῾Η ἀτμόσφαιρα εἶναι πολύ καυθρή.**	
very clear.	ee atmosfera eene polee katharee	
Is it cold here in the	**Κάνει κρύο ἐδῶ τόν χειμώνα;**	
winter?	kanee kreeo edho ton kheemona	
I love	**᾽Αγαπῶ**	
	aghapo	
the spring/the	**τήν ἄνοιξη/τό καλοκαίρι/τό φθινόπωρο.**	
summer/the	teen aneeksee/to kalokeree/to ftheenoporo	
autumn.		
What does the	**Τί λέει τό βαρόμετρο;**	
barometer say?	tee leee to varometro	

Vocabulary

breeze	**ἡ αὔρα**	ee avra
cloudburst	**ἡ νεροποντή**	ee neropondee
cloudy	**συννεφιασμένος**	seenefyazmenos
drizzle	**τό ψιχάλισμα**	to pseekhaleezma
dry	**ξηρός**	kseeros
forecast	**ἡ πρόγνωση καιροῦ**	ee proghnosee keroo
hail	**τό χαλάζι**	to khalazee
meteorological office	**ἡ μετεωρολογική ὑπηρεσία**	ee meteoroloyeekee eepeereseea
mist	**ἡ ἐλαφρή ὀμίχλη**	ee elafree omeekhlee
pressure	**ἡ (ἀτμοσφαιρική) πίεση**	ee (atmosfereekee) peeesee
rain	**ἡ βροχή**	ee vrokhee
sleet	**τό χιονόνερο**	to khyononero

snow	τό χιόνι	to khyonee
sunny	ἡλιόλουστος	eelyoloostos
temperature	ἡ θερμοκρασία	ee thermokraseea
weather report	τό δελτίο καιροῦ	to dhelteeo keroo
wet	βροχερός	vrokheros

About Families

This is	Ὁρίστε oreeste	
my wife/my husband/my daughter/my son.	ἡ γυναίκα μου/ὁ ἄντρας μου/ἡ κόρη μου/ὁ γιός μου. ee yeeneka moo/o andras moo/ee koree moo/o yos moo	
My son is an	Ὁ γιός μου εἶναι o yos moo eene	
architect/doctor/ student/teacher/ engineer.	ἀρχιτέκτων/γιατρός/φοιτητής/ καθηγητής/ μηχανολόγος. arkheetekton/yatros/feeteetees/ katheeyeetees/ meekhanologhos	
My daughter is at school.	Ἡ κόρη μου εἶναι στό σχολεῖο. ee koree moo eene sto skholeeo	
She is taking her examinations.	Δίνει τούς διαγωνισμούς της. dheenee toos dhyaghoneezmoos tees	
Then she will go	Ἔπειτα θά πάει epeeta tha paee	
to university/to art school/to a teacher's training college.	στό πανεπιστήμιο/στή σχολή καλῶν τεχνῶν/στήν παιδαγωγική ἀκαδημία. sto panepeesteemeeo/stee skholee kalon tekhnon/steen pedhaghoyeekee akadheemeea	
She learnt some Greek at night school.	Ἔμαθε κάτι Ἑλληνικά σ' ἕνα νυκτερινό σχολεῖο. emathe katee eleeneeka sena neektereeno skholeeo	

My wife is Scottish, but her mother is Greek.	Ἡ γυναίκα μου εἶναι Σκωτσέζα, ἀλλά ἡ μητέρα της εἶναι Ἑλληνίδα. ee yeeneka moo eene skotseza ala ee meetera tees eene eleeneedha
My father was a teacher.	Ὁ πατέρας μου ἦταν δάσκαλος. o pateras moo eetan dhaskalos
The children prefer to have holidays on their own.	Τά παιδιά προτιμοῦν νά κάνουν διακοπές μόνα τους. ta pedhya proteemoon na kanoon dhyakopes mona toos
They prefer camping.	Προτιμοῦν τίς κατασκηνώσεις. proteemoon tees kataskeenosees
My eldest (youngest) daughter is married and lives in . . .	Ἡ μεγαλύτερη (πιό μικρή) κόρη μου εἶναι παντρεμένη καί ζεῖ εἰς . . . ee meghaleeteree (pyo meekree) koree moo eene pandremenee ke zee ees
Would you like to see some photos of our family?	Θά θέλατε νά δεῖτε μερικές φωτογραφίες τῆς οἰκογενείας μας; tha thelate na dheete mereekes fotoghrafeees tees eekoyeneeas mas
The younger children stayed at home with their grandparents.	Τά μικρότερα παιδιά ἔμειναν στό σπίτι μέ τόν παππού καί τή γιαγιά. ta meekrotera pedhya emeenan sto speetee me ton papoo ke tee yaya
Are these your children?	Εἶναι αὐτά τά παιδιά σας; eene afta ta pedhya sas
The boy/the girl	Τό ἀγόρι/ἡ κοπέλλα to aghoree/ee kopela
looks like his (her) mother/looks like his (her) father.	ὁμοιάζει μέ τή μητέρα του (της)/ὁμοιάζει μέ τόν πατέρα (της). omyazee me tee meetera too (tees)/omyazee me ton patera too (tees)

How old is he/she?	Πόσο χρονῶν εἶναι poso khronon eene αὐτός/αὐτή; aftos/aftee
My daughter is fourteen.	Ἡ κόρη μου εἶναι δεκατεσσάρων χρονῶν. ee koree moo eene dhekatesaron khronon

VOCABULARY

aunt	ἡ θεία	ee theea
birthday	τά γενέθλια	ta yenethleea
builder	ὁ οἰκοδόμος	o eekodhomos
computer expert	ὁ σπεσιαλιστής γιά τά κομπιοῦτερ	o spesyaleestees ya ta kompyooter
cousin	ὁ ἐξάδελφος, ἡ ἐξαδέλφη	o eksadhelfos, ee eksadhelfee
daughter-in-law	ἡ νύφη	ee neefee
divorce	τό διαζύγιο	to dhyazeeyeeo
journalist	ὁ δημοσιογράφος	o dheemoseeoghrafos
lawyer	ὁ δικηγόρος	o dheekeeghoros
marriage	ἡ παντρειά	ee pandreea
mother-in-law	ἡ πεθερά	ee pethera
relatives	οἱ συγγενεῖς	ee seenggenees
salesman	ὁ ἀντιπρόσωπος πωλήσεων	o andeeprosopos poleeseon
technician	ὁ τεχνικός	o tekhneekos
uncle	ὁ θεῖος	o theeos
wedding	ὁ γάμος	o ghamos

About Homes

We have a house in town/in the country.	Ἔχουμε ἕνα σπίτι ekhoome ena speetee στήν πόλη/στήν ἐξοχή. steen polee/steen eksokhee

It is	**Εἶναι**
	eene
a two-storey house.	**διόροφο σπίτι.**
	dheeorofo **speetee**
a detached house.	**μονοκατοικία (μιά βίλλα).**
	monokateekeea (mya veela)
a semi-detached house.	**ἕνα σπίτι προσκολλημένο στή μία πλευρά μέ ἕνα ἄλλο.**
	ena **speetee** proskoleemeno stee **meea** plevra me ena alo
a cottage.	**ἕνα ἐξοχικό σπιτάκι.**
	ena eksokheeko speetakee
a maisonette.	**ἕνα διαμέρισμα σέ μονοκατοικία.**
	ena dhyamereezma se monokateekeea
a flat.	**ἕνα διαμέρισμα (σέ πολυκατοικία).**
	ena dhyamereezma (se poleekateekeea)

We have	**Ἔχουμε**
	ekhoome
a large garden/a patio.	**ἕνα μεγάλο κῆπο/μιά βεράντα.**
	ena meghalo keepo/mya veranda

There are two living rooms. One has a French window, the other a bay window.	**Ἔχει δύο σαλόνια. Τό ἕνα ἔχει μιά πόρτα βεράντας μέ τζάμια, τό ἄλλο ἕνα ἡμισφαιρικό παράθυρο.**
	ekhee **dheeo** salonya. to ena ekhee mya **porta** verandas me dzamya, to alo ena eemeesfereeko paratheero

There is a fireplace in the dining room.	**Ἔχει ἕνα τζάκι στήν τραπεζαρία.**
	ekhee ena dzakee steen trapezareea

The house	**Ὅλο τό σπίτι**
	olo to **speetee**
is centrally heated/has air conditioning.	**ἔχει καλοριφέρ/ἔχει κλιματισμό.**
	ekhee kaloreefer/ekhee kleemateez**mo**

We have two garages.	**Ἔχουμε δύο γκαράζια.**
	ekhoome **dheeo** garazya

The back garden has a lawn and swimming pool.	Ὁ πισινός κῆπος ἔχει γρασίδι καί μιά πισίνα. o peeseenos keepos ekhee ghraseedhee ke mya peeseena
In our village there are many old houses.	Στό χωριό μας ὑπάρχουν πολλά παλιά σπίτια. sto khoryo mas eeparkhoon pola palya speetya
We prefer an old/a modern house.	Ἐμεῖς προτιμοῦμε emees proteemoome ἔνα σπίτι παλαιοῦ στύλ/ἕνα σπίτι μοντέρνου στύλ. ena speetee paleoo steel/ena speetee modernoo steel
What kind of house have you got?	Τί εἶδος σπιτιοῦ ἔχετε ἐσεῖς; tee eedhos speetyoo ekhete esees
I like Greek-style houses.	Μοῦ ἀρέσουν τά σπίτια σέ Ἑλληνικό στύλ. moo aresoon ta speetya se eleeneeko steel
Do you cook by gas or electricity?	Μαγειρεύετε μέ γκάζι ἤ ἠλεκτρισμό; mayeerevete me gazee ee eelektreezmo
In a warm climate tiled floors are delightful.	Σ' ἔνα θερμό κλίμα τά πατώματα μέ πλακάκια εἶναι πολύ ὡραῖα. sena thermo kleema ta patomata me plakakya eene polee orea
Wall-to-wall carpeting makes a house warm in winter.	Μέ τάπητα σ' ὁλόκληρο τό πάτωμα ἔνα σπίτι εἶναι ζεστό τό χειμώνα. me tapeeta solokleero to patoma ena speetee eene zesto to kheemona
Built-in cupboards make a room seem larger.	Οἱ ἐντοιχισμένες ντουλάπες κάνουν ἔνα δωμάτιο νά φαίνεται πιό μεγάλο. ee endeekheezmenes doolapes kanoon ena dhomateeo na fenete pyo meghalo
Old furniture is lovely but very expensive.	Τά ἀρχαῖα ἔπιπλα εἶναι ὡραῖα ἀλλά πολύ ἀκριβά. ta arkhea epeepla eene orea ala polee akreeva

Vocabulary

balcony	τό μπαλκόνι	to balkonee
bathroom	τό λουτρό	to lootro
brick (made of)	τούβλινος, -η, -ο	toovleenos, -ee, -ο
ceiling	τό ταβάνι	to tavanee
chimney	ὁ καπνοδόχος	o kapno**dho**khos
door	ἡ πόρτα	ee **porta**
drains	ἡ ἀποχέτευση	ee apo**khe**tefsee
floor	τό πάτωμα	to **pa**toma
foundations	τά θεμέλια	ta the**me**lya
gable	ἡ τριγωνική πρόσοψη	ee treeghonee**kee** prosopsee
mains electricity	τό ρεῦμα κεντρικῆς παροχῆς	to **re**vma kendree**kees** paro**khees**
mains gas	τό γκάζι κεντρικῆς παροχῆς	to **ga**zee kendree**kees** paro**khees**
plumbing	ἡ ὑδραυλική ἐγκατάσταση	ee eedhravlee**kee** enggatastasee
roof	ἡ σκεπή	ee ske**pee**
stone (made of)	πέτρινος, -η, -ο	**pe**treenos, -ee, -ο
terrace	ἡ βεράντα, ὁ ἐξώστης	ee ve**randa**, o ek**so**stees
thatch	ἡ ψάθινη σκεπή	ee **psa**theenee ske**pee**
tiles	τά κεραμίδια	ta kera**mee**dhya
wall	ὁ τοῖχος	o **tee**khos
wallpaper	ἡ ταπετσαρία τοίχου	ee tapetsa**ree**a **tee**khoo
window	τό παράθυρο	to pa**ra**theero
window frame	ὁ σκελετός τοῦ παραθύρου	o skele**tos** too para**thee**roo
window pane	τό τζάμι	to **dza**mee
wood	τό ξύλο	to **ksee**lo

Looking After Your Money

The Bank

Where is the nearest bank?
Ποῦ εἶναι ἡ πλησιέστερη τράπεζα;
poo eene ee pleeseeesteree trapeza

Do you accept travellers' cheques at this bank?
Δέχεστε τράβελερς τσέκ σ' αὐτή τήν τράπεζα;
dhekheste travelers tsek saftee teen trapeza

Can I use a Eurocheque card?
Μπορῶ νά χρησιμοποιήσω μιά κάρτα Eurocheque;
boro na khreeseemopeeeeso mya karta Eurocheque

Do you issue money against a credit card?
Χορηγεῖτε χρήματα βάσει κάρτας πιστώσεως;
khoreeyeete khreemata vasee kartas peestoseos

I am expecting a remittance.
Περιμένω ἕνα ἔμβασμα.
pereemeno ena emvazma

I have a letter of credit.
Ἔχω μιά πιστωτική ἐπιστολή.
ekho mya peestoteekee epeestolee

I would like a draft to send away.
Θά ἤθελα μιά ἐπιταγή γιά ἔξω.
tha eethela mya epeetayee ya ekso

What is the rate of exchange for
the pound/dollar/ Australian dollar?
Τί εἶναι ἡ τιμή συναλλάγματος γιά
tee eene ee teemee seenalaghmatos ya
τή λίρα Ἀγγλίας/τό δολλάριο/τό δολλάριο Αὐστραλίας;
tee leera anggleeas/to dholareeo/to dholareeo afstraleeas

What is your commission charge?
Τί προμήθεια παίρνετε;
tee promeethya pernete

204   Money Matters

I will have it all in 50 drachma notes.	**Θά τά πάρω ὅλα σέ χαρτονομίσματα τῶν 50 δραχμῶν.** tha ta paro ola se khartonomeezmata ton peneenda dhrakhmon
Please give me 500 drachmas worth of change.	**Μπορεῖτε νά μοῦ δώσετε 500 δραχμές ψιλά, παρακαλῶ;** borete na moo dhosete pendakosyes drakhmes pseela parakalo
Can you split this cheque into several currencies?	**Μπορεῖτε νά ἀλλάξετε αὐτό τό τσέκ σέ διάφορα συναλλάγματα;** borete na alaksete afto to tsek se dhyafora seenalaghmata
I will have	**Θά πάρω** tha paro
some German marks, Swiss francs and Greek drachmas.	**Γερμανικά μάρκα, φράγκα Ἑλβετίας καί Ἑλληνικές δραχμές.** yermaneeka marka franggа elveteeas ke eleeneekes dhrakhmes
Can I open a temporary bank account?	**Μπορῶ ν' ἀνοίξω ἕνα προσωρινό τραπεζιτικό λογαριασμό;** boro naneekso ena prosoreeno trapezeeteeko logharyazmo
Can you arrange for some money to be sent from my bank in Britain?	**Μπορεῖτε νά κανονίσετε νά στείλουν χρήματα ἀπ' τήν τράπεζά μου στή Βρεττανία;** borete na kanoneesete na steeloon khreemata apteen trapeza moo stee vretaneea
I seem to be 10 drachmas short. Can you please count it again?	**Μοῦ φαίνεται ὅτι λείπουν 10 δραχμές. Μπορεῖτε νά τά ξαναμετρήσετε παρακαλῶ;** moo fenete otee leepoon dheka dhrakhmes. borete na ta ksanametreesete parakalo
Have you a card showing current exchange rates?	**Ἔχετε ἕναν πίνακα πού δείχνει τίς σημερινές τιμές συναλλάγματος;** ekhete ena peenaka poo dheekhnee tees seemereenes teemes seenalaghmatos

VOCABULARY

Bank of England	'Η Τράπεζα τῆς 'Αγγλίας	ee trapeza tees anggleeas
cashier	ὁ/ἡ ταμίας	o/ee tameeas
cheque book	τό βιβλιάριο ἐπιταγῶν	to veevleeareeo epeetaghon
coins	τά κέρματα	ta kermata
credit	ἡ πίστωση	ee peestosee
debit	ἡ χρέωση	ee khreosee
deposit slip	τό ἔντυπο καταθέσεως	to endeepo katatheseos
foreign exchange regulations	οἱ κανονισμοί ξένου συναλάγματος	ee kanoneezmee ksenoo seenalaghmatos
manager	ὁ διευθυντής	o dhyeftheendees
notes	τά χαρτονομίσματα	ta khartonomeezmata
signature	ἡ ὑπογραφή	ee eepoghrafee
Treasury	Τό Ὑπουργεῖο Οἰκονομικῶν	to epooryeeo eekonomeekon

Bureau de Change

Are you open outside banking hours?
Εἶναι τό κατάστημα ἀνοικτό ἐκτός ἀπ' τίς κανονικές ὧρες ἐργασίας τῶν τραπεζῶν;
eene to katasteema aneekto ektos aptees kanoneekes ores erghaseeas ton trapezon

Does the rate of exchange alter outside normal hours?
'Αλλάζει ἡ τιμή συναλλάγματος τίς μή κανονικές ὧρες ἐργασίας;
alazee ee teemee seenalaghmatos tees mee kanoneekes ores erghaseeas

Are you open on Sundays?
'Ανοίγετε τήν Κυριακή;
aneeyete teen keeryakee

Can you show me your rates of exchange?
Μπορεῖτε νά μοῦ δείξετε τίς τιμές συναλλάγματός σας;
boreete na moo dheeksete tees teemes seenalaghmatos sas

Do you give the same rate for notes as for travellers' cheques?	Δίνετε τὴν ἴδια τιμὴ γιά χαρτονομίσματα ὅπως γιά τά τράβελερς τσέκ; dheenete teen eedhya teemee ya khartonomeezmata opos ya ta travelers tsek

On Losing Travellers' Cheques or Credit Cards

When this happens you should immediately notify the company that has issued the cheques or card, but you may need help from a local hotelier or banker.

I have lost	Ἔχασα ekhasa
my travellers' cheques/my credit card.	τά τράβελερς τσέκ μου/τήν κάρτα πιστώσεώς μου. tra travelers tsek moo/teen karta peestoseos moo
May I ask them to communicate with me through you?	Μπορῶ νά τούς προτείνω νά 'ρθοῦν σ' ἐπαφή μαζί μου μέσω ἐσᾶς; boro na toos proteeno narthoon sepafee mazee moo meso esas
Have you a British representative?	Ἔχετε ἀντιπροσωπεία στὴ Βρεττανία; ekhete andeeprosopeea stee vretaneea
I hope they will be able to refund the cheques quickly. I have no other money.	Ἐλπίζω ὅτι θά μπορέσουν νά ἐπανακαταθέσουν τά τσέκ πολύ γρήγορα. Δέν ἔχω ἄλλα χρήματα. elpeezo otee tha boresoon na epanakatathesoon ta tsek polee ghreeghora. dhen ekho ala khreemata
I will ask my bank at home to send some money to you.	Θά ζητήσω ἀπ' τήν τράπεζά μου νά σᾶς ἀποστείλουν χρήματα. tha zeeteeso apteen trapeza moo na sas aposteeloon khreemata

Will you accept a British cheque in payment of the hotel bill?

Θά δεχόσαστε ἕνα τσέχ μιᾶς Βρεττανικῆς Τραπέζης πρός ἐξόφληση τοῦ λογαριασμοῦ τοῦ ξενοδοχείου;

tha dhe**kh**osaste **e**na **tsek** myas vretan**ee**k**ee**s trap**e**zees pros eks**o**fl**ee**see too logharyaz**moo** too ksenodho**kh**ee**oo**

Reference Section

Numbers

1	ἕνα	ena
2	δύο	**dheeo**
3	τρία	**treea**
4	τέσσερα	tesera
5	πέντε	**pende**
6	ἕξη	eksee
7	ἑπτά	epta
8	ὀκτώ	okto
9	ἐννέα	enea
10	δέκα	**dheka**
11	ἕντεκα	endeka
12	δώδεκα	**dhodheka**
13	δεκατρία	dheka**treea**
14	δεκατέσσερα	dhekatesera
15	δεκαπέντε	dhekapende
16	δεκαέξη	dhekaeksee
17	δεκαεπτά	dhekaepta
18	δεκαοκτώ	dhekaokto
19	δεκαεννέα	dhekaenea
20	εἴκοσι	eekosee
21	εἴκοσι ἕνα	eekosee ena
22	εἴκοσι δύο	eekosee **dheeo**
23	εἴκοσι τρία	eekosee **treea**
24	εἴκοσι τέσσερα	eekosee tesera
25	εἴκοσι πέντε	eekosee **pende**
26	εἴκοσι ἕξη	eekosee eksee
27	εἴκοσι ἑπτά	eekosee epta
28	εἴκοσι ὀκτώ	eekosee okto
29	εἴκοσι ἐννέα	eekosee enea
30	τριάντα	treeanda
31	τριάντα ἕνα	treeanda ena
40	σαράντα	saranda

50	πενήντα	peneenda
60	ἐξήντα	ekseenda
70	ἑβδομήντα	evdhomeenda
80	ὀγδόντα	oghdhonda
90	ἐννενήντα	eneneenda
100	ἑκατό	ekato
101	ἑκατόν ἕνα	ekaton ena
110	ἑκατόν δέκα	ekaton dheka
200	διακόσια	dhyakosya
1000	χίλια	kheelya
1001	χίλια ἕνα	kheelya ena
1100	χίλια ἑκατό	kheelya ekato
2000	δύο χιλιάδες	dheeo kheelyadhes
1,000,000	ἕνα ἑκατομμύριο	ena ekatomeereeo
1,000,000,000	ἕνα δισεκατομμύριο	ena dheesekatomeereeo

first	πρῶτος	protos	sixth	ἕκτος	ektos
second	δεύτερος	dhefteros	seventh	ἕβδομος	evdhomos
third	τρίτος	treetos	eighth	ὄγδοος	oghdho-os
fourth	τέταρτος	tetartos	ninth	ἔνατος	enatos
fifth	πέμπτος	pemptos	tenth	δέκατος	dhekatos

once	μιά φορά	mya fora
twice	δυό φορές	dhyo fores
three times	τρεῖς φορές	trees fores
half	μισός, μισή, μισό	meesos, meesee, meeso
a quarter	ἕνα τέταρτο	ena tetarto
a third	ἕνα τρίτο	ena treeto
an eighth	ἕνα ὄγδοο	ena oghdho-o
a pair (of)	ἕνα ζευγάρι	ena zevgharee
a dozen	μιά ντουζίνα,	mya doozeena,
	μιά δωδεκάδα	mya dhodhekadha

Time

Greenwich Mean Time	**Ὥρα Γκρήνουϊτς** ora greenooeets
Central European Time	**Ὥρα Κεντρικῆς Εὐρώπης** ora kendreekees evropees
Atlantic Time	**Ὥρα Νέας Ὑόρκης** ora neas eeorkees
Greek Time	**Ὥρα Ἑλλάδος** ora eladhos
Date line	**Ἡ γραμμή ἀλλαγῆς ἡμερομηνίας.** ee ghramee alayees eemeromeeneeas
a.m./p.m.	**π.μ. (πρό μεσημβρίας)/μ.μ. (μετά μεσημβρίαν).** pee mee (pro meseemvreeas)/mee mee (meta meseemvreean)
24-hour clock	**ρολόϊ εἰκοσιτετραώρου** roloee eekoseetetraoroo
summer time	**καλοκαιρινή ὥρα** kalokereenee ora
it is	**εἶναι** eene
12.15/12.20/ 12.30/12.35/ 12.45/1.00	**δώδεκα καί τέταρτο/δώδεκα καί εἴκοσι/δώδεκα καί μισή/μία παρά εἴκοσι πέντε/μία παρά τέταρτο/μία ἡ ὥρα** dhodheka ke tetarto/dhodheka ke eekosee/dhodheka ke meesee/meea para eekosee pende/meea para tetarto/meea ee ora
midnight, midday.	**μεσάνυχτα/μεσημέρι.** mesaneekta/meseemeree

Phrases Referring to Time

What time is it?	**Τί ὥρα εἶναι;**	
	tee ora eene	
It is late.	**Εἶναι ἀργά.**	
	eene argha	
It is early.	**Εἶναι ἐνωρίς.**	
	eene enorees	
Are we on time?	**Εἴμαστε στήν ὥρα;**	
	eemaste steen ora	
At what time shall we meet?	**Τί ὥρα θά συναντηθοῦμε;**	
	tee ora tha seenandeethoome	
At what time are we expected?	**Τί ὥρα μᾶς περιμένουν;**	
	tee ora mas pereemenoon	
On the hour.	**'Ακριβῶς στήν ὥρα.**	
	akreevos steen ora	
By the minute.	**Μέ τό λεπτό.**	
	me to lepto	
Every second.	**Κάθε δευτερόλεπτο.**	
	kathe dhefterolepto	
At regular intervals.	**Κατά τακτικά χρονικά διαστήματα.**	
	kata takteeka khroneeka dhyasteemata	
Day by day.	**Μέρα παρά μέρα.**	
	mera para mera	

VOCABULARY

days	ἡμέρες	eemeres
weeks	ἑβδομάδες	evdhomadhes
years	χρόνια	khronya
Sunday	ἡ Κυριακή	ee keeryakee

Monday	ἡ Δευτέρα	ee dheftera
Tuesday	ἡ Τρίτη	ee treetee
Wednesday	ἡ Τετάρτη	ee tetartee
Thursday	ἡ Πέμπτη	ee pemptee
Friday	ἡ Παρασκευή	ee paraskevee
Saturday	τό Σάββατο	to savato
daybreak	ἡ χαραυγή	ee kharavyee
dawn	ἡ αὐγή	ee avyee
morning	τό πρωΐ	to proee
afternoon	τό ἀπόγευμα	to apoyevma
evening	τό βράδυ	to vradhee
night	ἡ νύκτα	ee neekta
today	σήμερα	seemera
yesterday	χθές	khthes
tomorrow	αὔριο	avreeo
the day before yesterday	προχθές	prokhthes
three days ago	πρίν τρεῖς ἡμέρες	preen trees eemeres
the day after tomorrow	μεθαύριο	methavreeo
the following day	τήν ἐπομένη ἡμέρα	teen epomenee eemera
weekday	τήν καθημερινή ἡμέρα	teen katheemereenee eemera
a day off	μία ἡμέρα ρεπό	meea eemera repo
birthday	τά γενέθλια	ta yenethleea
Christmas Day	ἡ ἡμέρα τῶν Χριστουγέννων	ee eemera ton khreestooyenon
New Year's Day	ἡ Πρωτοχρονιά	ee protokhronya
All Saints' Day	ἡ ἡμέρα τῶν Ἁγίων Πάντων	ee eemera ton ayeeon pandon
May Day	ἡ Πρωτομαγιά	ee protomaya
weekend	τό σαββατοκύριακο	to savatokeereeako
last week	τήν περασμένη ἑβδομάδα	teen perazmenee evdhomadha
next week	τήν ἐπομένη ἑβδομάδα	teen epomenee evdhomadha
for two weeks	γιά δύο ἑβδομάδες	ya dheeo evdhomadhes
January	ὁ Ἰανουάριος	o eeanooareeos
February	ὁ Φεβρουάριος	o fevrooareeos

March	ὁ Μάρτιος	o marteeos
April	ὁ Ἀπρίλιος	o apreeleeos
May	ὁ Μάϊος	o maeeos
June	ὁ Ἰούνιος	o eeooneeos
July	ὁ Ἰούλιος	o eeooleeos
August	ὁ Αὔγουστος	o avghoostos
September	ὁ Σεπτέμβριος	o septemvreeos
October	ὁ Ὀκτώβριος	o oktovreeos
November	ὁ Νοέμβριος	o noemvreeos
December	ὁ Δεκέμβριος	o dhekemvreeos
calendar month	ὁ ἡμερολογιακός μήνας	o eemeroloyeeakos meenas
lunar month	ὁ σεληνιακός μήνας	o seleneeakos meenas
monthly	μηνιαίως	meeneeeos
since January	ἀπό τόν Ἰανουάριο	apo ton eeanooareeo
last month	τόν περασμένο μήνα	ton perazmeno meena
next month	τόν ἐπόμενο μήνα	ton epomeno meena
the month before	τόν προηγούμενο μήνα	ton proeeghoomeno meena
the first of the month	τήν πρώτη τοῦ μηνός	teen protee too meenos
the first of March	τήν πρώτη Μαρτίου	teen protee marteeoo
spring	ἡ ἄνοιξη	ee aneeksee
summer	τό καλοκαίρι	to kalokeree
autumn	τό φθινόπωρο	to ftheenoporo
winter	ὁ χειμώνας	o kheemonas
equinox	ἡ ἰσημερία	ee eeseemereea
solstice	τό ἡλιοστάσιο	to eeleeostaseeo
midsummer	τό θερινό ἡλιοστάσιο	to thereeno eeleeostaseeo
midwinter	τό χειμερινό ἡλιοστάσιο	to kheemereeno eeleeostaseeo
leap year	τό δίσεκτο ἔτος	to dheesekto etos
BC	Π.Χ. (πρό Χριστοῦ)	pee khee (pro khreestoo)
AD	Μ.Χ. (μετά Χριστόν)	mee khee (meta khreeston)

Temperature Equivalents

FAHRENHEIT		CENTIGRADE
212	Boiling point	100
100		37·8
98·4	Body temperature	37
86		30
77		25
68		20
50		10
32	Freezing point	0
0		−17·8

To convert Fahrenheit to Centigrade subtract 32 and divide by 1·8.

To convert Centigrade to Fahrenheit multiply by 1·8 and add 32.

Pressure

The barometer tells you the air pressure of the atmosphere: 15 lb. per sq. in. is normal air pressure at sea level. This equals 1·06 kg. per sq. cm.

A tyre gauge tells you the pressure of your car tyres.

POUNDS PER SQUARE INCH	KILOGRAMS PER SQUARE CENTIMETRE
16	1·12
18	1·27
20	1·41
22	1·55
24	1·69
26	1·83
28	1·97

Measurement of Distance

One kilometre = 1000 metres = 0·62 miles

One hundred centimetres = 1 metre = 3·28 ft.

One centimetre = 0·39 inches.

The following table gives equivalents for metres and feet. The figure in the centre column can stand for either feet or metres and the equivalent should then be read off in the appropriate column.

Metres	Metres and Feet.	Feet
0·30	1	3·28
0·61	2	6·56
0·91	3	9·84
1·22	4	13·12
1·52	5	16·40
1·83	6	19·69
2·13	7	22·97
2·44	8	26·25
2·74	9	29·53
3·05	10	32·81
3·35	11	36·09
3·66	12	39·37
3·96	13	42·65
4·27	14	45·93
4·57	15	49·21
4·88	16	52·49
5·18	17	55·77
5·49	18	59·06
5·79	19	62·34
6·10	20	65·62
7·62	25	82·02
15·24	50	164·04
22·86	75	264·06
30·48	100	328·08

MILES	MILES AND KILOMETRES	KILOMETRES
0·62	1	1·61
1·24	2	3·22
1·86	3	4·82
2·49	4	6·44
3·11	5	8·05
3·73	6	9·66
4·35	7	11·27
4·97	8	12·88
5·59	9	14·48
6·21	10	16·09
15·53	25	40·23
31·07	50	80·47
46·60	75	120·70
62·14	100	160·93

For motorists it is useful to remember that

30 miles is 48·3 km.   70 miles is 112·7 km.
but
70 km. is 43·5 miles   100 km. is 62·1 miles

To convert kilometres to miles, divide by 8 and multiply by 5.

To convert miles to kilometres, divide by 5 and multiply by 8.

Measurements of Quantity

Weight

POUNDS	POUNDS AND KILOGRAMS	KILOGRAMS
2·21	1	0·45
4·41	2	0·91
6·61	3	1·36

POUNDS	POUNDS AND KILOGRAMS		KILOGRAMS
8·82	4		1·81
11·02	5		2·27
13·23	6		2·72
15·43	7		3·18
17·64	8		3·63

OUNCES	GRAMS	OUNCES	GRAMS
0·5	14·18	6	170·10
1	28·35	7	198·45
2	56·70	8 (½ lb.)	226·80
3	85·05	12	340·19
4	113·40	16 (1 lb.)	453·59
5	141·75		

One kilogram = 1000 grams = 2·2 lb.
Half a kilogram = 500 grams = 1·1 lb.
When shopping for small items, it is useful to remember that
    100 grams is about 3½ oz.
One metric ton is 1000 kilograms.

Liquid Measures

U.K. PINTS	U.K. PINTS AND LITRES	LITRES
1·76	1	0·57
3·52	2 (1 quart)	1·14
5·28	3	1·70
7·04	4	2·27
8·80	5	2·84
10·56	6	3·41
12·32	7	3·98
14·08	8 (1 gallon)	4·55
15·84	9	5·11
17·60	10	5·68

1 litre = 1·76 pints
One tenth of a litre is a decilitre or 0·18 of a pint.
One hundredth of a litre is a centilitre or 0·018 of a pint.
One hundred litres are a hectolitre or 22 gallons.
One gallon = 4·55 litres.
One quart = 1·14 litres.
One pint = 0·57 litres.

Clothing Sizes

Measurements for clothes are made according to the metric system in Greece. Here are the equivalent sizes for the main articles of clothing:

Women

DRESSES AND COATS

British	34	36	38	40	42	44	46
American	32	34	36	38	40	42	44
Continental	40	42	44	46	48	50	52

Men

SUITS

British and American	36	38	40	42	44	46
Continental	46	48	50	52	54	56

SHIRTS

British and American	14	14½	15	15½	16	16½	17
Continental	36	37	38	39	41	42	43

Index to Phrases